Belle's Best Bits

A London Call Girl Reveals her Favourite Adventures

BELLE DE JOUR

PHOENIX

This book, an abridged edition of THE INTIMATE
ADVENTURES OF A LONDON CALL GIRL and
THE FURTHER ADVENTURES OF A LONDON CALL GIRL,
was first published in Great Britain in 2010
by Phoenix, an imprint of the Orion Publishing Group Ltd.

An Hachette Livre UK company

3 5 7 9 10 8 6 4

ISBN 978-0-7538-2794-9

Typeset at The Spartan Press Ltd,
Lymington, Hants

Printed and bound in Great Britain by
Clays Ltd, St Ives plc

The Orion Publishing Group's policy is to use papers that
are natural, renewable and recyclable products and made
from wood grown in sustainable forests. The logging and
manufacturing processes are expected to conform to the
environmental regulations of the country of origin.

The Orion Publishing Group Ltd
Orion House
5 Upper Saint Martin's Lane
London, WC2H 9EA

www.orionbooks.co.uk

Praise for Belle de Jour

THE FURTHER ADVENTURES OF A LONDON CALL GIRL

'Full of frank humour and even more frank action'
Daily Mirror

'Her writing [is] full of refreshing comedy and eye-watering advice . . . Belle's candid humour is compulsive'
Independent

'Whether she's describing peculiar fetishes or handing out agony aunt style advice, it's Belle's witty, stylish writing, rather than her salacious subject matter, that really stands out. Although more Bridget Jones in a brothel than Catherine Deneuve in Chanel, this tongue-in-cheek delight will nonetheless leave a smile on your face'   *Heat*

'Full of agony aunt letters and advice from her days as a call girl, Belle de Jour's diary is bold and funny. It's a book full of insightful observations written by a woman working hard to find her place in the world'   *Waterstone's Books Quarterly*

THE INTIMATE ADVENTURES OF A LONDON CALL GIRL

'She lists like Hornby. She talks dirty like Amis. She has the misanthropy of Larkin and examines the finer points of sexual technique as if she is adjusting the torque on a beloved but temperamental old E-type . . . [A] clever and candid new voice . . . Whoever the author is, she should give up the day job'   *Independent*

'A voyeuristic glimpse into the glamour and revelations of [Belle's] life. A really gripping read'   *B Magazine*

'Belle is quick-witted, funny and keen to establish her academic credentials'   *Sunday Telegraph*

'Belle is a natural-born blogger, her style is witty and compact, with the right mixture of intimacy and disassociation . . . Her entertainment value is huge . . . because she writes about sex with a mind behind it'   *The Times*

Belle de Jour rose to prominence with her award-winning blog about her life as a London call girl. Her diaries, *The Intimate Adventures of a London Call Girl* and *The Further Adventures of a London Call Girl*, have both been bestsellers and adapted for a hit TV series.

Many, many thanks to all the fantastic people who have supported my writing, including Helen Garnons-Williams, Genevieve Pegg, Michael Burton and Mil Millington. And of course, with grateful appreciation for Patrick Walsh – the most trustworthy man in London.

To the readers

The first thing you should know is that I'm a whore.

I don't mean that in a glib way. I'm not using the word as an analogy for working a desk job or toiling away in new media – many of my friends will tell you how temping for a year or ending up in sales is equivalent to prostitution. It's not. I know this because I've been a temp *and* I've fucked for money, and they are in no way similar. Not even the same planet. Different solar systems altogether.

The second thing is that I live in London. These two facts may or may not be related. London is not a cheap city. Like almost all of my friends, I moved here after university with the hope of getting a job, if not a well-paying one, at least something interesting, or populated exclusively by handsome, eligible men. However, such positions are thin on the ground. Almost everyone is studying to be an accountant now, including my friends A2 and A3, who are respected in their academic circles. Good God – a fate worse than death. Accountancy trumps even academia in the unsexiness stakes.

Prostitution is steady work but not demanding. I meet a lot of people. Granted, they're almost all men, most of whom I'll never see again, and I'm required to fuck them regardless of whether they're covered in hairy moles, have a grand total of three teeth or want me to recreate a fantasy involving their sixth-form history teacher. But it's better than watching the clock until the next scheduled tea break in a dismal staff room. So when my friends pull out the tired analogy of corporate-employment-as-whoring yet again, I nod and commiserate with them and we down cocktails and wonder where all our youthful promise went. Theirs is probably on a trunk road to the suburbs. Mine is spreading its legs for cash on a regular basis. Having said that, the leap to prostitution didn't happen overnight.

As I say, I ended up in London like thousands of other recent graduates. With only a small student debt and a bit saved, I thought I was set up for a few months but my surplus was quickly drained by rent and a thousand trivial expenses. My daily routine consisted of poring over the job pages, writing enthusiastic and sycophantic covering letters, although I knew I'd never be interviewed, and masturbating furiously before bed every night.

London wasn't the first city I'd lived in, but it was certainly the largest. Anywhere else, there's always the chance of seeing someone you know, or at the very least, a smiling face. Not here. Commuters crowd the trains, eager to outdo their fellow travellers in an escalating privacy war of paperbacks, headphones and newspapers. A woman next to me on the Northern Line one day held the *Metro* just inches from her face; it was only three stops later that I noticed she was not reading but crying. It was hard not to offer sympathy and harder still not to start crying myself.

As buying a Travelcard became the highlight of each week, so I watched my mean savings dwindle away. And while I have a crippling lingerie-buying habit, even cutting down the intake of lacy things was not going to solve the problem.

Not long after moving, I had a text from an acquaintance, known through my friend N. This is N's city and he seems to know everyone. He's at least four of my six degrees of separation. So when he went out of his way to introduce me to this lady, I paid attention. 'Heard you're in town – would love to meet when you're free,' the text said. She was a completely sexy older woman, with a cut-glass accent and impeccable taste. When we had first met, I'd thought she was out of my league. But as soon as her back was turned, N indicated in half-whispers and furious hand gestures that she went like a train and liked women, too. I dumped a gusher in my knickers, as they say. Like, instantly.

I saved that text for weeks as my imagination grew more heated and restless. Before long she had morphed into the latex-clad hell-bitch-boss of my nocturnal reveries. The wenches and sex-crazed office drones in my dreams were developing faces, and they were all hers. I texted back. She rang almost immediately to say that she and her new man would love to see me for dinner the next week.

I panicked for days about what to wear and splurged on a haircut and new underwear. On the night itself I tore my wardrobe apart, changing outfits a dozen times. Finally I decided on a tight aqua jumper and charcoal trousers – a little office-temp, perhaps, but modestly sexy. I arrived at the restaurant half an hour early, even after half an hour of trying to find the restaurant in the first place. The staff said I could only be seated when my party arrived. I spent the last of my money on a drink at the bar and hoped they'd cover the cost of the meal.

The sound of couples talking in the narrow rooms mingled with the burbling background music. Everyone looked probably older than me, definitely better off. A few might have just come from work; others had clearly been home to refresh. The door, each time it opened, let in a blast of chilly autumn air and the smell of dry leaves.

The couple arrived. We were seated at a table in the corner, well away from the attention of the staff; I was tucked between them. He looked down the front of my jumper while she talked about art galleries and sport. As I felt his hand creep onto my right knee, her stockinged foot started to slide up the inside leg of my trousers.

Ah, that's what they're after, I thought, and hadn't I known it all along? They were older, libertine, gorgeous. There was no good reason not to fuck or be fucked by them. I followed their lead in ordering: rich, buttery dishes. A mushroom risotto so thick it could barely be torn away from the shallow bowl, so glutinous the only way to dislodge it from the spoon was with teeth. Fish with the head still attached and its heat-glazed eyes staring up at us. She licked her fingers and I had the feeling this was a purposeful gesture rather than a lapse in manners. My hand slid over her skintight trousers to her crotch, and she clamped her legs together around my knuckles. At that particular moment the waitress decided our table needed more attention. She brought over a sampler of tiny pastries and chocolate treats, and the man fed his girlfriend with one hand, gripping my hand in the other, while my fingers crawled in her lap. She came easily, almost silently. I brushed her neck with my lips.

'Excellent,' he murmured. 'Now do it again.'

So I did. Straight after the meal we left the restaurant. He asked me to strip to the waist and sit in the front passenger seat while she drove. From the back seat he grabbed my breasts and pinched my nipples as we travelled the short distance to her house. I walked from the car to the door topless and, once inside, was ordered on my knees. She disappeared into the bedroom as he put me through a few basic obedience lessons: holding uncomfortable positions, holding heavy things in uncomfortable positions, holding heavy things in uncomfortable positions with his cock in my mouth.

She returned with candles and whips. While I have had both hot wax and the business end of a riding crop applied to my flesh before, it was a new experience to have it done with my legs in the air and lit candles plunged into me, dripping over my torso. After two hours, he entered her and, using his cock like the domme in my fantasy, drove her face-first into my pussy.

We dressed, she showered. He walked me out to find a black cab. His arm threaded through mine. Father and daughter, any passing stranger might have thought. We looked a comfortable pair.

'Quite a woman you have there,' I said.

'Whatever it takes to keep her happy,' he said.

4

I nodded. He waved down a taxi and gave the driver instructions. As I stepped into the back, he handed me some money and said I was welcome any time. I was halfway home before I unfolded the wad of notes and saw it was at least three times as much as the cab fare would cost.

My mind made the calculations: rent due, the number of days in a month, the net profit from the night out. I thought I should feel a pang of regret or surprise at being used and paid for, but it was nothing like that. They'd enjoyed themselves and to a wealthy couple the expense of dinner and a taxi was nothing at all. And, truth be told, I hadn't exactly found it a chore.

The idea of selling sex festered and grew, but for a while I buried my curiosity about prostitution. I borrowed money off friends and started a serious realationship. This was pleasantly distracting until the first overdraft statement from my building society arrived, suggesting I see them about a loan. The festering whispered and itched with every job application rejection and failed interview. I couldn't stop thinking how it felt, swept away in the back of a black cab in the middle of the night. I could do it. I had to see.

And it wasn't too long after I decided to do it that I started keeping a diary . . .

Novembre

samedi, le 1 novembre

A client was fondling my nipples. 'Careful there, I'm pre-menstrual,' I said, gently guiding his hands elsewhere.

'Tell me something you fantasise about,' he said.

'I'm abducted by four men, stripped and tied up in the back of a car. They park the car and get out and masturbate on me through the open windows.'

'Are there horses nearby?'

'There are a lot of horses nearby. We're in the middle of the country. We're on a farm. They're farmers.'

'Can you smell the horses?'

'I can smell the horses, they're making noises in their stalls and getting very excited. Horses have giant cocks, don't they?'

'Oh yes. Yes, they do.'

'When the farmers are finished, they take me to the stables.'

'Don't fuck the horse.'

'Oh no, I don't even get close. It's too big! And the horse . . . the stallion . . . is out of control, too excited. I think it's far too big. It sounds like it's going to break down the stall door.'

'Urrrrrrrr . . .'

dimanche, le 2 novembre

A few things I have learned on the job:

In a world of twelve-year-olds in sexy boots and nans in

sparkly mini-dresses, the surest way to tell a prostitute walking into a hotel at Heathrow is to look for the lady in the designer suit. Fact.

The build-up to my appointments is almost always the same. The clients contact the agency after seeing the website. The manager then rings me, she re-confirms with them, then they wait. I usually need two hours' notice. One hour of plucking, showering, making up and hair; one to call a minicab and get to the meeting point.

The make-up sits apart from the rest of my toiletries on its own shelf. I stand in front of a full-length mirror as the layers go on: powder and cologne; knickers, bra and stockings; dress, shoes, make-up and hair. Three outfits in the rotation: a modest but slinky grey jersey dress, a white-on-white checked suit, a tailored black linen dress with smart jacket. An infinite choice of underwear and shoes.

The last three seconds before entering the hotel are vital. Are their doors glass? If so, scan quickly for the lifts. Don't go in and just stop, don't ask the staff for directions. Sweep through, acknowledge them with a slight nod. If the lifts or toilets aren't obvious, go for the nearest hallway then get your bearings. If you leave an impression at all, it should be of a well-dressed lady. You are a businesswoman.

Not strictly untrue.

Lifts are useful. Time to dig through the bag for a phone, text the agency – they'll want to know you arrived on time. If you're running late they'll let the client know when to expect you. Freshen lip gloss if needed; arrange clothing. Never be sweating or looking rushed. Find the door and knock briefly, firmly. On entering the room you say, 'Darling, hello, pleased to meet you . . . Sorry to keep you waiting', whether late or not. Even if you make it bang on time, the customer will have been counting the minutes. If anyone is nervous it mustn't be you. Coat off, sit down. The client usually offers a drink. Never say no. If nothing else have a sparkling water.

Collect the money before anything starts. One time I forgot to do this. The client laughed. 'You must be new to this,' he said, and when I went to the bathroom to clean up afterwards, he stuck the notes in the toaster in his flat. Don't count it in front of him; there'll be time later if you're suspicious. Leave on time. If he wants you to stay longer, he has to ring the manager, arrange the price, and pay you right then. On leaving, a quick kiss. 'An absolute pleasure. I hope to see you again.' Out the front, nod to the staff, as quickly gone as you arrived. Text or ring the agency once out of the hotel. If the manager can't get through she'll ring the client, then the hotel, her own security if they're nearby, then the police. She knows. She's been in your shoes too.

My manager is sweet, an absolute doll. When she asks how it went, I always reply that the client was lovely, a gentleman, even if it's stretching the truth. I wouldn't want her to worry.

lundi, le 3 novembre

I had a meeting yesterday near Leicester Square. It was an overnight job: staying until sunrise. The manager has received such positive feedback about my skills as a disciplinarian that she lists it prominently in the website portfolio. I'm not naturally dominant, but I don't mind doing it. Now it seems all clients want the treatment.

He: 'There's nothing quite like the buzz from fucking strangers.'

Me: 'Can I quote you on that?'

'Yes,' he pauses, 'what are doing with your hands?'

My fingers were tented, bearing my weight above him. 'I don't want to knock the paintings off the wall.' I gritted my teeth.

'Good idea. Try not to, then.' Cripes, mate, it's not as if it's your own house. Hmph. Pretty demanding for a submissive, I thought.

Later still . . .

He: 'You're a class act, my dear.'

Me: 'I didn't know anyone actually said that, outside the movies.'

'Have to get my lines from somewhere.'

N met me outside the hotel just before sunrise. He's a close friend, we used to date, he knows what I do, and can double for George Clooney in the right light. As in pitch black. N was smirking. 'Have fun in there?' I opened my coat to show him two whips tied to the inside lining. 'You brought The Persuaders. So you were having fun.'

'Sort of. Yes. He couldn't stay hard so we drank the minibar and watched Channel Five for the last hour.' We got into N's car, which was parked on the pavement. 'And he gave me a silver bubble-blower.' I took the gift out of my bag. It was in a wooden box wrapped with gold and black ribbons, and shaped like a tiny champagne bottle.

I wasn't feeling tired and neither was he. 'You want to blow bubbles?' N asked, as we drove over a bridge. We turned and went up the leafy Embankment, and the growing light of the morning made the water glint darkly. We ended up at Charing Cross Station as the sun rose, blowing soapy scraps of bubble-juice diluted with manky Thames water onto the first commuters of the day.

mardi, le 4 novembre

Small handbags, bah. The magazines can tout this or that tiny purse of the season. But considering what I typically leave the house carrying,

a pair of folding scissors (stray threads are the enemy)
a pen (my memory is good, but not that good)
phone (to phone agency on arrival and leaving)
condoms (polyurethane as well as latex, some people have allergies)
a spoon
bottle of lube
lip gloss (reapplying lipstick after a blowjob is too complicated)
compact and mascara
small vial of scent (anything with a citrus note is nice)
tissues
spare knickers and stockings
keys, bankcards, other normal detritus
and sometimes, nipple clamps, ball gag and a multi-tailed rubber whip,

a capacious holdall is the order of the day. Packing all that into a Fendi baguette is a black art not even Houdini could master.

jeudi, le 6 novembre

My parents are nice. I know I'm biased, but it's true. In spite of having left home years ago, I'm still in contact with one or both of them on an almost daily basis.

Officially, they don't know what I do. They know I'm in the sex trade but that's it. Knowing my mother and her middle-class sensibilities, she probably tells her friends I'm a sales rep for Myla or something.

So while they officially don't know, I suspect they unofficially do know. Or at least have a clue. They're not stupid.

I rang home for no particular reason.

'Hello, honey,' Daddy said. 'Still beating the streets?'

'Ha,' I bleated flatly. 'Mum there?'

He grunted and handed the phone over.

13

'When are you coming home?' she asked. No hello. No asking after my health. No one in her family has bothered with polite pleasantries since antediluvian times. Straight to the point, that's them.

'Couple of weeks?'

'How's the job search going?'

I ummed and erred. I couldn't remember what I'd last told her. That I was looking for work, or starting on a research project? 'Not bad, a few things out there, no interviews yet.'

Actually, it's not quite all lies, I had a job interview.

Don't get too excited – it wasn't a real one. I was instructed to meet a client at a hotel, and was emailed his specific requirements for my interview technique. He required a shy, almost virginal secretary who would be powerless under his persuasion.

My mother seemed satisfied with the evasion of her question. 'Let me know when you're visiting, yes? And if you're bringing anyone? So I can make up the rooms.'

'Of course,' I lied. Setting a date would have been pointless, because she inevitably forgets.

She put Daddy back on the line. 'Tell that nice boy of yours with the glasses I said hello!' he chirruped. That was a boy called A4, a lovely young lad who was very clever and always smiled. My father still says from time to time that he hopes we'll marry. I don't know if this is a sign of senility or a misguided attempt at match-making. A4 was three relationships ago. We're still friends, though. I sighed, wished them a pleasant weekend and rang off.

dimanche, le 9 novembre

Prostitution isn't my first foray into sex work. Perhaps my unusual CV did lead to the current job. Here's the executive summary:

- As a student, was rather short of money.
- Someone suggested stripping. By 'someone' I mean my then boyfriend Al. By 'suggested' I mean 'used to date a stripper and would take me to the fleshpots with his friends', which I rather liked.
- It was not terribly hard work; the girls were frightening.
- Couldn't stop giggling at the men talking to me between sets. Who wants to go over the finer points of Greek tragedy with a girl in a see-through bra?
- Scratch that – I completely see the appeal. BBC3 take note.
- But it was a stopgap and I was dead scared of a tutor walking in. I left.

Then, a couple of years later:

- Was at a vaguely witchy party with a housemate.
- Dressed in black and carrying a whip (mine). The housemate was dressed as Miss World, which is not relevant, but interesting.
- A woman approached us, talked to me a bit, she had a place and all the kit.
- It paid far more than stripping; I managed to control the impulse to laugh.
- Stopped when I landed a 'legit' job in a bookshop on weekends, less well-paid, but access to loads of free books.
- In retrospect, did not choose wisely.

But enough reminiscing. Today's my birthday, and I mean to celebrate in style.

lundi, le 10 novembre

At 9 pm yesterday, while readying ourselves for my birthday night out (all shaving shaven, all brushing brushed, all scrubbing scrubbed), the Boy and I finished off a sex quiz from a glossy women's magazine.

Yes, I am a call girl with a boyfriend. A boyfriend who knows what I do. We've been together about a year. He doesn't live in the city, though.

Yes, it causes friction. Mmm, friction. Not always a bad thing. Especially in bed. He doesn't like my job but he has some abominable social habits, too, like sneaking rum into people's drinks when they're not looking and voting Conservative.

He buttoned up a soft dark-blue shirt, a gift from his mother. I sat at a dressing table, crossed my legs and read out the questions in my sauciest voice. 'At what time is a man most likely to be aroused – A, morning; B, midday; or C, night?'

He raised an eyebrow at his reflection in the mirror. 'Is there a D, "all the time" option?'

10 pm: met A2 (one of my exes), A4 (the clever boy) and other friends at the Blue Posts, commandeered the big leather seats by the fire. Set about attempting to fill the greater percentage of my stomach with alcohol.

Midnight: a club nearby, I think. It all grows a bit hazy. Multiple shots imbibed containing schnapps, which is evil. I lost a pair of gloves.

2 am: emboldened by recent gym-going, asserted that I was strong enough to pick the Boy up. Wobbled on my heels and we both fell back on the floor. Certain if I wasn't so drunk, I would have felt a right twat.

3 am: Oxford Street, everyone marching along and singing 'Seven Nation Army' in unison.

Sometime after that, minicab. We collapse in the approximate location of my bed twenty minutes later.

9 am: I get up to use the toilet. When I come back, the Boy is standing in the door. 'Close your eyes,' he says. I do. He puts one arm under my arms and one under my knees and carries me to the bed. Gently, he sets me down, I feel the

softness of fleece under my back and toes. 'Open them,' he says, and I see that he has spread the bed with a soft white sheepskin blanket identical to the one on his bed. 'Happy birthday,' he whispers, and we make love three times.

A happy birthday indeed.

mercredi, le 12 novembre

The manager rang. 'Darling, is verrrry nice gentleman who loves your pictures. Are you free?'

'I'm afraid not, no,' I say, hoping the Boy doesn't overhear.

'But he is verrrry nice.'

'Sorry, no.'

A few months after the encounter with the older woman and her boyfriend, I located what sounded like a small, discreet agency on the internet. The miracle of information interconnected by technology means that any site is only three clicks away from an escort service, really. The website was modestly designed compared to some others, but the girls were attractive and straightforwardly described. Most of them looked extremely normal – not scary robo-women and not shudderingly unattractive amateur cam girls, either. Just reasonably normal women, but, you know, naked and straddling a garden wall. After email contact and sending my photos, I finally rang to make arrangements to meet the manager at the dining room of a central London hotel. She sounded very young and had a very strong Eastern European accent. Polish, maybe? Should I ask?

'How will I know you?' I asked. 'What do you look like?'

'When I was younger everyone used to say I looked like Brooke Shields,' she said.

'Ah, you must be very beautiful then.'

'No, I am old and decrepit. Now people say I look like Daryl Hannah.'

I ended the call feeling disloyal. After all, my relationship with the Boy at that stage was fairly new, and here I was arranging to meet a madame and work as a whore. Would we have a problem with it? Stupid question, girl. My mind worked through the possible outcomes:

- He chucks me instantly, and tells all his friends.
- He chucks me instantly, and is too embarrassed to tell his friends.
- He doesn't chuck me, but becomes scary and unbalanced as the result of dating a whore.
- He doesn't chuck me, but becomes scary because he actually likes the idea.
- He offers to join in, pro bono.
- He offers to join in, and earns better money than me.
- He's okay with it, and things go on as normal.

The first three seemed likely enough, while the last four varied from 'no way' to 'really no fucking way'.

I could have backed out at any time before meeting the manager, of course, but I didn't. A few days passed between making first contact through email and the interview. I went out and re-stocked make-up supplies. On the day of the appointment I spent all morning getting ready. This involved no small amount of eyelash curling, hair straightening and wardrobe panicking. Sexy, but not slutty? You'll be wanting the dark silk top, then. Young, but serious? Well-cut coat. As much cleavage as I could muster. Boots, of course – it is autumn in London after all.

On the way to the meeting point, I passed a movie poster and convinced myself that I looked not unlike Catherine Zeta Jones. Pull the other one.

I arrived early. The manager rang and asked me to take a table near the window. Was this so she could spy on me and run off if I didn't fit the bill? Was it some kind of sting? More likely, she was just covering her back.

She arrived, as described. Long blonde hair. Horsey face. Tight dress and killer brocade boots that matched her handbag – my chocolate high-street clompers were dull in comparison.

'Darling, hello.' Air kisses.

She had to take a few calls during lunch, when I learned she speaks fluent German and Arabic. Domineering. God, the punters must love that. She asked about my experience. Some dominatrix work, some stripping, no sex with clients, all ages ago. She asked if I had a partner; I said yes. She told me about hers, and how he didn't know what she did for a living. I found that incredible – her phone had gone off three times already.

She ordered herbal tea. I had a coffee. I could feel the full weight of her gaze as I tipped a spoonful of sugar into the cup. Whether longing or disapproval, I wasn't sure. 'So now we have to talk about services.' She pronounced the word like it had twelve vowels: suuuuuuuuvices. 'Have you done A levels?'

Well, yes, but that was years ago. Who knew that academic achievement was a prereq for the job? Maybe the customers were more discerning than I thought. 'A levels?'

'You know,' her voice dropped to a whisper, 'anal.'

'Oh, right. Yes, I can do that. Provided I haven't been out for a curry the night before.' We laughed.

The manager said she needed more up-to-date photos for her portfolio. The ones I had sent were unsuitable, as they were nothing like the usual glamour shots, showing me in various states of inebriation at the clubs. More air kisses and she was away, sticking me with the bill: eight quid. Probably a bargain at the price.

I packed the Boy into his car and waved until he reached the end of the street. Before he even could have reached the motorway, he texted a kiss.

It's been the better part of a year since starting this work, and he's still with me. Not that it was easy at first, especially when I had to tell him.

The Boy had come up to London for a job interview. I was unsure how to bring up the subject of my new employment. Gently, blurring the edges of truth if necessary? 'Darling, I want you to know, I've been seeing men for money, but I do it fully clothed and they come in Bacofoil in another room. Every time. Did I mention I love you?' Or, be blunt and see what happens. 'My dearest one, I'm a ho. Did you somehow fail to notice the bling?'

He gabbled about his family and work through sandwiches, coffee, and our walk down the road to buy a pastry. Over a morsel of baklava I finally blurted it out. He didn't say anything, just pursed his lips and nodded. But he didn't object outright. I took a deep breath. 'Of course if ever you want me to stop, I will.'

He still didn't say anything. We left the shop and walked in the sunshine. Falling leaves spiralled on the pavements; crunching underfoot, they smelled of earth and dust. My step fell in with his: we run together and are accustomed to the same length of stride. He put an arm around me, started to speak, but stammered. He tried again. 'You'd be surprised. I've been thinking about it and I think it's okay.'

mercredi, le 19 novembre

I crouched between the man's legs. His inner thighs were smooth and I brushed the skin with my fingertips. 'How was your holiday?'

'Good, good. Japan is an interesting place. Have you ever been?' he asked, leaning back on the bed.

'No.' I took the hardening cock in my hand and pulled on its foreskin gently. It stiffened and lengthened in my palm. 'What is your favourite thing to do there?'

'They're an odd people, they have these places,' he said, pausing slightly as I took his member between my lips. 'Simulating a crowded underground carriage. Where people's bodies rub up against each other . . .'

He slipped out of my mouth; I began pumping the shaft with my fist. 'I've always had a fantasy like that. A crowded student pub, short skirt, leaning over the bar to get a drink, someone comes up behind me. And there's no space to move, so not only can I not get away, no one else can tell it's happening.'

'Mmm, that sounds good.'

'Will you promise me something?' I asked. 'If you ever see me after this at a bar, will you just come up and do that?'

'You have my word,' he said, angling his erection back into my mouth.

vendredi, le 21 novembre

The Boy is in town, so I am seeing no clients. We went to the gym, ostensibly so I could show him off, but mostly so he could show himself off.

First event was the rowing machine. I hate the rowing machine. Hate hate hate it. It is the Devil's Bicycle. It is my nemesis and wants me dead. However, I will gladly sit alongside the Boy as he thrashes the metal beast into fly-wheeled submission. After five minutes, droplets of sweat appeared on the back of his neck. After ten, the rippling ribbons in his forearms were driving me to distraction. A glorious half-hour later I was aching to jump his bones.

Suitably panting, we headed for the bench press (which I can't do) and the bench pull (which I can). Suffice to say I am not fit to hold the man's towel.

For the pièce de résistance, I goaded him into chin-ups. Four sets of six, shirt off, ensuring that even the resident thick-necked gym bunnies were suitably humbled.

In order to reassert control, we did something I am good at – stretching. I have always been able to put my legs behind my ears. A long session of contorting hamstrings ensured that, fragrant with sweat and lusting as only long-distance lovers can, we never got past the car park. Well, we did. But our clothes didn't. And our dignity came nowhere near.

Ah, young love.

samedi, le 22 novembre

Of all the services the manager and I had discussed at our first meeting, there was one neither of us mentioned. Oral. But there on the website for all to see, I am advertised as OWO. Oral Without. Without condom, that is.

To tell the truth, if she had asked, I would have said yes. I've done the deed with condoms in the past and my lips react badly to the latex and spermicide, swelling and tingling. And like all other sex acts, there is some risk involved, but nothing near what most things entailed. I wouldn't do it if I had cold sores, for instance. Or if I was especially concerned about the staying power of my lipstick.

But I'm a swallower and always have been. Once it's in

22

there it doesn't taste any better to spit it out, and to be frank, it's no worse than the taste of a woman. A girl I went to school with once described semen as tasting of 'an oyster on a two-pence piece'. I wouldn't know, having never eaten either, but she's probably not far off the mark.

mercredi, le 26 novembre

It's a public health issue, I know.

I understand such feelings perfectly. This job I do, the number of people I come in contact with. Living in a city where disease flies in from all over the world. And the time of year – the festive season when people are out partying, splurging, doing things they wouldn't normally do because they think, hey, it's the end of another year, I deserve a treat. Then they wake up the next morning unsure of what they got and whom they were with. And even if you do remember, you never know at the time who has it and who hasn't.

I'm a disease-spreading vector. No one is safe, sure, but some of us are more at risk than others, even with all the precautions available these days: the free clinics, the vaccinations, the public awareness campaigns.

And it's important to me. There's no such thing as paid sick leave for call girls. And God forbid you end up in hospital.

So I want to set your minds at ease as much as I can. I want you to know.

I have had a flu jab.

A late text from the Boy last night: 'We were taken out for free drinks after work. Am now in a tree.'

It's cold out there. I hope his rapidly shrinking boyparts make it home safely and are up for warming again soon.

The first time we met it was his birthday, about one year ago now. He was tearing up the dance floor in a club, almost literally – the bouncers had their hackles up the moment he and his equally large, drunken friends came in the door. They weren't the only ones. I couldn't take my eyes off this man who moved like water and threw his limbs around as though they were only nominally attached to his body.

The otherwise crowded floor cleared a wide circle around their group. They took turns chucking each other around, laughing, like little boys. His eyes were shining, probably from alcohol. His curly hair and freckles stood out in a room of pale poseurs. I demanded a mutual friend introduce us. The club was too loud, he looked down and smiled at me, but didn't hear a word we were saying. I stayed on the fringes and waited. When he went out in the hall to join the queue for the toilets, I followed him.

'Happy birthday,' I said.

'Thank you,' he smiled. He didn't appear to recognise me. He did seem quite interested in staring down my top, however. Hey, I thought, it's a start.

I stood on tiptoe and kissed him. He seemed puzzled but didn't resist. I pulled at the sleeve of his shirt to drag him to the smaller, quieter room. We found a corner of a red velvet sofa and snuggled together.

'You can't do this,' he said.

'Why not?'

'You don't know me at all,' he said. 'My name, where I'm from. You know nothing about me.'

'I want to know you,' I said, squeezing my hand around

his arm, which was roped with thick muscles. His hands, resting lightly on my waist, were easily the largest and finest I'd ever seen on a man.

Just then another woman – maybe biologically not female, it was difficult to tell in the dark – interrupted us.

'Love the boots, honey,' she said.

'Cheers.' I was wearing leather knee-highs with vertiginous heels. They were practically hobbling me, but worth it.

The Boy looked down. 'They are actually rather good,' he said, fingering the skin just under my knee. I melted. 'But I don't think we should go back to the others. You'd likely break an ankle dancing in those.'

'Guess we'll have to find something else to do?'

'I suppose,' he smiled, and we groped a bit longer, until I caught a glance at my watch. It was time for Cinderella to make her escape. 'Come home with me,' he growled in my ear, fiddling with the zip of my left boot. It was the kind of order a woman dreams about. Irresistible.

'I have a boyfriend,' I said. It seemed only fair to mention it. The Boy said he didn't care. I was technically in an open relationship, but knew this man was not one-night material. He was far more interesting than that, there was too much crackling energy around him.

'Well,' I said, 'you can have me one night or see me again. Which will it be?'

'I can't not see you again,' the Boy said. I shrugged – *tant pis*. 'Shameless trollop.' But he was smiling, and took my phone number. He followed me as far as the bouncers. The rest of his friends were still inside. There was a pause. I could have invited him back and wanted to, but also knew, as I walked out the glass doors, he'd be watching me go.

I went home and told the housemates I was in love. The fact that I was also blind drunk and trying to balance four candles in a fir wreath on my head is by the by.

The Boy and I met for drinks later that week but nothing happened. I felt uncomfortable following up on the promise of that first evening. He did try at first – a lingering glance here, a trailing hand there – but soon learned the boundaries. He may have been a fully paid-up member of the *bon ton*, but he was no cad. Or perhaps he was biding his time. The relationship I was in was clearly not healthy. By the time I split with that boyfriend and moved to London, the Boy had new digs in Brighton. He drove up to meet me and moved everything in to my new flat. We fucked for the first time among the scattered boxes and suitcases and piles of books on the floor. Wooden planks . . . I had friction scars for weeks after.

samedi, le 29 novembre

In the beginning I thought this job would just be a stopgap, but it's been months now. It's become almost routine, but I remember when it didn't always seem like that.

Preparing for my first appointment had felt like making up for the stage. I showered and dried myself carefully in the bathroom, looking for stray hairs missed by waxing and shaving. A quick blast of deodorant. Applied a drop of cologne to my cleavage and inside elbows. Put on a white lace bra and knickers, stockings, dried my hair. Part it here or there? Which way should it fall? Hair up or hair down? Fluffy or straight? Small pearl earrings.

I put the dress over my head then started on make-up. Foundation, no powder. Violet eyeshadow – only a touch. A dab of white eyeliner just at the inside corner of my eyes. Cat eyes or not? Vamp or girlish? My hand was shaking.

I lined my lips, wondering how much to use and how much would come off on him. What would I have to take with me, would there be time to reapply? With the tip of my little finger I dabbed a liquid blusher on as lipstain. Gloss. I thought of the manager's advice: 'Men love glossy lips.' I suppose it doesn't take a genius to realise why.

A touch of gel to keep the hair off my forehead and cheeks. A clip to keep it back. I put the shoes on and buckled them at the ankles. Black, patent-leather stilettos showing a long stripe of instep. Incredibly high heels, but I'd once run for a bus in them and had danced till morning in them many times. Fuck-me shoes.

My mouth had gone dry. Went to the kitchen and poured a drink. Was alcohol a bad idea? Didn't know. One couldn't hurt. My lips left a crackling pink half-moon on the rim of the glass. Packed a handbag. Still ten minutes until the taxi. Looked at the location for the appointment again in the A–Z.

Went downstairs and stood outside. The cold wind tickled the hair at my neck. Looked down my road. No one was out walking. A bus paused at the bus stop. A car came up behind it, a man looking out the window. That must be the cab, I thought. Focus. I'm working as of now. Smile, wave, give him the address. From here on, I am not me.

We found the house. Paid the driver. Up the walk, brass knocker on the door. A light on inside. My hair was falling in my face. I took the clip out and shook the hair loose. Smiled. Rapped at the door. No turning back.

The next morning I woke up in my own bed. Held my hand up, stared at it for ages. Was something supposed to be different? Should I have felt victimised, abused? I couldn't say. The finer points of feminist theory didn't seem to apply. Things felt as they always had. Same hand, same girl. I got up and made breakfast.

dimanche, le 30 novembre

The Boy has been casting around for a new position for some time (working position that is, not sexual, though all offers gratefully received). He's been unhappy at work for so long, but it's secure and so on and so forth. His workmates are the same crowd he ran with at university. But now one of them has been made redundant and he's starting to feel the full focus of the upper echelons of administration looking carefully at what he does. I keep suggesting military service, and not just because I think he would fill out a uniform in a most attractive manner. So he emailed me his CV to see if there was anything I could do.

I returned it within the half-hour. Almost immediately the phone rang. It was the Boy, and he was laughing.

'This is great stuff, kitty . . . but I don't think I can use it.'

'No?'

'For one thing, I don't think the army cares either way about the size of my member.'

'You don't know that for sure. You could get anyone interviewing you. I hear the services are really very modern these days.'

'Nice thought.' I heard him scrolling down the email from the other end of the phone. 'Recovery time between ejaculations should not be in the Other Qualifications section.'

'It's important to me, sweetie.'

'Doubtless. And "Oral Sex: Giving and Receiving" under Interests and Activities?'

'Are you saying they're not?' We laughed.

It occurred to me to recommend my own line of work, not that he'd ever bite. The Boy is as strait-laced as a whalebone corset. I, by contrast, am widely considered among our acquaintances to be amoral. Even by the ones who don't know what I do for a living.

Décembre

jeudi, le 4 décembre

There is someone in London who just paid to lick the pucker of my arse for one hour. Isn't that what everyone really wants in life, someone who'll kiss your grits and enjoy it?

If someone had only told me from the outset such perfect clients existed, I would have jumped in straight away.

vendredi, le 5 décembre

'Have you ever been with a woman?' the client asked, stroking my breasts.

'Yes,' I said. He sighed. 'Many. Outside of work.' It has been a while since the last. The Boy grumbles and pouts sometimes because he knows about my past and has never had a threesome. I am wary of the problems that picking up a spare girl can introduce to a relationship. Better to go pro, I think. Maybe sometime in the future. Not now.

'Are you gay?'

'No, I just like women.' Probably equally to men for sex. But I would rather be in a relationship with a man, which I think reads as essentially straight. This was a conclusion won over much heart-rending identification nonsense during university. I'll fuck women, but I don't want to go home to one.

I've been looking through the agency website again. The manager rearranges the profiles from time to time, to give this or that girl a lift in business, or to emphasise a new arrival.

My own profile compares reasonably against the other girls on the site and pictures around the web. Nothing to stand out particularly; just like hundreds of others. It's always stunning to see just how many call girls are working in London. There seems to be a leggy blonde or brunette sex goddess for every potential horny businessman on earth.

I remember the first time I saw myself on the site. The profile turned out decently enough. I hadn't thought it would, considering the way the photo shoot went. There had been some selective cropping and Photoshop magic, but the woman in the images was very definitely me. Would someone recognise me? Don't be silly, I scolded myself. No one who knew you and spotted you while perusing escort sites would ever confess to it. Perhaps, I thought then in horror, they might go one worse and book an appointment!

The photographer for the escort agency had arranged to meet me at a hotel. Cute until she opened her mouth. She started in on me straight away. 'Hair – not big enough,' she said, and pulled out a teasing comb that looked as if it had served time in some of the country's finer dog-grooming facilities. Her own pink lipliner was enlisted in the quest to make my lips look fuller, poutier. The lingerie I had brought, still in its store wrapping, was judged unsuitable which is to say it was far too tasteful. 'You would suit something . . . purple,' she said, throwing a cheap lace vest at me. At least it was unworn; it still had the tags on. This is how I found myself in colours I'd never wear, with make-up I'd never use, hair ten times its normal size, writhing on the hotel furniture. 'Keep those legs straight up in the air,' she said, as my thighs shook from the exertion of holding pose after pose. 'And . . . relax!'

We worked through a dozen standard glamour shots.

'Pity about the bikini lines. So seventies porn star.' This from someone who put me in pink latex hotpants? She changed the film and shot through another roll. I couldn't imagine there were any more impossible contortions to exact. After an hour I'd had enough and got up to change back into my civvies.

Surprisingly, the manager seemed pleased with the results. 'Darling, the pictures, they are fabulous,' she purred. I've noticed she never introduces herself on the phone but launches straight into conversation. Must be an alumna of the same charm school as my mother.

'Thank you, I was worried about not looking relaxed.'

'No, they are perfect. Can you do something for me? Can you write something about yourself for the portfolio?'

Cripes.

I am a tall, luscious . . . ah, no. *Amusant, savoir faire?* Save me. Self-motivated, works well in groups . . . perhaps closer to the truth. Where are the CV clinics for whores?

In the end I was pleased with the result. I had liked the look of the agency's website from the beginning, and especially the descriptions of the women. They seemed more honest than most – there was no messing about a girl's size and what she did – but also less pornographic. The tawdry outfits from the photographer's wardrobe looked unexpectedly sexier and more subtle in a photograph than they had in person.

There is certainly an art to the glamour shot. On the one hand, perfection is expected and nothing less is tolerated, so who wouldn't consider pixel manipulation her best friend? On the other, those of us who do like the way our bodies look feel at a distinct disadvantage to those who would airbrush their way onto a catwalk if they could. Perusing the pictures revealed these trends.

The bending-over bumshot: everyone looks good like this. If you don't see the full-on wobbly face-up, don't be surprised if it turns out to be rather less (or rather, more) than you expected in the flesh.

The tit-grab: a double-A could take on Jordanesque proportions given the right tilting of the chest flesh. What is the point? Many men like small breasts. As someone once said, more than a mouthful's wasted (mine are a perfect handful, but I'm not saying whose hands).

The deep-cleavage angle from above: see previous.

The toe point: she's not a trained ballerina; she's trying to make her legs look longer. I reckon if God had meant us to point our bare feet in mid-air he wouldn't have invented stilettos.

The evening wrap/well-placed fur: fat arms, okay?

The turned-up collar/long hair obscuring the cheek: for double chin, or lack of any chin at all. Julie Burchill pulls this trick, which I think says it all.

Knee-high boot and pencil skirt combo: in real life this is immensely sexy. Who hasn't wanted to stroke the milky white strip exposed on a lady's leg? In sexy photos, anyone willing to show only an inch of thigh at a time has issues.

Bubble bath: good for hiding a multitude of sins.

Bending backward: like the bending-over bumshot but in reverse. Poochy tummy extremely likely. Personally I'd rather see an inch to pinch than force someone to suck it for an hour on the trot.

Crossed legs: hasn't waxed.

Ankle socks: ditto.

Girlish bunches and teenage clothing sense: is actually thirty-four.

dimanche, le 7 décembre

N, the hub of all gossip, was meeting me at the gym and coming back for supper afterwards. He has a keen interest in porn and the magazine collection to prove it. He told me about his plans for a trip to Amsterdam with a friend from work.

'Why not pick up some girls for a threesome while you're there?' I asked. The threesome is his longest standing fantasy.

I feel bad for N. Having tasted the fruits of group sex once or twice, it has become my full-time obsession.

'Why, do you think Dutch women are any more willing than the English?'

'No, I mean you could hire some.'

'Mmph,' he said. While supportive of the concept of prostitution, I don't think he'd actually sample a professional. Once in the distant past he and I had a threesome and so far as I know, he hasn't had another shot since.

He was smiling. 'Any chance you might—'

'Sorry, darling, that train left the station years ago.' Eww, friends hiring me for sex. Must make a mental note to nip all future suggestions in the bud. Especially as they are not all at the same level of knowledge about my work. A2 knows outright, A1 and A4 know the general outline but not the details, and the less A3 knows, the better. N, of course, gets the full skinny, warts and all. Literally.

He drove me back to my house. It wasn't late, but the city was already as dark as midnight. 'How much do you tell that man of yours?' he said after a long silence. N and the Boy know and don't approve of each other, but since they live in different cities, rarely meet.

'Enough.'

'Can't imagine he's happy with it.'

'Can't imagine he has a choice,' I said, affecting more bravado than I felt. If he turns out to have major objections, I'll find something else to do.

Probably.

lundi, le 8 décembre

Have a booking with a banker at a hotel near Bond Street. We drank some coffee, chatted about New York briefly, then got down to business. And, as they say, business is good.

He: 'That was my first anal.'

Me: 'Really? I'm surprised.' Perhaps not that surprised, since there have been more than a few first-time anals in my past.

'Well, I enjoyed it.'

'I would tell you it's my first time too, but you'd know I was lying.'

He (laughing): 'So, how did I do?'

'Excellent – just remember, lots of lube, and use fingers first. As you did.'

'Thanks – you're too nice.'

'Well, you did all the hard work. So to speak.'

Later . . .

He: 'I don't understand why my colleagues would have an

affair with some girl in the office, and risk a marriage, when they could have someone like you.'

I nodded, didn't have anything to add.

'It must be a power thing, or to show off to other men. Still,' and he shuddered slightly, in the manner of a man whose faint tan line from a removed wedding band is still visible, and he knows it, 'I just couldn't risk some little temp ringing my wife up weeks or months afterwards.'

mardi, le 9 décembre

I walked into the hotel, large coat bundled tight around me. It was more insurance against the tools of the trade falling out than protection against the sharp weather. The client undressed while I laid out the things he had requested: blindfold, The Persuaders, choke chain collar and nipple clamps.

'I've never done this before,' he said, eyeing the whips.

Doubtful. Still, his fantasy, not mine. 'I'll be gentle with you, then,' I said. I was lying, and we both knew it.

We were finished in exactly an hour. Sometimes the job seems too easy to be believed.

jeudi, le 11 décembre

I've always been attracted to strong, tall men. And they have not ever forced anything on me. Except for one. But I begged him to do it.

It was GBH with kissing. I'll call him W. When we met, we were both in love with other people but it didn't matter. What we did could only loosely be called sexual congress anyway.

37

W was tall and nicely built, the result of a career in sport. We flirted over the course of a week and agreed to go out on the Friday night. I dressed and thought about W, his long, thick limbs and large hands, knowing something odd was happening. I couldn't imagine myself in this man's arms so much as on the end of his fist. He looked capable of breaking me into small pieces and crushing those pieces into a ball. I could not stop thinking of him hurting me, and the thought made me sick. It also turned me on.

Our meeting place was just south of the river. We stood at the crowded bar of a pub for a while before going on to a comedy club where I got legless on gin and tonic. The acts ranged from bad to criminally awful. I began fantasising about having W's bulky shoulder rammed into my face. I went downstairs to the ladies'. W followed me in.

'You're not going to corner me in the loos, are you?' I asked, pawing his shirt. My head came to not quite the middle of his chest. I could smell the sour waft of a day's sweat on him and was aroused.

'I'm not stalking you,' he said. 'Much.'

I bit him as discouragement. The layers of fabric felt fuzzy on my tongue. My teeth closed just hard enough to make it hurt. But he didn't flinch. 'Now then,' he said, taking my face in his hands, 'you'll pay for that. I'll see you outside.'

I was unstable on my heels, leaning heavily on his arm all the way to the corner of my street. We stopped and I looked up. He lifted my body easily, standing me on a bench. From that height we had our first kiss.

'Get a room,' yelled some teenagers from the other side of the road.

We didn't. Not that night, anyway. The night after.

The location was a pastel-decorated chain hotel in Hammersmith. I didn't even take an overnight bag. He pushed me down on the bed as soon as we were inside and straddled my waist. Pulling out his cock, he aimed it not for my mouth or my cleavage but at my cheek.

So it began. After that first time, when he hit the side of my face so hard with his erection that there were blisters inside my mouth afterwards, there was no going back. 'I've never made a woman cry before,' he said. 'I liked that.' No pretence of romance. Just us, anywhere we could be together alone, and his open palm. On cold days in parks where the biting weather would make it sting all the more, he'd stop the car suddenly, and we'd get out and he'd smack me one. My knickers were always sopping wet after.

I couldn't explain the bruises. 'Ran into the door,' I shrugged. 'Hard session at the gym.' Or, 'A bruise? Where?'

W was as mystified by the attraction as I was. 'What do you think when I'm hitting you?' he asked one afternoon. We were sitting on a bench in Regent's Park, watching the geese and swans. Every few minutes, satisfied no one was coming down the paths, he'd hit me again.

'Nothing,' I said. There was only the moment when his hand would stop stroking my cheek and I knew the smack was coming; the first hard impact of his palm against the side of my face; the eye-wetting sting of pain; the warm glow of heat there afterwards. It was perhaps the only time when there was nothing else in my head. It hurt, but the pain was neutral: there was no hate or disgust behind it. It was pure and exhilarating, like any other physical experience. Like the moment of orgasm when you forget yourself, you partner, the world.

The relationship felt too tightly wound to survive, destined for a break-up, a spell in prison or, worst of all possible worlds, a suburban marriage with occasional light S&M. W couldn't bear the thought either, so one night we engineered, on the flimsiest excuse, the demise of our affair. And I – polite yet firm, like a woman in film noir – smacked him.

'You've been wanting to do that since we met,' he said.

That never stopped me wanting him. Two weeks later I sent a note: 'There are still marks on my left breast from your fingernails. I miss you.'

39

vendredi, le 12 décembre

Phone call from the Boy last night. At last. It consisted of the usual moaning and gnashing of teeth at our fate of being star-crossed lovers with the A23 betwixt us.

Towards the end of the conversation, things turned prosaic. 'My dad's going to be in London this week. I know he's dreading it. I mean, what is there to do when you're stuck in the city by yourself and don't know anyone?'

One thing came to mind immediately. Dear God, I hope he doesn't call an escort. And please don't let it be me.

My logical mind knows it's statistically unlikely. Still, I have three hotel visits in the next two days and can't help wondering. If time has taught me anything, it's that a) cheating is a common human condition and b) the stars always align against me.

dimanche, le 14 décembre

The manager rang to deliver the details of a client to meet near Waterloo. 'This man, he is verrrrry nice,' she said.

I decided on top-to-toe white, mainly because I had a new lace basque that had never seen the light of day (or night, for that matter), also because all my other stockings had ladders. He'd booked two hours, which I took to mean that he wanted something odd or that he wanted conversation.

It was the latter. I rattled the brass door knocker and a shortish man answered. Older, but not ancient. Deep characterful grooves on either side of his mouth. Charming house and nicely decorated. I tried not to look as though I was assessing the interior. We drank our way through two bottles of chardonnay, discussed the Sultan of Brunei's gambling habits and listened to CDs. 'I suppose you're wondering when we're going to get down to it,' he smiled.

'I am.' I looked up at him from the floor, where I was sitting barefoot. He leaned down and kissed me. It felt like a first-date kiss. Tentative. I stood up and pulled the dress over my head.

'Just like that,' he said, running his hands over my hips and thighs. The thin fabric of my basque whirred against his dry palms. Standing up, he turned me around and bent me over a table. His mouth pressed to the gusset of my knickers and I felt the hot steam of his breath through the fabric. He stood again to slip on a condom and, pushing the gusset to one side, took me from behind. It was over quickly.

'I'll take you on my next holiday, baby,' he said. 'You deserve to get out of the city.' I doubted this, but it was nice to hear.

lundi, le 15 décembre

We sat in the car, silent. The light was on inside.

'I thought he was supposed to be out,' I said.

'He was,' the Boy said. 'At least, I thought he was.' He looked as though he might start crying. 'Please, come in. You're my guest, I want you here and I'm sure he can stand it for a minute if he's on his way out anyway.'

I knew there was a reason why the Boy always comes up to see me instead of the other way round.

Taking my bags, we went to the door. The Boy opened it and put his head round the corner carefully. 'Why, hello, you're still in situ?' he cheerily queried of the Housemate. 'I just wanted to let you know, I'm here with the lovely—'

'NO,' bellowed the Housemate. 'I will not have THAT WOMAN in my house.'

Ostensibly, the Housemate dislikes me because of my job.

He hasn't always hated me. In fact, I have another theory altogether: he is annoyed because I am one of a very few women he could never, ever have. Not even if he paid for it.

For the Housemate is young, attractive, smart and healthy. Has no trouble with women at all and knows it. He has cracked on to me at least ten times in three years with no luck whatsoever. I could never go off in secret with the Boy's ersatz best friend.

'Listen, she's leaving quite early in the morning, and you won't have to—'

'I said NO, didn't I?'

The Housemate can do this – he owns the house. The conversation continued in this tedious vein for the better part of ten minutes. Less than charmed, I went to the car and waited. When the Boy returned, we nipped to the chip shop for a snack and, certain the Housemate must surely be gone, snuck back after an hour. But my temper and libido had suffered from the episode. Nothing a few cups of chocolate and an hour-long massage couldn't cure, of course.

'What are we going to do, kitty?' he said, half asleep. 'What are we going to do?'

'Come up to London and live with me,' I blurted. It's time I moved to a more sociable area of the city anyway, one where the crack addicts may stagger by the door but don't collapse just inside.

'Money's an issue,' he said.

'You can live off me while you look for a better job up there, then,' I said. 'I can afford it easily.' Oh, cringe, shouldn't have said that, don't remind him!

'This is all rather out of left-field,' he said.

'You don't have to decide now. I won't take offence if you say no. But it's an offer, anyway.' Ah, negotiating the terms of modern cohabitation. Who said romance was dead?

It would solve one problem – that of the belligerent Housemate. Though perhaps faced with the day-to-day of my comings and goings, the Boy would soon go off the idea.

But I sure could use a friendly face and a foot rub with the beating my stiletto-clad feet take on a daily basis.

mardi, le 16 décembre

As I am paid in cash, I find myself at the bank rather often and tend to use the same one every day. Cashiers are naturally curious people who would have to be brain-dead not to wonder why I come in with rolls of notes several times a week and deposit into two accounts, one of which is not mine.

One day I presented the deposit details with a slip, on the back of which the Boy had been sketching. He studied art, at some long-forgotten time in the past, and still tends to doodle and scratch at odd pieces of paper. The cashier turned it over, looked at the drawing and at me. 'This is good. Did you do this?' she asked. 'Yes, well, I'm a . . . cartoonist,' I lied. The cashier nodded, accepted this. Which is how the people at the bank came to believe that I draw for a living. Whether they took the next logical leap of questioning why any legitimate artist would demand payment in cash is unknown to me.

One advantage of this job is not being limited to the lunch hour for running errands. Therefore, I tend to go shopping in mid-afternoon.

'Live close to here?' the grocer by the tube station asked one day, as I picked out apples and kiwifruit.

'Just around the corner,' I said. 'I work as a nanny.' Which is blatantly unbelievable, as I never have children visibly in tow and, unless the Boy is staying over, am only buying for one. Still, he now occasionally asks how the kids are doing.

I tend to bump into neighbours very seldom, except in the evening, at which time they see me dolled up in a dress or suit, full make-up and freshly washed hair, meeting a cab. 'Going out?' they ask.

'Best friend's engagement party,' I say. Or, 'Meeting people from work for drinks.' They nod and wish me well. I slip out the door and wonder what story I'm going to tell the taxi driver.

mercredi, le 17 décembre

Met the As for lunch today. They don't always hunt in a pack, but when they do, no eating establishment is safe.

A1, A2, A3 and A4 were already waiting at a Thai restaurant. I was unexpectedly the last to arrive – at least three of them are tardy by nature. We exchanged kisses and settled at a corner table.

A1 squeezed my knee and affected a dirty-old-man cackle. A2 winked over his menu. A3 glowered in the corner – as is his custom – and A4 grinned brightly into middle distance.

'So what are you lads up to today?' I asked.

'Nothing very much,' said A1. His measured words were like those of a schoolteacher.

'Nothing much at all,' said A2.

A4 smiled towards me. 'Wasting as much of your time as possible.'

'Don't you fellows have jobs to go to?' They don't all live in London, but business brings them through on a semi-regular basis.

'Theoretically, yes,' grumbled A3. He's the ginger one. Dour northerner. And I mean that admiringly.

'Rubbish,' said A2, turning to me. 'And your good self? Things to do, people to see?'

'Not until later,' I said. The waitress came by to take our orders. A1 ordered the special for everyone. None of us knew what it was. Didn't matter. A3 seemed reluctant to give up his menu. A2 asked after the Boy.

'I've asked him to come up here and move in with me,' I said.

'Mistake,' said A1.

'Big mistake,' A2 said.

A3 mumbled unintelligibly.

A4 continued smiling for no good reason. That's why I like him best.

My phone buzzed in my pocket. It was the manager of the agency. She asked if I could be in Marylebone for four.

'The time or the number?' She meant the time. I checked my watch. Very doable. The As pretended not to eavesdrop.

Most people raise an eyebrow when they find that my closest friends are mostly men, and for the most part, men I've slept with. But whom else are you going to sleep with besides the people you know? Strangers?

Don't answer that.

I count the time I've spent enjoying sex from the first time I slept with A1. I remember the afternoon clearly. His large frame blocked the light from the single window of his flat. I smiled up at him. We were naked, entwined in each other's limbs. He reached down, put his hand round one of my ankles, and moved my leg until it crossed my body. He bore down on my doubled body and entered me.

'What are you doing?' I squeaked.

'I want to feel the fullness of your arse against my body,' he said. Though it was not my first time – far from it – it might as well have been. Here was a man, finally, who knew what he wanted and, better still, knew what to do to get it.

A1 and I dated for several years. It was not an easy relationship, except for the sex. Once our clothes were off so were all bets. I knew I could ask him for anything and he could ask the same. For the most part, we always said yes to whatever the other wanted, but took no offence if the suggestion was rejected. He was the first man to tell me I was pretty whom I believed, the first person outside of a gym shower I could walk in front of unclothed. And I adored him physically: A1 is tall but not too tall, muscular, hairy. His dark, straight hair and gravelly voice were deliciously anachronistic. He was the sort of man who should have been around in the 1950s as a captain of industry.

We would have unbelievable rows. The passion I felt for him was something I didn't know how to handle. It felt too intense and slippery for me, liquid mercury pouring out of my hands. We made it up in the bedroom, of course. Or on his kitchen table. Or his desk at work, after his boss had gone. In an elevator. In a university post office.

And we did it every way we could imagine, from the exotic (double penetration, restraints, golden showers) to the embarrassingly prosaic (missionary while he watched a football match on telly). I've done more and dirtier with other people since then, but never felt such a sense of stretching my own boundaries.

He was the first person to take a paddle to my behind; in return, I administered a doubled leather belt to his bottom while he bent over a sofa, holding his genitals away from the strikes. His impressively varied collection of pornography was the first hardcore I'd ever seen, and we acquired new magazines and sorted them into categories with glee. The things he did like – watersports, anal, women with frog-spawnish come dripping off their faces – took their place; even things he didn't like such as bestiality and lesbian sex got a look in because he was a collector. The explicit permission just to look at someone's body, as opposed to a surreptitious glance in the gym or a furtive peek before the covers came up and the lights went out, was delightful.

I started seeing A2 several years after A1 and I split. He was a sensitive lover. Not gentle as such, but strong and slow. He seemed to me to make no unnecessary movements, and I was enthralled by his long, measured steps. Sometimes, with his pale skin and fair hair, he still looked a teenager. Or even younger – an overgrown boy. From the beginning of our affair to the end, no body and no touch ever felt so right every time as his did. No fingers and no tongue ever came so close to being what I imagined the perfect lover was like. His body was spare but muscular. Tall but not excessively so. Not an ounce wasted.

He had a washing machine at home, I didn't. I went round one day with laundry and found a pair of my own knickers in the otherwise empty drum. 'What are these doing in here?' I asked.

'I missed you when you went home last weekend, so I wore them,' he said.

I examined the elastic. His hips were so narrow they didn't seem to have torn the underwear. 'Maybe we should get some for you,' I kidded.

'Maybe we should,' he said, not joking.

I had his key. After waking and breakfasting (poached eggs on toast if hungry, cappuccino and a slice of challah if not), I would cycle to A2's house. He usually rose late and was showering when I arrived. The bedroom door would be open and I would head to the bureau drawer, which contained almost two dozen pairs of knickers. I would choose a pair and leave them in the drawer of his bedside stand and return to the front room. He would come out and dress. No comment on the knickers, which were for later.

We spent most of each day together. He worked from home; at the time I had odd hours in the bookshop nearby. While I was working he'd take a break, bringing me take-away cups of coffee and tea. We read the literary supplements; I gave him bound proofs of upcoming books from the back room. My workmates were a mad, absinthe-drinking, middle-aged woman and the often-absent, never-happy boss. Almost every week I ended up covering half of their hours but didn't mind. There were books and plenty of them. And it was exciting the few times an author of note came in the shop. I noticed, though, that most of them breezed in the door and went to check for their titles on the shelves before coming back to the front to greet me.

After work A2 would be waiting at home. No words, just through the door and straight to his sofa. He sat, arms thrown over the back, as I opened his jeans with my teeth. Always a harder trick to pull off than I remembered. Then the first flash of silk or lace, and his hard cock distorting the fabric. I put my face in his crotch and smelled the odour of a day's worth of sweat, piss and pre-come through the knickers. I nibbled him, licked the underwear until it stuck to him.

A2 loved to pull at me, flip me over with his hands. He stripped me bare but kept his girly pants on. When he entered me – almost always anally – it was with the knickers pushed to one side, constricting the base of his penis, clinging to his balls.

After a few months the knickers weren't enough. I bought a summer dress, short, brightly coloured. He tried it on. I laughed and fucked him in the dress and was only slightly depressed that A2 had thinner hips and better legs than mine.

'Let's go to the sales,' he said one weekend. I didn't have to ask if the purchases were going to be for him or for me. Soon, several short, pretty dresses joined the knickers in the drawer.

I knew there was another woman. He'd told me before we ever slept together. I probably fooled myself into believing it was almost over, for she lived hours away and, from what I knew, had always treated him badly. But one week he went to see friends in the city where she lived. While I tried for a few days to ignore the itching weight of his key in my pocket, in the end I could not resist. I tore his house apart looking for evidence of her: email, pictures. There was one in particular that broke my heart: her gorgeous face cracked in a smile and pink satin pyjamas open to the waist. I found her name, her number, and rang her. There was no answer. I left a message on the answerphone: 'This is a friend of A2's,

48

I just wanted to talk to you – don't worry, it's not an emergency.'

She rang back. 'Hello,' she said, sounding tired.

It was hard to keep from screaming. The pulse in my neck was throbbing. 'Do you know who I am?' I asked.

'I've heard your name,' she said. I told her about me and A2. She was very quiet. 'Thank you,' she said at the end. The day after he came back I used his key to go in but he wasn't in the shower.

He was waiting for me. I'd upset her, he said. What right did I have to do that?

There was no answer. I was shaking with anger. What right does anyone have to feel jealousy?

One of the teachers at school gave a talk to the girls in our year about his marriage. 'Love is a decision,' he declared to a room of hormonally charged teenagers. We scoffed. Love isn't a decision; the films and songs tell us otherwise. It's a force, it's a virtue. We were at the charmed age when you can suck off your brother's best friend in your bedroom and still believe in one true love.

Then I fell for someone who hurt me. Gradually I came around to the teacher's point of view. You have to open the door before someone can come in. That was no guarantee of control once they got there, of course, but it was comprehensible, if not entirely logical.

In control, that's what I thought. But first-time jealousy tore me to pieces the same way first love had. A2 and I argued and fucked, and fucked and argued, then we argued more and fucked less.

And when we did have sex, it had changed. Once he used to put knickers on and bend over the edge of his sofa. Laughing, I would apply a riding crop to his behind. After a few minutes we'd run to his bathroom where he'd excitedly pull down the panties and look in the mirror. If I hadn't yet imprinted the pattern of the fabric on his skin, we'd go back and try again.

49

After, I just whipped him and whipped him until his skin was raw and spotted with blood. Until he told me to stop.

The times we shared a bed, A2 slept with his arms tangled around me. I kick and struggle against sheets and blankets in the night; he held me in. I rub my legs together like a cricket; he warmed my cold feet between his. Whenever his hand rested on my belly, I would wake, wondering not only at his stillness – he was only slightly less animated asleep than awake – but also at his lack of self-consciousness. The body is so unarmoured: our species' success is dependent on what is inside our skin, not a thousand spikes mounted on it. I might have hurt him any time he was asleep. If he turned over, exposed his spine, I might have attacked him right then.

And once I woke before the alarm to find my curtains open on a perfectly grey morning. Hearing a sigh, thinking him awake, I turned toward A2. He still lingered in the twilight of sleep and his long arms were at strange angles under the displaced pillow.

'Why are you tucking your hands in like that?' I asked, for his elbows jutted out but his palms were jammed beneath the bedding.

'So you don't snap them off,' he murmured, and went into deeper sleep. The first starling of the morning started in a tree outside.

He broke things off with his other lover but I never quite believed it and we drifted apart, sleeping together less and less frequently until one day he was seeing someone else and so was I. We were each happy for the other.

vendredi, le 19 décembre

The manager is a doll, but easily confused. Case in point: I was sitting in the back of a cab while the driver tried to find the Royal Kensington Hotel (which, incidentally, doesn't exist). I was a quarter of an hour late. We finally decided she must have meant the Royal Garden Hotel, Kensington. The driver waited outside while I checked the name and room number at reception. It was indeed correct. I gave the cabbie the thumbs up and he drove off.

The client was freshly showered and wearing a white towelling robe. We walked through to the suite's front room, where another woman sat drinking wine, already topless. She was a small blonde cutie from Israel.

I took off her skirt and shoes and undid the ribbon ties on her black silk knickers with my teeth. I had been told she was his girlfriend but something about it didn't quite jibe. He seemed to know her no better than I did. If she was a working girl, she definitely wasn't from my agency. Instincts can be wrong, though, and in threesomes with someone's girlfriend the best course of action is to lavish attention on the woman. It was no hardship – she smelled of baby powder and tasted of warm honey.

We moved on to the bedroom. He went at me from behind while she kneeled down to work at me with her tongue, fingers and a mini-vibe. I found his exceptionally smooth body fascinating – someone's been spending plenty of time down the waxing salon, I thought – an effect compromised by his rough, untrimmed beard. The whiskers tickled and scratched as he lapped at my girl-parts.

'I don't know what you had in mind,' I said, as my time started drawing to a close, 'but I think it would be great if you came all over both our faces.'

The Israeli girl licked her lips and winked at me. A pro. Had to be, had to be.

Afterwards I produced a small bottle of apricot oil, and she gave both me and the client the most luscious massages. If I hadn't enjoyed it so much, I would have been jealous of her skill. I gathered my clothes from the rooms while she pummelled and kneaded his back.

The client went to collect my coat. I gave the girl a kiss

51

and nodded at the bottle of massage oil in her tiny hand. 'Keep it – you'll make better use of it than I will.' He came back and put a possessive arm around her, and my mind switched over again. Escort? Girlfriend? I couldn't be sure. The tip he slipped me was equal to the fee.

samedi, le 20 décembre

I am heading home to see friends and family, as is my custom. The Boy has gone to spend a few weeks with his parents, as is his custom. I think some things should be sacrosanct from the intrusion of couplehood, and watching your family get drunk and pass out in the toilet is one of them.

Train travel is a most exciting wonder of the modern age. Having invented no shortage of faster, cheaper and more comfortable ways to travel, we insist on perpetuating an outdated and, dare I say it, wildly inconvenient method of transport. What other modes of carriage would expect you to make your own way to the start and terminating stations, wait until the company's convenience to commence your journey, sit so long without even a free warm soda, and set up seats and tables so that you are inadvertently rubbing thighs with every pervert between King's Cross and Yorkshire?

I love it, you know I do.

Having made this journey so often, I know when we are one minute from my stop – seconds before the conductor's voice breaks over the tannoy – and which carriage will put me closest to the exit. Even when no one is waiting for me, and there is a twenty-minute queue for a taxi, the effect of stepping onto the platform is vivid delight. I would conduct a tour of the station blindfolded. And the glow of being on my own ground lasts until I pull into my parents' drive.

dimanche, le 21 décembre

Daddy and I went for a walk just after sunset. He claimed his legs were cramping from so much sitting around, but I suspect it was to get away from my mother, who has gone into celebratory overdrive. She's an equal-opportunity party animal, juggling five or six seasonal holidays at a go. The last we checked she was trying to whip up familial enthusiasm for an Eid firework party. Having only a vague notion of what Eid is, who celebrates it or what shoes would be appropriate for standing in a back garden and craning my neck at multi-coloured gunpowder, I decided in favour of the walking option.

There was a nip in the air, just enough to set the cheeks and ears tingling. We walked past a cottage with smoke from the chimney. 'Coal,' Daddy said, authoritatively. We had a wood-burning stove when I was small. We used to cook the family meals on it. When it went and the new electric cooker and fake fire came in, I was very sad.

We returned to a dark house and a worried-looking man pushing his car off ours. He did the little foot-to-foot dance of trying to look innocent, which is especially tough when your front bumper is entangled in someone's estate car.

Daddy did a low whistle. 'Ooh, the woman's not going to be happy,' he said to the strange man, as if the threat of my mother's displeasure alone could convince a perfect stranger not to do a runner. He circled the scene of the accident, which even I could see wasn't serious. But the stranger had clearly had a bit of Christmas cheer and was panicking.

'Don't know, now,' Daddy said, sucking his teeth. 'Could be a lot of damage.' The man pleaded for leniency. The usual story – points on his licence, poor insurance, wife at home about to give birth to a multi-headed hydra and only his being home on time could save her.

'Tell you what,' my father said, stroking his chin. 'Let's have two hundred off you and call it even.'

'I only have one-twenty on me.'

'One-twenty and that bottle of whisky in your front seat.'

A curt nod and the man handed over the goods. My father crouched low and, with a coordinated effort, they disentangled the bumpers. The man got in his saloon and drove off slowly, mumbling gratitude. We waved him round the corner.

'Well, that was potentially exciting,' Daddy said, unlocking the front door. He handed me half of the notes. 'Let's not tell your mother, shall we?'

mardi, le 23 décembre

Long coat: check

Dark sunglasses: check.

One hour's alibi to the parents: check.

I'm out of the door and free.

I was on time for the rendezvous. He was late. I sipped a coffee and pretended to read the paper. He slid in the door unnoticed, sat across from me. I nodded hello and pushed the package across the table.

A4 lifted the lid discreetly and looked in the box. 'You sure these are the goods?' he asked.

'None finer,' I said. 'Guaranteed results. If you don't mind my asking, do you really need so much product to get through a week with your family?'

'They'd kill me otherwise. Soon as they start to smell blood in the water, I can throw these chocolate truffles their way. That buys me at least a few hours.'

A4 and I dated for some years, we even lived together for a time. We didn't have a pot to piss in, as they say, but it was a comfortable domestic arrangement. It lasted until I moved away in the first of several unsuccessful attempts to gain useful employment. I was upset, recently, to find that he thought the post-student house we'd shared was 'a hovel'. I always remembered it fondly.

'You're a lifesaver,' A4 said. He's the one my father still asks after, as if we're still an item. He's the one I have the most pictures of.

mercredi, le 24 décembre

I miss living in the north. The stories are all true. People really are friendlier up here. The chips really are better. Everything really is cheaper. The women really do go out in mid-winter wearing less.

I miss getting pissed for less than a fiver.

jeudi, le 25 décembre

I have been waiting absolutely weeks to say this:
Happy Christmas, ho ho ho!
It made me laugh anyway. It's Chanukah, and I am eating white chocolate gelt at the moment, which is cooler than cool. And no sign of a gift from the Boy, which is less than cool.

vendredi, le 26 décembre

My first diary was a seventh birthday gift. Fortunately, most of the intervening volumes have been lost. This morning, bored to death, I set about cleaning out a desk and found some old ones from a few years back. They were written in soft cover exercise books with flowers drawn on the covers. They date from the time N and I met a few years ago. We hit it off immediately (a coy way of saying 'grabbed a room in the first hotel we could find'). A couple of days later, when we came up for air, he mentioned his female friend J and the possibility of a threesome. He'd had threesomes with her several times before and vouched for her beauty and over-whelming sexuality.

We were sitting in his car, looking at the river near Hammersmith. 'Sure,' I said. I hadn't been with many women, but considering all the ground he and I had covered in a weekend it seemed impossible to refuse. He rang her to arrange a meeting, and this is how the diary entry continued:

We met J at her place and went for brunch. Food was nice, talked about sex and underwater archaeology. Back at hers I made hot cocoa for N and me. When he went out of the room she kissed me and asked how many women I'd been with. Lied and said eight or nine. We drank the cocoa in the front room and N said he might have a nap. J took me to her bedroom, which held a big white bed and pillowcases that spelled 'La Nuit' in a serif font. We kissed and touched. J seemed tiny until I took off my shoes – in fact, we are the same height. Her bum looked so good in the cream striped trousers, but even better naked. The night before, N had said I had the best arse he'd ever seen but J's, I think, is better. Her neck, skin and hair all smelled so nice I was suddenly aware of my own sweat. 'Did N do that?' she asked of the deep scratches on my shoulder. I showed her the dark bruises on my thighs and the faint marks from his cock on my face. She told me to lie down and blindfolded me and tied my hands.

She dragged a soft, multi-stranded whip across me. 'Do you know what this is?' 'Yes.' 'Do you want it?' She saved the hardest lashes for my breasts and fucked me with a double-headed dildo. When I pressed my face in her crotch, she untied me and took the mask off. I licked her through the knickers and then took them off – J was shaven down below.

It was easy to get her off with my fingers. After which I noticed N watching from the open door. Asked how long he'd been there. 'Since the mask went on,' he said. 'I could smell the two of you before I even got to the door.'

At this point J's boyfriend turned up and the diary gets a little vague. To make a long story short, he had a problem with N – namely, he didn't want N to touch J. Out of frustration N blurted that if that was so, J's man couldn't touch me either. Instead, N tried unsuccessfully to fist me. I was so distracted I couldn't come. J sucked her partner off, we all showered separately, exchanged numbers, and N and I left. He dropped me at King's Cross and asked if I needed anything before the journey. Something meaningful to live for, I quipped. Food and sex, he said immediately, and I laughed. I've reminded him of this flash of philosophy several times since, but he never remembers saying it. Walking through the station, I felt lighter than air, dazed. Happy.

'Well,' he shrugged just before the train doors closed, 'I guess four in a bed is too many.'

I remember masturbating on the ride north. It wasn't easy, the carriage was crowded and people kept sitting next to me. I didn't want to do it in the toilet. But I had hours to do it in and unbuttoned my trousers as slowly as needed for perfect silence. It happened with an Asian girl sitting next to me, turned talking to her friend a few rows back. I had a coat thrown over my lap and pretended to be asleep. Afterwards I rang N to let him know. It was somewhere around Grantham, I believe.

dimanche, le 28 décembre

Ah, the bosom of home. So comforting. So convivial.

So stiflingly the same as it is every year. I'm off down south again, before Mum notices the dent in the side of the car.

lundi, le 29 décembre

The phone rings.

Me: 'Hello?'

Manager (for it is she): 'Darling, are you asleep?'

'Umn, no?'

'I have a booking for you right away. I don't know what it is all of a sudden, but everyone has gone mad for you.' They say that madames are known to play favourites with the girls, promoting some more heavily than others according to personal whim, but I have not yet noticed this. The business seems to have up weeks when I'm turning down offers and down weeks when I wonder if there'll be anyone at all. But the manager always seems uniformly businesslike.

'Um, good?'

'Verrrrrry good, darling. I will text you the details.'

The client offered me a drink. I love English archetypes: public schoolboy, thirties, MD of his father's company. The sort of person who says 'chin chin' before a drink. I'm a fan of Boris Johnson. I stripped down to underwear at the bottom of the stairs and he watched me slowly walk up.

I paused at the top of the steps, turned and looked over my shoulder. 'So what do you want to do?'

'I want to make love to you.'

'Like the full-on Barry White kind?'

'Oh yes.' We wrestled in the bed sheets for the better part of an hour. His hair was soft and thick and smelled slightly metallic. 'What can I do to make you come?'

'It's very complicated. We'd be here all night.' I don't come with clients. Some people don't kiss, which I think is rubbish. It's just lips after all. But orgasms I save for some-one else. This isn't difficult – I've never reached orgasm too easily.

'That sounds ideal.'

'Yes, but do you have a drill press and six goats? Also, the planets are not in the correct alignment.'

'Fair dues. I'll know for next time.'

mardi, le 30 décembre

'There is a client, he wants to pee on you,' the manager said. I swear if someone ever got hold of transcripts of my phone calls, they'd probably think I was a – oh wait, I am.

'He wants to what?' I asked, knowing very well what she said.

'Pee. On you. Don't worry, darling, not in your clothes. You will be in a bath.'

'A bath of what? Urine?'

'No, just a normal bath.'

I sighed weakly. 'You know I don't do degradation.' Not at work, at any rate. I know it sounds odd, but even when W was treating me worst, I knew it was because he cared. I'd be reluctant to let a stranger do anything similar.

'Oh, no, not like that at all, darling,' she said. 'He doesn't want you to be degraded. He wants to pee on a girl who enjoys it.'

Eventually I agreed, but only with a significant mark-up in the usual fee. The client was rather nice and seemed exceedingly shy. We talked for a little while and had a drink – spirits for me and a large beer for him. The better to fill the bladder with, I suppose. When it came time to do the deed, I stripped him from the waist down, got all my kit off and knelt in an empty bathtub.

He looked at me, looked at the wall above me and sighed. Nothing happened for a couple of minutes. I was starting to get cold. 'Is everything okay?' I asked.

'It's not going to happen. I'm too turned on,' he said. He

looked down again. 'If I look at you, I'll get hard. If I look away, I'll think of what's going to happen, and get hard.'

'Try thinking of something that doesn't turn you on.'

'Such as?'

'Your mother shopping for underwear for you. With you in tow. Aged thirty-five.' He started to laugh. I felt the first trickle hit my neck, roll down my breasts.

mercredi, le 31 décembre

In London alone for New Year's Eve.

The Boy was supposed to visit – at least that's what I was told. Last night he rang after midnight to say he couldn't come up. In fact, he had gone skiing; perhaps I could fly out and join him instead? With less than twelve hours' notice. On 31 December.

I hadn't even known he was on holiday. Why couldn't he get here? Because it would be too expensive to change his ticket, of course. I'm amazed that someone who professes so little cash can throw a pile together to hit the European slopes but not to see in the New Year with his girl. Nevertheless I scoured the web to see if by some miracle I could be waking up in France. BA were booking no flights before 2 January. It was even too last-minute for Lastminute.com.

So I regretfully declined. He didn't seem that bothered, to be honest. Suspicious? Of course. His travel companion on this little jaunt is none other than the housemate who hates me.

Janvier

jeudi, le 1 janvier

N and I met in town last night for mutual holidaytide misanthropy. I hate going out on New Year's Eve, but being alone is infinitely worse. As I lifted my drink, a woman we knew pushed past, spilling half of it on my jeans.

'What's her problem?' I sniffed.

'Nothing a fortnight in a Turkish brothel wouldn't fix,' N said. Thus inspired, we spent the rest of the evening compiling a list of people whose attitudes we thought would be much improved by such a holiday:

Naomi Campbell
Penelope Keith
Princess Anne
Cherie Blair
Jordan (though she may actually enjoy it)
(E)liz(abeth) Hurley
Myleene Klass
Any Jagger ex or offspring
Theresa May
Tara Palmer Tompkinson
any blonde for whom the descriptors 'It Girl' and 'double-barrelled' apply.

vendredi, le 2 janvier

Regarding orgasms at work:

I don't equate number of orgasms with the level of enjoyment of sex, nor good sex with the ability to produce an orgasm. At the age of nineteen, I realised that sex was about the quality of your enjoyment and that doesn't always mean coming.

Let's be honest, this is a customer-service position, not a self-fulfilment odyssey.

They're paying for their orgasm, not mine. Plenty of the men – more than you might think – never even come at all. They never imply it's a failure on my part. Sometimes they're just after human contact, a warm body, an erotic embrace. Most times, come to think of it.

The inability of punters to produce an orgasm in me is no way a comment on their shortcomings. So far as their part of the bargain goes, they're doing a great job, and I enjoy sex far more than the merely physical tingle. Being desired is fun. Dressing up is fun. No pressure to either experience physical release for fear of damaging someone's ego, or to give someone an orgasm for fear of never hearing from them again, is wicked.

Sometimes a race is a good day out – regardless of where you finish.

samedi, le 3 janvier

Text from the Boy: 'Are you okay? Feeling sad because I'm afraid you don't want to talk to me.'

I wonder if I'm abnormal sometimes. A little cold for love, slightly lacking in sentiment. As soon as someone's interest flags, my own feelings start to go that way too. As Clive Owen said in *Croupier*, 'Hold on tightly – let go lightly.'

I don't give people enough chances. But maybe I know when it's not right anyway. All romance is narcissism, A1 told me once. I'm doing us both a favour by not responding to the Boy's text.

dimanche, le 4 janvier

N jewelled my arm for a formal dinner last night – purely platonically, you understand. I was still angry with the Boy and taking the hard line that 'all men are twats, unless they're paying, in which case they're twats who are paying'. N understood and accepted his appointment as 'twat' with grace. This probably meant he was trying to get me into bed.

We stopped for a pre-revelry drink at a bar that was cunningly hidden under another bar. Several dozen other celebrants were there as well and N introduced me. A chirpy, raven-haired Nigella-alike planted herself to my left.

'Why, hello there,' she twanged. 'My name's T—' Her dress was doing a reasonable job of keeping her breasts restrained, but I didn't reckon on its chances for surviving the night.

I gave N a 'Do you know this woman?' look. He shot me a 'No, do you think she'll sleep with me?' reply.

She put her perfectly-manicured hand on my knee. 'I just love your accent!' she enthused. 'Where are you from?'

'Yorkshire,' I said. 'And yourself?'

'Michigan.'

Charming. But the crowd grew restless, and we moved on to the venue. Unfortunately T and her date were sitting three tables from us.

The speeches were the highlight of the evening. A multiple-medalled paralympian with a seemingly endless supply of sex jokes, followed by a sport personality, followed by a punchy silver-haired man. The quality of the speakers was such that even I, a rank amateur at anything smacking of non-sexual exertion, could pretend to be interested for twenty minutes.

Then it all broke down for the disco. I danced, I drank, I danced some more. Out of the corner of my eye, I noticed N on the sidelines bending T's ear. Good lad, I thought. After she went off to dance with her date, I sought him out.

'You sly dog. So did you get her number?'

'Actually, she was more interested in you.'

'Really?' I looked back at the dance floor, where she was being spun round and round by three men, an experiment in centrifugal force and its effect on fabric strain. So far as I could see, the dress was still refusing to budge – whether due to magic or double-sided tape, I didn't know.

'Yeah, I think I ruined your chances though.'

'How's that?'

'I said you'd only do it with her if I came along.'

'You complete twat!' I punched his shoulder, hurting my fist more than him.

He kissed the top of my head. 'Just saving you from yourself, dear.'

mardi, le 6 janvier

I rang the bell of the building. No answer from the speaker – he buzzed me straight up. The client opened the door of the flat and disappeared into the kitchen for a drink. Inside it was clean, almost sterile. Smoky glass mirrors everywhere – rather incredible digs for someone the manager said was a student. Postgraduate bursaries probably extend far enough for a few piss-ups each term, but I doubt they cover a lady of the night.

He: 'Don't be so nervous.'

Me (startled): 'I am relaxed. So what is it you study?'

'I'll tell you later.'

He told me his name. 'Really?' I said. It was an odd, old-fashioned moniker.

We discussed the client's desire to move – to north London, which apparently has 'the highest density of psychotherapists in the world'. Knowing a few people who live there, I understood perfectly.

He: 'You're an odd one, I can't quite figure you out.'

Me: 'I'm fairly straightforward.'

'An open book, right?'

'Something like that.'

Later . . .

Me: 'What is it you do again?'

He: 'Psychoanalysis.'

Which made us comrades, if not exactly colleagues. The conversation strayed to evolutionary biology and the role of pheromones in attraction. How well you like someone's smell is, apparently, related to likelihood of producing children together with as few congenital defects as possible. Not the usual overture to inciting romance but it works well enough on me. He liked the sex intense, sensual, tongue-centric. I liked the mirrors. He held me open and took me anally, slithering in and out.

Me: (dressing): 'I enjoyed that. And you smell nice.'

He: 'Excellent, that means we can have children.'

We both laughed. 'Not quite yet.'

mercredi, le 7 janvier

He: 'White wine, I presume?'

Me: 'Why, how very thoughtful.' He presents a glass; we toast and sip.

'Rather drier than usual.'

'Thought I'd give it a try.'

As a regular becomes more regular, rules slip a tiny bit. They're not supposed to be under the influence during an appointment – and neither are we – though a little alcohol isn't expressly forbidden. Having seen this particular man several times, I know that he must indulge in a spliff before he sees me. I can smell it, and am surprised it doesn't affect his performance. Last night I arrived a few minutes early – Tuesday night, light traffic – and caught him in the act.

Another of his habits is using an inhalant during my visits. Now, I realise this isn't illegal (at least, I don't think it is), and I'm not opposed to drug-taking as such. Live and let live, victimless crime and all that. I only rarely take anything stronger than a stiff drink – though those who knew me at uni would probably attest to the contrary.

Last night on his bedroom floor, I was sitting astride him. He, eyes closed, reached for the familiar small brown bottle and took a direct sniff. And then he offered it to me. What's the harm? I thought, and sniffed, and did so again when he picked it up ten minutes later.

And what a rush it was. I felt my scalp, face and ears pounding, like when you blush but more so. Every sound seemed intensified, a little tinny. My fingertips felt like paws, a foot wide.

Thank goodness it only lasted a minute or so. The inhalant, that is. The sex was rather longer.

jeudi, le 8 janvier

This job makes several things difficult to take seriously.

First: Public transport. Perhaps in normal jobs, arriving twenty minutes late is excused with the 'Northern Line, you know' routine. But when a neglected husband has sixty minutes between lunch hour and his next meeting, has taken Viagra and seriously has the horn, you cannot be late. The taxis and I are old friends now, darling.

Second: People giving you the eye on public transport. Maybe they think I'll follow them to a hidden love nest? Or that they'll follow me off and it will be love at first crowded, southbound delays sight? No chance.

Third: One-night stands. Like the army, I have fun and get paid to do it. Sometimes it's not as fun but I always get paid. I clock more oral sex in a week from customers than I did in my entire time at uni.

Fourth: Boyfriend troubles. I don't want to be single and a prostitute. I don't want to be without the Boy in my life. We called a truce. Yes, really.

Fifth: Fashion. Flat boots, short hair, cropped trousers, ra-ra skirts? I'd never get work again.

vendredi, le 9 janvier

It was the Boy's birthday, so he came up to visit. He was clean, polite and clearly on best behaviour. For most of the night, things were easy, relaxed even. I leaned more and more heavily on his arm and he responded with an arm around me. Thank goodness, I thought. Just a blip. Nothing to fret over.

We decided to leave our friends in Wimbledon early (the better to strain the bed, my dear) with the flimsiest of excuses, only to run into epic stoppages on the Tube. After being stuck at Earl's Court for an hour, Himself nodding off on my shoulder, a change of route was announced for our train. So we leapt off at Gloucester Road to make a transfer. Alas, the Piccadilly Line was also toast.

I made an executive decision and dragged us outside to flag down a black cab. 'How much is this going to cost us?' the Boy asked.

'Don't worry, I'll cover it,' I said. He leaned in to quiz the driver himself. 'Oh, come on, you silly,' I scolded, bundling him into the cab.

I directed the driver first to an appropriate bank to withdraw cash. The Boy was sulking when I got back in the car. 'The meter went back on while we were waiting,' he grumbled. 'Probably added at least a pound to the fare.'

When we were about two miles from home, he said, 'I think we should get out here, we're close enough.' The meter had just ticked over £20, but I was in heels and uninterested in spending half an hour in the cold when we could be in bed making sweet lurve.

I looked at him sharply. 'If you want to get out and walk, I won't stop you.' I had no intention of going anywhere.

The light turned green. The driver nervously checked his mirror. 'Um, are you getting out here, mate?' he asked.

'No.' The Boy crossed his arms and sunk lower in the seat.

We were at mine inside five minutes, safe and sound. I unlocked the door and stepped inside, mortified at the scene we were having.

'Are you going to apologise? Because I am livid.'

'I can't believe you let him fleece you like that.'

'I can't believe you acted like that. It's only money.'

Cue a night-long argument in which, ironically, the whore bears the standard for Money is Meaningless, while her boyfriend recounts favours done and expenses incurred by him throughout the past year. It ended rather abruptly with me writing a cheque for something approaching my hourly fee and shoving it into his hand. 'Will that do?' I asked. 'Does that make you happier?'

We were exhausted from arguing all night. He had a train to catch at London Bridge and I was meeting friends, so we left the house at the same time. At the Tube station, we sat with an empty seat between us.

A Northern Line train arrived. I jogged up and hopped on. Looked around – he hadn't followed me on. Popped my head out the door. The Boy wasn't there. The doors closed.

I sat down again, sighed. A couple of stops passed. I got off to change at Euston and momentarily thought about going back. No, I figured, he'd be long gone. But I stood on the platform, waited through a few arriving trains, just in case. After ten minutes I gave up and got on a train. Sat down opposite a bored-looking blonde with her shopping.

Just before London Bridge a face popped in front of mine. I jumped. It was him. I was surprised.

'Where did you come from?' I asked.

'What do you mean? I've been here all along.'

'On this train? In this carriage?'

'Yes. I was standing right next to you the whole way.'

'No, you can't have been.'

He stepped off the train, onto the platform. A stream of people parted to flow around him. 'If you want to talk to me, get off and talk to me.'

'I can't. If you want to talk to me, get on.'

'No, you get off.'

The doors started to close. I said his name, strained, my voice sharp and high. 'Don't be stupid. Come on.'

The doors closed, we pulled away. Last time I saw the Boy he was waving.

I sighed. The train was almost empty. The blonde woman with the bags leaned across. 'He was lying to you,' she said. 'He got on at Bank.'

dimanche, le 11 janvier

Anal sex is the new black.

Hands up if you remember when big-name porn stars didn't go there, when no one said it out loud, when the only people who made regular trips up the poop chute were gay men and prostate examiners. A man who suggested his wife grab her ankles and take it like a choirboy was probably courting divorce, or at the very least burnt suppers for a month.

As with the mass amateurisation of everything, though, anal has gone mainstream in a big way. Girls who used to ask whether you can go down on a boy and still be 'technically' a virgin now wonder whether opening the back door still leaves you theoretically pure.

Hurrah, I say, because anal's wonderful. Then again I had the benefit of being introduced to the practice gently and considerately over a matter of weeks, by a man whose desire for me to be able to take him inspired the necessary patience to persevere. He started with massaging and stimulating the anus, then moved on to inserting his own well-lubed fingers. It wasn't long before small vibes were introduced. When we finally got to the main event, I was begging him to do it.

And other folks must be catching on too, because simply everyone does it these days. By the time it was mentioned on *Sex and the City*, all my friends shrugged. 'So what?' they said. 'We've been doing that for yonks.'

I know anal sex is the new black because my bloody mother just rang to talk about it.

But so long as I had her on the phone I thought I could break the news about the Boy. To her credit, she didn't say a thing until I was finished. 'Poor little creature,' she said, and it was just at that moment I felt the first tears dropping. Yes. Poor, poor me. What luck I have such a sympathetic mother.

Who then made me wait on the line as she turned to tell the whole story to my father, verbatim.

They agreed I should go home for a couple of days. I was powerless to argue.

lundi, le 12 janvier

My head fell further towards the surface of the table. I didn't want the steaming mug of tea in my hands. My mother sighed. 'I suppose at least each failed relationship raises my standards for the next one,' I grumbled.

'Honey, don't you worry that some day your standards will get so high no one will satisfy them?'

If I had the energy to lift my forehead off the rim of the mug, I would have given her the evil eye to end all evil eyes.

'I don't even know why it happened,' I groaned. 'I mean, I know why it happened, but not globally why.'

Father rattled his paper and looked concerned. 'Don't worry, sweetheart,' he said. 'He was probably seeing some other girl and just looking for a reason to end it.'

'Oh, that helps very much, ta.'

Come to think of it, maybe he was. Oh, there were a few times, a few texts, a few phone calls that seemed odd at the time. And one big thing, several months back. You never surprise me, he used to say. He said it often.

I was in an expansive mood one morning in December. For reasons I cannot put a finger on, I woke with the birds. Never surprise you? We'll see. I walked down to Kentish Town station and waited for a train on the southbound platform.

A taxi dropped me at his doorstep at the other end. The air was damp and smelled salty. It was still before nine in the morning. The back door is usually unlocked and I didn't want to wake his housemate. I crept up the stairs and put a hand on the handle of his door.

Turned. No luck. Turned harder. Regency house; sometimes the weather makes the fixtures stick. No. Locked. I tapped on the door. Already my heart was sinking.

There was a noise of whispering inside. The creaking bed. 'Hello?' came a whisper from the other side of the door.

'It's me,' I said.

'Oh.' More muffled talking.

'Wait in the back garden. I'll meet you there.'

'No,' I said, raising my voice. 'Let me in.' He came outside – very quickly. Shut the door behind him. I lunged for the door. He held me off easily.

'For goodness' sake – don't embarrass me,' he said. His eyes pleaded with me.

No way, I thought. There's someone in there. But there was no getting past him. He started to walk down the stairs, taking me, struggling, with him.

'What the hell is going on?' I shrieked. I could hear the other bedroom doors in the house opening, and his housemates coming out to see what was happening. He bullied me into the kitchen. There was a girl in there, yes, he said. Friend of his housemate. In the spare foldaway bed? No, in his bed. Who was she? I screamed. Don't embarrass me, he kept saying. She was a medic, he said. An army officer. A friend of a friend, but nothing happened. Like fuck it didn't, no one shares a bed and look – you're not wearing anything under that dressing gown, are you? It was true, he wasn't.

'Trust me,' he pleaded. 'Go to the café at the end of the road. We'll talk about it later.'

'Trust you? Trust you? Can I trust you?'

He made accusations. He played the Whore Card.

I lost my rag.

'You have never found me in bed with someone else. You never will. This is the price I pay for honesty?' I am digging

74

my own grave, I thought. No one values the truth over perceived fidelity. I fuck other people for a living and yes, I tell him as much as he wants to knows, but, oh. Oh. Oh. My heart has always been in the right place, I think.

I left. I went to the shore, waited for the shops to open and bought a bag of coconut-covered marshmallows. The water was high and the wind against the tide made white horses on the sea. My phone rang – the Boy. I turned it off. He left messages. Nothing happened, he swore. The medic (blonde, thin – I waited long enough in the bushes over the road to see her come out – but not pretty) was very drunk, she fell asleep in his bed in her underwear, he was too tired to go down and sleep on the sofa. Whatever. I didn't ring back. I caught a train home and took three appointments that day. We made it up through texts, over a few days.

Still sat at my parents' breakfast table, the mug of tea cold in my grip. Daddy refolded the paper and left it at my elbow. Go home, go to work, get over it, I said to myself.

samedi, le 17 janvier

These are a few of my favourite things (that punters never ask for):

For me to come for real: Why should they? With someone I've just met, who doesn't know the unspoken road map to my body, it'll take a geological age, with his tongue propelled by more drive than an industrial bandsaw. Of course I fake it, when asked at all.

Glass marbles: Infinitely better than the rubbery love-bead variety. The sound they make when they come out is as delicious as the change of temperature going in.

Food sex: I have never, ever been paid to lick chocolate sauce off someone or have it licked off me. (NB: Does not include the insertion of vegetables, which you don't eat afterwards anyway.)

To turn up in my regular clothes: Random person sex is cool. Random person sex with someone who looks random is even better. Also I'm very lazy.

Bathing him afterwards: I love soaping a man's body. Plenty want to wash me, though, so perhaps they are acting on the same desire.

Rimming: Given a thorough wash with hot soapy water beforehand, I will do this. The tiniest flicker of your tongue goes further there than anywhere else. It's cunnilingus on the miniature scale. As with the last one though – they do it to me all the time. I shouldn't complain really.

To imitate an animal: For some reason I imagined they would. They don't.

dimanche, le 18 janvier

I haven't had a proper first date in ages. He's an acquaintance of N's, which gave us a conversational springboard, but I quickly grew addicted to his looks, his voice and his sense of humour. It surprised me to feel just as awkward flirting with someone as it always had. Did I get nervous having to leave a message on his answerphone? Check. Did I deliberate over what I was going to wear on our date? Check. Obsessing over the details, including Googling his name? Too right I did. Did my heart speed up just a tiny bit on seeing a text or email from him? You betcha.

So we went out – the details are meaningless – and talked around and around each other, and around the topic of how mutually attracted we were. I kept looking at his hands when I thought he wouldn't notice. He must have been looking at mine because all of a sudden, on the train, we were holding hands (dear God, we were holding hands) and he was exploring the spaces between my fingers with his lips (just shiver) and I put my head on his shoulder (yes, it fitted perfectly) and he smelled my hair (oh, yes, please).

Then we went and fucked it up by fucking.

Maybe it was the glass or three of wine. Perhaps it was the music, which was just at the right bpm to make my head spin. But I did what I should not have done – I went straight from cuddling and kissing into Whore Mode.

And this poor thing, he got the works. The little squeals. The wrist restraints. The full-on, sweat-soaked, bed-rattling, neighbour-waking, deep-throating, dirty-talking, facial-cum-shot works. He fell asleep straight after but I couldn't close my eyes because I knew what had just happened. I had had utterly hot, but completely soulless, sex with someone who – up to that point – I actually wanted to see more of. There's that line about the likelihood of buying the cow when the milk's on sale, you know the one I mean?

So we woke early and dressed. He escorted me to the station and I caught the first train home. I couldn't look at him and felt like an utter idiot. Note to self: never have sex on a first date.

mardi, le 20 janvier

They say when it rains, it pours, but is there a saying for the complete opposite? Perhaps 'When it's dry, it's arid'?

The most recent bookings have all been time-wasters and mind-changers. There is always a certain amount of this at work – like the man who wanted to book an overnight but didn't ring the manager when he got to the hotel. So while I knew first name, time, and location, I wasn't about to turn up and go round all the floors, knocking at each door.

Can you imagine? 'Room service? No? I'll try next door then . . .'

He did contact the agency a few days later to apologise. Seems he simply didn't write our number down and couldn't ring again. Of course.

Other times the cancellation comes from my end. I get nervous if someone changes time and location more than once. Too many overly specific requests also tend to put me on guard. Dressing up is fine. Dressing up like your septuagenarian grandmother and being asked to bring my own mortuary foam is not. A finely tuned Creep Radar is a necessary part of the business. This is, after all, an occupation that ranks somewhere between nuclear core inspector and rugby prop for job safety. Except I'm issued neither a foil suit nor a pair of spiked boots for protection.

I have also learned never to trust a booking made more than three days ahead, as these people almost never call back to verify the appointment details. At first I imagined my work diary filling up weeks ahead. But the most reliable calls come six to twelve hours in advance, even from regulars. It seems the longer someone has to think about it, the heavier guilt weighs on them. Or maybe they decide to DIY the situation. A copy of the *Sunday Sport* isn't exactly going to give you a blowjob and a backrub – then again, it's more likely to be found hanging around your local newsagents and can be had for under a quid.

Lame excuses, cancellations, aggressive patients, dubious over-the-counter remedies. Now I know how a GP feels.

N is approaching the one-year anniversary of a break-up. I am of the belief that it usually takes as long as the relationship itself for the pangs to subside, which means he should have been over this one about nine months ago. His ex was a flighty girl. Frankly I never thought they'd make it. I was right, but this isn't the sort of thing you go telling your friends straight after the fact. Example:

'I sent her a Christmas card and a birthday card and she hasn't so much as texted me.'

I'm thinking: Well, of course not, silly boy. She's probably married to an oil tycoon and has a litter of children by now. I'm saying: 'How dare she. That is so profoundly unfair.'

N has a charming ability to think the world of his exes. Naturally, I'm not complaining. 'Pedestal-worthy' is a modifier that more of my acquaintances should use. In the wake of his ex's refusal to contact him, N is seeking out every other immortal beloved to have crossed his path – very *High Fidelity*. It started last month with His First.

They exchanged phone calls for a few weeks. He was sweet about it. Talking to her seemed to bring a lot of memories to the fore – how they met and courted, secretly, over several years. Why she never wanted to marry or have children. The last time he saw her in person, the sad, strained final farewell. Like everyone else, I love a good passion. I love a good story even more.

Then N arranged to meet His First in person, and his reminiscences went from the rosy-hued to the frankly sexual. He's never had a woman since with bigger breasts. She taught him everything a man ever need know about going down on a woman. How she reacted to the taste of come. And so on.

'God, if she'll let me, I'd love to have her again. Just once, just for old times' sake.'

I'm thinking: There isn't a single ex I would take back. I'm at least 95 per cent sure of that. Usually. Depending on which way the wind's blowing. I'm saying: 'Darling, great idea. I bet it's even better than before.'

'You mean they're even better than before,' he said, making a groping gesture in midair with his hands.

'Of course. Of course that's what I meant.'

He looked at me and smiled. 'So if I manage to get her in bed, and she's up for it, would you do a threesome with us?'

I'm thinking: Not a chance, hon. She'll never say yes, and even if she did, I wouldn't. I'm saying: 'Go for it, sweetie. The more the merrier!'

N put his arm around my shoulders. 'You're the best woman ever, you know that?'

Happily he will continue to believe so for the time being. I am informed that His First didn't let him get any more intimate than an awkward hug at the end. He can go on thinking I'm a sexual saint and it'll never be put to the test.

vendredi, le 23 janvier

To my great surprise, First Date rang back. He hadn't taken my guilty conscience as a hint – in fact, he'd been hiking in the north and simply not been able to ring.

He invited me out to a play. Unfortunately, I do like to keep evenings free for work, and haven't been terribly in the black of late. Must be that pesky habit of spending all my money on smalls. I politely declined, but said we must get together later in the week.

'You can brush me off, I won't take offence,' he said.

'Oh no, I'm not at all,' I back-pedalled. 'I really would like to see you soon.' It's not every man who offers to take you out on the town after knowing he can score with you regardless. Most would take first-date sex as an excuse to crack open a can of cider and watch Grand Prix on all forthcoming dates.

But First Date, I suspected, was nicer than that. Much nicer. 'You promise?' I could hear the smile in his voice.

'Guarantee,' I said, smiling back.

lundi, le 26 janvier

N has a friend, Angel, who is also a working girl. I see her around occasionally – we share some of the same haunts.

I've always admired her figure but never really wanted it. All womanly curves have been banished in favour of narrow thighs and a perfect arse. She's a sculpted triumph of engineering, all legs and long hair, and toned to within an ounce of her life. It wouldn't be the worst thing in the world to wake up one day in her Versace-clad body. It possibly would be the worst thing in the world to try to achieve that shape.

I was out and about a few nights ago and nipped to the Ladies to reapply lipstick. Unhappily, it was one of these ultra-modern places with a trough-like sink where the water splashes everywhere, and a too-narrow mirror lit obliquely from below, which reflects the space between your collar-bone and chin. Flattering to exactly no one.

Having ascertained that the toilet was designed by some-one who hated women, I turned round to see Angel crouched on the floor, sobbing. I almost didn't stop. She hadn't seen me yet. But something about the fragile bow of her heaving shoulders made it impossible to walk away. 'Are you okay?' I whispered, kneeling beside her.

It all came out in fits and starts – first man trouble, then family problems, then a recent surgery gone wrong, then the reason for the surgery. It turned out Angel was the victim of a notorious attack several years ago. It was the anniversary of the incident.

'That was you?' She nodded. 'I'm so, so sorry.'

She showed me the cuts from the reconstructive surgery she'd been undergoing, just at her hairline. I hugged her gently. I told her about my last few years, losing family and futures, how sometimes you feel like a cork tossed around on an ocean. How being told to buck up and stiff-upper-lip it often makes things worse. Yes, the world really is an unfair place. Yes, these things are sent to try us. No, you don't have to smile all the time, every day. How it wasn't her fault.

I stayed in there for almost an hour while people walked in, walked out, stepped over and around us. Then Angel stood up, straightened her clothes, ran a brush through her hair. And while I didn't expect this was the start of something beautiful between us, I thought perhaps a connection had been made. Not mates watching telly on a Friday night and scarfing Milk Tray, but maybe a gentle, unspoken acknowledgement. A subtle nod across the room. A sorority of two.

So I saw her again last night. Another club, another toilet. I said hello. And she utterly blanked me. I ran straight to N, wounded by the snub. 'Yeah,' he said. 'I would have a lot of time for her, but she can go from needy to brittle in about ten seconds, and you never know which one you're going to get.'

mercredi, le 28 janvier

Last night I had friends over – not so much a celebration as an excuse to clear the pantry of bottles that have been hanging around since time out of mind. Rang a few people, sent a few emails, all very last-minute. Happily *Chez Jour* is just large enough to accommodate the dozen or so who saw fit to turn up.

By 3 am I was left with two rather drunken but helpful guests who collected bowls and glasses, loaded the dishwasher and shooed out the neighbour's cat. But they were clearly not in any condition to drive. Sleeping arrangements had to be sorted. Unfortunately, the two remainders were N and First Date, the fellow I disastrously slept with last week.

We hung onto the last shreds of conversation until it was far too late to do anything else. N was clearly not going anywhere in a hurry, and neither was First Date – I expect he wanted to get me alone again. It was well past my accustomed bedtime and I hoped one or the other of them would give up and go home, but they did not. 'Well,' I said, 'the bed sleeps two and there are three of us – so it's the sofa for some unlucky soul, I believe.'

They looked at each other. They looked at me. Neither volunteered for the sofa. Neither volunteered for the bed.

'Seeing as the two of you are both tall, why don't you boys take the bed? I'm the only one short enough to sleep here easily.'

'I'll have the sofa,' First Date offered. We took turns changing in the bathroom and I brought out a quilt and two blankets before turning in.

N and I went up to the bedroom. N shut the door. 'Don't do that,' I whispered. 'He'll think we're having sex.'

'Why do you care? Besides, he's probably already asleep.'

I didn't know why I cared. It just seemed a bad idea.

A few hours later I woke, mouth dry from too much alcohol. Walked down to the kitchen for a glass of water. First Date was curled tightly on the couch and looked very cold indeed. I went back up to the bedroom, took out the sheepskin, and wrapped it around his feet. He didn't wake.

People are either more trusting than I expect them to be or I appear more trustworthy than I am. Recently I strong-armed the landlady into a spot of redecoration at my place. With the excuse that most of the kitchen fittings need replacing anyway, I have made the case for a full-on Chintz Removal.

In the meantime, I will be experiencing minor household disturbance. Not unliveable, mind, just inconvenient. I was talking to one of the A's about the impending re-design recently.

'Well, I'll be at a conference the next fortnight. Do you want the keys to mine?'

'Surely, darling, but aren't you afraid I'll spill something on the carpet?' A is notoriously fussy about his home.

'I trust you,' he said.

Another case in point: a recent customer booked me for an evening at his own home. Having exhausted most of a bottle of gin, the springs of his bed and all reasonable conversation, he slipped away for a quick shower.

Most customers are wary. When visiting a home instead of a hotel, they often put off the bathing ritual or suggest a joint shower, so as not to leave me alone. I'm not offended. But this client scampered off to the bath. I sat on the couch. Considered pawing through his CD collection, but decided that would be rude. With nothing more to do, nothing to read, I did what any reasonable person would do.

He emerged from the bathroom to find me washing up.

Perhaps I am more trustworthy than I thought.

Février

dimanche, le 1 février

First Date and I agreed to meet to see a play. No big-budget West End production, this: he suggested we go to a show put on by some of his friends at a pub. It was something by one of my favourite Renaissance playwrights and I was dubious of the adaptation. 'You'll be amazed what they've done with it,' he assured me. 'A real two-hander.'

I giggled. I think perhaps the phrase means something different to luvvies than it does to call girls.

The two-hander was in an upstairs room. It was clear from the start that I was not going to like it much, but First Date's long muscular thigh was pressed against mine, and he laughed in the right places, and aside from the overacting going on 12 feet ahead of us, it was nice to be in a dark room together.

The audience filed downstairs for drinks afterwards. I saw the lead actor and joined the crowd in paying him lavish, undeserved compliments.

'What did you really think?' said one of First Date's friends, looking at me with a canny smile, when the actor had walked away.

'Bloodless,' I said. 'Without passion.'

'Example?'

'I can do better than that,' I said. Turning to First Date, I quoted a line from the play, a line given by the lead actor. I pawed his shirt as if he were Helen of Troy. And he played it well, moving off my advances archly.

We both turned towards the friend. 'Point made,' he said. First Date and I emptied our glasses and left.

He offered me a lift. We talked about everything and nothing. I outlined how things had ended with the Boy. He told me about his recent ex-girlfriend. My mind wandered to A2, and I found myself saying, 'I suppose it was a revelation to learn that just because someone loves you, you don't have to love them back. And you can't tell that person their loving you is wrong.'

There was a pause. 'That's good,' he said, zipping round Hyde Park Corner. 'Because I love you.'

I felt trapped by my own words. 'Thank you,' I said. And I knew right at that moment I didn't feel the same. Not yet. Maybe never. We went back to mine, had sex, slept. He woke early – habit of an honestly employed person, I suppose. We had a quiet breakfast and he went home.

lundi, le 2 février

Client: 'May I take your picture?'

Me (spotting the palm-sized video camera nearby): 'No.'

'Please? I won't include your face.'

Hmph. Thanks. 'No, I'm sorry – it's not our policy to allow photographs or recordings.'

'I just want to see you spreading those lips while my dick goes inside.'

'Good, we can do that. We'll use a mirror. But no pictures.'

'Other girls do it.'

'I'm not other girls.'

(Pouting): 'Other girls from the same agency do it.'

Is that supposed to swing my vote? Mister, I don't care if you have snaps of my mother going down on your dog. 'Terribly sorry, no.'

'Not even a photo? It'll be mostly me anyway.'

'No.' This was getting tedious, and more to the point,

taking up quite a lot of our time. I smiled sweetly, stood right against him and played with the top button of his shirt. 'Shall we?'

So we did, though he peppered the talk during our session with comments such as 'Wow, that's amazing, wish I could get a picture of that' and 'You really should be in porn, you know?' There was the time N and I toyed with the idea of funding a sabbatical in Poland by working in Eastern European skin flicks, but that's another story for another day.

He just didn't let up. To the point where bucking enthusiastically and making all the right moves was becoming difficult because I couldn't escape the feeling of being watched. At the end of the hour I was so spooked I couldn't help scanning the room for hidden cameras. At least it was a hotel room and not a private house, but when he went to use the toilet I still opened all the drawers and looked under the bed.

It's a good idea to stay suspicious, in my experience. It hasn't served me badly yet. No one has ever taken advantage and I want to ensure it never does happen. That's part of why I work through an agency.

I know my place in sex work is a privileged one, as far as having sex with strangers goes. Many prostitutes are addicts, in damaging relationships, abused by clients, or all of the above. It is probably a measure of my naivety that I do not ask the few other WGs I meet if they are happy in their work. Honestly, I did not even notice that streetwalkers existed until well into my teenage years. Sometimes it's hard to tell a girl heading for a club from one who's, er, not.

mercredi, le 4 février

Client (setting the dresser mirror on the floor): 'I want to watch you watching yourself masturbate.'

Well, this makes a change. 'What with?'

'Your hands first. Then a vibe.'

'And then you . . . ?'

'No, I just want to watch.'

He provided a chair and I sat. Wriggled out of my knickers and drew the skirt of my dress around my hips. There it all was, on display, as I'd rarely seen. Yes, I usually do a spot check after waxing and before going out, but this was different. And hand mirrors feature strongly in both work and sex at home, but this was just me, alone, inviolate. Belle from a fly on the wall. And being a self-obsessed creature, I was possibly as fascinated as he was.

I watched my lips grow fuller, redder, wetter. Much darker than I imagined, almost purple, as I've seen the head of a penis do so many times. The aperture itself widened and gasped. I could hear its gentle smacks like a mouth opening and closing as my hand rubbed faster and my hips moved less gently.

The effect was of watching myself on television. I suppose it must have been for him as well – he paid far more attention to the reflection than to me in the chair. I wondered why bother paying someone to masturbate when there was no interaction, then I realised. He wanted to be the director.

But as I approached the point of no return, I would slow down and readjust my position – ostensibly to give him a better look or varied position, but really to keep myself from coming.

It was remarkably difficult to keep from setting off the hair-trigger for most of the hour. He sat on a bed, then knelt on the ground, coming closer and closer to the mirror, occasionally making requests regarding the speed and action of the vibe or the location of my free hand – but didn't touch. When he came, it hit the glass, sliding thickly over my reflected image onto the carpet.

N came round after the gym to help with the cushions. By 'help' I mean 'sit on them while I boil the kettle', which is helpful in its way, I suppose. Someone has to make the first stain on the upholstery. By which I mean nothing ruder than spilled tea. You sick creatures.

One of N's other exes, the one who broke his heart, has started turning up at the gym. I notice it's never a time he's likely to be there. Sometimes I linger in the locker area, listening in case she talks to anyone. If she knows who I am, she hasn't acknowledged it. I'm not certain whether to tell him yet or not. We were only halfway through the tea before the conversation turned, as it inevitably does, to her.

'I don't know whether just to call her,' he said. 'If she's seeing someone new, I'll feel rubbish; if she isn't, I'll wonder what was the point of us breaking up.'

'When someone decides it's over there's nothing you can do.'

'I know. I just thought, finally I have everything sorted, finally I – holy fuck.'

'What's wrong?'

'Look out your window.'

I did. A residential street, cars parked on the opposite side. Droplets of rain blown sideways, showing up as a shower of orange under the streetlight. 'Yes?'

'It's his car. It's your ex's car.'

I squinted. Yes, it looked awfully like the Boy's car – Fiat, V reg, half a block down.

An inadvertent shiver. It was cold by the window and I pulled the drapes. 'Lots of cars like that around.'

'Wasn't there when I parked,' N said. 'None of your neighbours has one.'

I turned back towards the sofa and sat down. 'Mmm. I don't think so. I don't know.'

When N left an hour later, the car was gone, anyway.

mercredi, le 11 février

In the last week I have been set up on three more dates. This might mean my friends are concerned about my emotional well-being, or afraid of what might happen if I am single for too long, or both. And I don't want to get attached to First Date too quickly. He's a nice person and we get on well, but the more I think about him the more I find his intentions a little . . . intense.

None of the intended gents, however, were quite what I had in mind for a love match.

Bachelor number one was a lovely bloke – tall, strange dark eyes, devastating Welsh accent. If there's anything that drives me batty it's the mellifluous tones of men from the Valleys. Superficial, I know, but we all have our weaknesses.

Alas, halfway through the starter he related an elaborate anecdote, which essentially came down to ridiculing his best friend for 'dating a whore's sister'. Ah. Well. Pity. The meal was nice, though.

Bachelor number two met me at a pub and was already drunk. Another fine figure of manhood, but having distinct problems negotiating the relationship between his body and the force of gravity. Inside of half an hour he was clinging to the bar for support, having discovered I am unsuitably small to support 15-odd stone of wavering man.

A couple of hours later we were in the queue for a club. In spite of the rain they were operating a one-in, one-out door policy when the place itself was clearly nowhere near full. Bachelor number two took umbrage and decided to address the bouncers on the matter. They, quite reasonably, chucked the lad out on his ear. I peeled him off the pavement, got him back to his in a taxi, located a bag of peas in his freezer and slapped it on his swelling cheek before making my excuses. Being already unconscious, I doubt he noticed.

Bachelor number three was the sort of person for whom the mantra 'better to keep quiet and be thought dim than open your mouth and remove all doubt' was created. After a solid hour of my bright chatter, he finally came out with a few winners: 'I can't say I'm a fan of [the subject I studied at uni].'

Wiping out an entire academic discipline with a single sentence. That's fine, that's okay, I'm not precious about such things. So off again the conversation went, this time to music, a subject about which he was somewhat more animated.

'I'll listen to anything except country and western.'

What, a life without Dolly? Without Patsy? The Flying Burrito Brothers? To paraphrase the country and western diva, I waxed my legs for this?

jeudi, le 12 février

In a taxi, sort of drowsing off in the back. I'd had the sort of day when you wake up already tired and it never quite comes together from there. My phone rang.

'Darling, I hope you're okay.' It was the manager. I'd forgotten to alert her on leaving the last client.

'Sorry, yes, I'm fine.' The taxi sped north, the streets were quiet. 'Everything was fine, he was very nice.'

'You always say they're very nice. You sound so happy.'

'Happy? I suppose so. I'm not unhappy.' I mean, the man was troll-like, but she's not interested in knowing.

'That's because you haven't experienced any aggression in the job yet.'

I laughed. Compared to real relationships, these men are absolute pussycats, and easily pleased pussycats at that. Even sleepy and disconnected, nothing I couldn't handle – so far. 'I suppose it just shows how well you take care of me,' I said.

Arrived home soon after and went to bed. I had my phone under my pillow just in case as I was expecting another call. It rang around midnight.

'Darling, are you still up? Can you do another appointment?'

'Mrrrrrf arrrrrm mmmmmmmmpf fhmmmmmmm.'

'Okay, you get some sleep. Stay happy, darling.'

samedi, le 14 février

But of course, the manager is wrong. I am not all that happy. 'Tis the blessed season of togetherness, when we honour the anniversary of the beheading of a Christian saint by exchanging overpriced tat.

The crass and obvious fakery of St Valentine's day is powerful enough to get even me down. It's not simply the fact of being alone, though I am not technically alone – in London, you really never are – I have friends aplenty and work enough. No, it's more the smug mutual pampering couples get to experience.

I don't begrudge anyone their good time. I've been known to smile at couples canoodling on the tube while pregnant women and little old ladies are forced to stand. If you have another, significant or somewhat less than, I wholeheartedly encourage you to lavish one another with lurve on that day.

What gets my goat is the shameless cashing-in by manicurists, hairstylist and purveyors of raunchy lingerie. I make an effort to keep myself baby smooth and silkily attired at all points in the year, and what's my reward? Nothing. Book a spoil-yourself spa weekend for two in February, though, and it's discounts ahoy.

Ahem. I think I deserve a little better here. Sure, Valentine's may be the lifestyle economy's equivalent of Christmas, but how about lending some sugar to the peeps who keep you afloat the rest of the year?

I brought up the subject with the woman lately charged with waxing my bush. She wasn't impressed by the logic.

lundi, le 16 février

A knock at the door this morning as I was drying my hair. It was one of the builders, holding a single pink rose.

'Er, um,' he said, charmingly.

'Is that for me?' I asked. The builders were meant to be finished by now, but there have been problems with the new dishwasher that they are either loath to describe to a delicate constitution such as mine, or are incapable of putting into words. Their morning requirement of tea and vague assurances that it will all be finished soon are becoming permanent features of my home life. If one decided to cement our union, I'm not sure I would be able to discourage him, except by engineering a tea shortage. 'How very sweet.'

'It's not from me,' he insisted. 'I mean, I mean . . . it's not from me, someone said to give it to you.'

'Lovely. And is there a note?'

'Didn't see one.'

'Whom did you say this was from again?'

'Dunno.' He thought a moment, scratching his chin with the tube of plastic wrapped round the rosebud. 'Some bloke?'

'And what did he look like?'

'Average size?'

It's good to know their general vagueness is not just an act to secure tea privileges. I suspected that plumbing for more detail, such as whether the suitor had come on foot or by car, would be met with similarly useless information. 'Well, thank you for delivering it,' I said, taking charge of the flower. The builder turned and trundled off to his van. I noticed the plastic bore a sticker from the florist and fruiterer around the corner so no clues there. Who said romance was dead?

mercredi, le 18 février

It used to be simple to buy faintly embarrassing items and hide them in the rest of my purchases. Of course, no shop assistant is fooled by an extra-strength deodorant hiding amongst the oranges.

On the other hand, put too many of these in at once, and you're cruising for jokes. A witness to my usual haul of cosmetic goods might suspect I'm buying for a minimum of six post-operative transsexuals. So there is one chemist I go to for normal things and another for everything else.

Typical shop at Chemist One:

- shampoo
- toothpaste
- bath salts
- cucumber gel masque

At worst, this might stimulate a solicitous, 'Ooh, a facial masque? Treating yourself?' As opposed to today's shop at Chemist Two:

- vaginal pessary (for irritation)
- condoms
- sugarless breath mints

- lubricant
- individual post-waxing wipes
- razor blades
- potassium citrate granules (for cystitis)

This was met with the vaguely uninterested, 'There are halitosis remedies on the far end of aisle two, if you're interested.'

Bitch.

lundi, le 23 février

The mystery car is back; I don't want to look but can't look away. I'm not convinced it's just paranoia; must remember to lock all the locks. The builders are giving me strange looks. Am thinking of investing in a bubble wig and giant pair of Jackie O sunglasses and not just for the sake of rocking the vintage look.

mardi, le 24 février

He: 'Um, you have a . . . I'm not sure . . .'

Me (looking over shoulder at man kneeling behind me): 'Is everything okay, sweetie?'

'There's a . . . I don't quite know how to tell you this . . .'

I was suddenly quite worried – what? Razor bump? Spare thicket of missed hair? Week-old tampon? The stub of a tail? 'Yes?'

'You have bruises on the backs of your thighs.'

'Oh, that. Just means you're not the first to tread this road vigorously, dear. Is it okay? We can do it another way.'

'Well, actually,' he said, growing harder and somewhat more forceful. 'You could tell me how they happened.'

mercredi, le 25 février

A1 hit a milestone birthday. His partner made the arrangements and booked a table at an over-rated Indian in Clerkenwell, which was acceptable, as she has no taste.

I was looking forward to getting out in a large group. Work can be intense. It's like having a series of blind dates over and over again, struggling to keep your end of the arrangement effortless and light, while knowing very little is going to come of it. Draining.

I arrived late, looking swish in a black silk shirt and tailored trousers. Hair pulled up, subtle pearl earrings. Okay, so I looked like a Goth PA. No matter. The table was lively, the drinks were flowing, the conversation was achingly, happily, beautifully normal. I sat across from N, who'd brought his friend Angel, the other working girl with whom I'd had a run-in last month. But she'd seemingly come to her senses and appeared lovely and chipper.

Halfway through the meal, Angel begged use of my phone – her battery had gone – to send a text. And yes, I'm a trusting soul, and was busily flirting with the blue-eyed Adonis on my right, so didn't check to see what she'd sent.

So I was surprised when First Date turned up as the gifts were being opened. He smiled at me. I smiled back. He looked round the table and sat next to Angel. Interesting. I should have known they knew each other, but never would have figured them for a potential couple.

The Adonis smiled, introduced himself across the table. First Date shook his hand. 'And you're with . . . ?' Adonis enquired.

'Her,' he said, nodding at me.

I laughed nervously. 'Are you?'

'Didn't you just invite me?'

I glared at Angel. 'I suppose it might look like I had,' I said. 'I'm not responsible – sorry for the confusion.'

The tail end of the supper I spent lavishing my attention on the pale, shy girl next to me while Adonis and First Date – whom, it turns out, had mutual acquaintances – chattered about university days. N begged off quickly, Adonis made his excuses, everyone at the other end of the table was going to some random's house to continue drinking and I was left with Angel and First Date. She went to collect her car.

First Date and I stepped into the street as she dashed round the corner. 'I'm sorry,' he said.

'Water under the bridge,' I said, though it was not.

'I didn't know that text wasn't from you. Am I in the way?'

I turned to him, angry at the situation, angry at feeling manipulated, even if he wasn't the cause. Most of all I was angry at his need to be needed by me.

'Because I love you.'

Yeah, that.

I sighed, closed my eyes. We stood on the pavement for a long time in silence. I looked at my shoes, he looked at me. The fear was coming over me, a black mist, the feeling of being trapped by well-meaning friends, by fate. 'I'm getting a cab home,' I said finally. 'Alone. You go meet Angel at the bar or she'll think we've deserted her.' Or gone home together, I thought.

jeudi, le 26 février

The next morning I woke to three missed calls and a text.

The first two calls were from numbers I didn't recognise. No voicemail. Not too unusual, but I smelled a rat. So I rang them back.

'Good morning. Did you by any chance ring my number last night?'

Both were confused, because they were clearly people who didn't know me but, if the call register was an impartial judge, had tried to call. Turns out Angel sent more than one text. And they tried to reach her on my number. At least they weren't international calls.

The third missed call was from First Date, sometime in the wee hours. The text was from him, too: 'Are you still seeing N? If so, are you aware I didn't know?'

Sigh. I rang him as well. 'I'm not seeing N. I haven't in ages.'

'You still seem so close, and with you both being single—'

'That automatically means we're more than just friends?'

'Well, no, it doesn't.' He paused. 'But Angel was very surprised when she found out you and I were a thing, and she said, didn't I know about you and N?'

'Excuse me . . . us two . . . we're a thing?'

'Umm.'

'That aside – someone you barely know is a more reliable source of information on my life than I am? Bullshit.'

'Hey, calm down. I love you. I care about you. I—'

Argh, those stupid words again. 'I don't feel the same way. If you didn't know that, you do now. I'm not going to belittle your feelings and say you shouldn't feel them, but you know nothing about me. Either way the things you feel entitle you to nothing.' I know I'm yelling but the sooner he understands this, the sooner he can go looking for someone he really loves.

'It's all just a misunderstanding, I'm sure we can talk about this with her—'

'Oh, just . . . quiet. I don't want to talk about this. I don't want to talk to her. Or you.'

'But I—'

'Goodbye.'

A pause. I could imagine his face, what I would and have

done in the same situation. Bargain for time or accept it gracefully? To his credit he chose the latter. 'Goodbye. Good luck to you. I'll miss seeing you.'

'Thank you.' I hung up. And went to the computer to send that woman a blistering email. I felt a coward hiding behind the inbox, but I was not sure I could keep from raising my voice on the phone. Then I ate breakfast, and felt a bit sad, and a bit of a twat, and even the thought that none of it mattered anyway didn't really cheer me.

dimanche, le 29 février

Yesterday Mum and I went shopping. We haven't been unleashed on a retail palace together in years, but believe me, the shop girls will be telling the tale to their children and their children's children. We're loud, we're efficient, we're armed with serious credit and cannot be stopped as we tear a smoking trail from shoes to lingerie.

She's after the Palm Beach look (well, what matron at her age isn't?). Lily Pulitzer-esque prints, bright brights, silky jumpers, white trousers. I'm genetically programmed to want the same, but live in a grimy city and you can't wear cream-coloured wool where there's any chance of sitting in schmutz.

We hit the shoes first. Same size, same taste; she cleaned three shops out of strappy sandals in spring green and blue; I did the same, with versions in camel and black. Handbags, suits, smalls: all fell before the might of our campaign of terror. She must have bought at least three outfits, as well as enough holiday gear to clothe an army of Mum-clones. I had forcibly to restrain her from beaded, flower-printed twinsets while she advised me my ankles 'look chubby' in vintage-style shoes.

Such is the power of unconditional love. Only a mother

can shriek 'VPL!' to her daughter at a volume loud enough to rock the foundations of the building and live to tell the tale.

She: 'Honey, you looked so adorable in the green! Are you not getting that?'

Me: 'I don't know, it makes me look too busty.'

(Thrusting her own ample chest to the fore): 'There's no such thing as looking too busty. What, you want to look like an adolescent?' And she threw the garment back on my pile.

I quiver in the shadow of a superior intellect.

Mars

mardi, le 2 mars

It is probably the lot of everyone to fear old age. When you are young, it does not seem possible that some day you will be as ancient as your relatives, and similarly impossible that they were even, in their turn, young.

Only recently I saw my own future. Or to be more precise, heard it.

I was at home. My mother and grandmother were talking in the kitchen, unaware that I, checking my email in a room around the corner, could hear every word. But I paid them no attention until my ears seized on one phrase: pubic hair.

Specifically, my mother saying to her mother, 'I feel old. Why, only the other day I noticed my pubic hair is now almost completely grey.'

To which my grandmother replied, 'You think that's bad? Wait until they start falling out.'

I think I had better top myself now, before it's too late.

mercredi, le 3 mars

Of the four A's, there's only one I haven't slept with. This is A3. When we first met, there was immediate, overpowering chemistry. We snogged but didn't go any further.

He lives in a neighbouring city, and when he went home, I was lonely. I confided in A2, and told him I'd fallen hard and had to see the man.

We devised a plan: I would turn up at A3's door at the

weekend as a surprise and see what happened. Meanwhile I had four days to plan and fret. So I did what any girl would do. I slept with A2.

I was seeing A4 at the time. We were on the outs, but still an item, just. Jumping ship was high on the agenda, and this looked like a good opportunity.

So, A4 is out of town on a conference, I'm sleeping with our mutual friend A2 and planning to throw myself at the feet of A3. When the weekend comes, I turn up at A3's door.

He had a girlfriend. I had no idea until she answered the door. Her confused smile said she had no idea what was going on, and I felt exactly as low as I was acting. I made like Paula Radcliffe on speed.

A4 and I split properly; A2 and I made a brief go of things and it didn't work out. But it's water under the bridge now – they're all friends with each other. Most people who meet us reckon A4 is my husband, A2 my brother and A1 our uncle – not because he looks old, we assure him, he just oozes manly authority. But there is the slight lingering problem of A3. After all these years, he's still seeing that girl. And sometimes on a night out he gets a bit pissed and overly friendly with me.

Too little, darling. Years too late.

We were all at a restaurant a few nights ago. A2 introduced me to a colleague of his. As if he had to point him out at all. I noticed the man as soon as he came in the door.

'Nice,' I whispered to A2. 'So where's he from?'

'South coast, originally.'

'Mmm. Where've you been hiding this one?'

'He lives in San Diego.'

'Ugh. Why?'

A2 shrugged. 'Job.'

I frowned. A 7,000-mile long-distance affair is out of the question unless handsomely remunerated for travel expenses. I've crossed the ocean for a heart of gold before, only to find it not worth the effort. But in the interest of social lubrication I flirted with him and the other boys over the meal. Afterwards A2 went home, leaving Dr California in the capable hands of me, A3 and A4.

We went to the pub. Dr California racked up a set of billiard balls. We four toured the table for a couple of hours, me on a team with Official Ex A4, he with Unofficial Crush A3. My eyes followed Dr C's lithe form around the room – eyeing the table, setting up a shot, the confident swing of the arm below the elbow on the follow-through. Competence so turns me on.

A few times, passing off the cue, I slid my hand over his lower back. Hard as.

A3 mumbled something about the last train home. On his way out the door, he put his arms roughly around my waist. He breathed hot against my ear. 'You be careful. Wouldn't want to damage that new lad,' he said, and left.

We put the cues away. The three of us finished our drinks. A4 gathered coats and went to the door.

I put a hand on Dr C's arm, holding him back until A4 had gone outside. I turned towards him, his bright open face. 'May I kiss you?'

'Please,' he said. We snogged in the open doorway, blocking the exit. 'I have a huge bed at the hotel,' he said.

'Perfect.'

A4 was outside and waved us off at the corner.

We went through the hotel's dim brown lobby and up to the second floor. The door was barely closed when we started grabbing at each other's clothes. Dr C was as fit in the altogether as he'd been dressed, and his hands as good as I'd imagined. I took his penis in my mouth. 'Ahh, that's fantastic,' he murmured. 'American girls don't know what to do with a foreskin.'

He felt right to me, he tasted and smelled amazing. The sex was good but not like at work. It was joyous, revelling in his body. I couldn't stop touching him, nibbling him, wanting him. He felt like someone I'd been with for ever. And he took me again and again with amazing intensity. Each time he came, the muscular spasms ripped straight through me like a sound wave, setting off my own alarms, starting an orgasm from the inside out.

We slept a couple of hours, woke up, shagged again. Listened to the morning news on the radio. The usual stories, bombs, death, foreign elections. There wasn't much conversation. I didn't know what to say. Thank you, that was luscious, you know we're not going to see each other again, don't you? I was going to London in a couple of hours; he'd be flying back to San Diego later in the day. And yet it was a comfortable silence, the kind I could imagine stretching indefinitely into couplehood.

I brushed my teeth. When I came out of the toilet he was dressed. He watched me put on my coat; I had to meet a train. 'Do you need a taxi?' he asked.

How many times have I heard that question? 'No thank you, I'll walk.'

He stood up, came over. Put his hands on my hips and kissed me tenderly. I'm reading too much into it, aren't I. It was a kiss that promised more if I wanted it. An open-ended question that already knew the answer. 'Safe trip,' he said.

'Goodbye,' I said, and left. California is thousands of miles away. I smiled. The morning was warmer and brighter than I had reason to expect it to be.

mardi, le 9 mars

The client was a young man, probably not much older than me. When I entered the room he was dressed casually, like any one of my friends, in a tight T-shirt and baggy trousers. Immediately I felt overdressed in my suit and make-up.

'Hello,' I smiled, and confirmed his name. There is always the slight possibility I might have knocked on the wrong door. Would someone turn away an unbidden hooker? Probably only when called on to pay before the sex.

'Hello,' he said. He had lovely, smooth brown skin and an American accent. The room was crowded with unpacked luggage and piles of books. Was he here on business? Yes, he said. Leaving tomorrow. He nodded towards the money in an envelope on the desk. I put it away without counting.

Many clients are in London on business. Most book a girl for the beginning of their stay rather than the end, and if they like her, book her again during their stay. If they don't get on, there's still time to try another. That he had waited until his last day made me think he wasn't expecting to have to pay for a liaison on this trip, and booked a girl out of desperation or boredom.

'Red or white wine?' he asked, perusing the contents of the minibar. To be honest I prefer spirits, but will only choose from what is explicitly offered. If they do not specify – as in 'What would you like to drink?' – I ask for either whatever they're having themselves or a glass of water. My mouth tends to go dry early on, and the first lip contact should be moist, welcoming, but not quite sloppy.

He held the glass out to me, we raised a half-ironic toast – 'To new friends' – and drank. I noticed the arm holding his glass was tattooed. A small dagger in black.

'Nice,' I said, reaching over to finger the inking. The first moment of contact can be hard to engineer. Men who kiss you at the door are easy to fall into physical intimacy with, but more often the client is nervous, and I make an excuse to reach across and make contact. Almost as if by accident, like the moment on a date when the other person's proximity is an implicit permission to grab and kiss.

He took my wine glass away and pushed me back on the bed. His forearms were stronger than his softening middle, suggesting a former athlete going to seed. I looked up at him, lips parted. His trousers were half-down and he was wearing no underwear. It occurred to me that there was something reckless about the way he handled me, and all the protection in the world would not stop him if he wanted to harm me. I leaned forward and took his cock in my mouth.

As a girl who is advertised as providing 'all services', I know many customers book me on the expectation of anal sex and am prepared for that. They typically let me suck them for a while first, move on to a brief encounter with vaginal sex, then either ask nervously about approaching the back door or accidentally-on-purpose start heading that way. This man did neither.

Pushing me back on the bed, he bent above me, moving my legs up above my head. He licked his fingers and worked three of them into my cunt. I reached forward to draw his hand out, and sucked the digits. I like to know what my own taste is, partly because I enjoy the flavour, partly to know what's going on down there.

I stopped him and rolled to the side, extracted a condom from my purse and pumped a heavy drop of lubricant on my finger. While he applied protection, I lubed my pucker. He burrowed his fingers back in and, using his wrist to pivot me backward, aimed his cock towards my back entrance. The full length sank straight in. He'd clearly worked it out beforehand – just the right angle for his member.

He pumped this way for half an hour, and literally pinned me to the bed; all I could do was moan and make encouraging noises. His hand furrowed inside me, rubbing the bottom of my vagina to feel his own cock through the muscle wall. I felt the first shuddering spasms and his come fill my arse.

He didn't want to be held. I went to the toilet and cleaned myself, came back and dressed. We discussed Iris Murdoch, and I left.

mercredi, le 10 mars

Today the builders left. The ginger one stood awkwardly in the kitchen as the landlady passed her eye over the white walls and clean pine cupboards. She didn't seem half as pleased as I was with the result, didn't say anything, just signed off an invoice and left.

The other one, the tall one, nodded towards the table where he'd left the spare keys.

'Thank you. I've become very used to you, you know,' I said as he reached the door.

'No, thank you,' he said (in a south London accent I wouldn't dare replicate in speech, much less writing – suffice to say they found my pronunciation of 'room', 'house' and 'year' as amusing as I found theirs). 'You're quite a lady, you are.'

I laughed. Lady, indeed. Lady in a green velvet thong.

dimanche, le 14 mars

The end of the affair was written from the beginning. He is a man who hires women for sex, I am the whore, and at some point his taste will move on.

I have grown accustomed to him, and while I do not love him I admit to being just as interested in staying up all night talking as in the carnal transaction.

In the upstairs bathroom is a large tub with gold-coloured taps and four drawings on the wall of a village in France. He says these are gifts from the artist. I have looked at the pictures so many times while bathing afterwards that when the painters who whitewashed the walls put them back in the wrong order, I noticed before he did.

'So they are,' he said. 'Well spotted.'

He knows a great deal about me, this one. He knows my real name and what I studied, and often mentions – he works in a related area – that should I ever need employment in the future, well . . . and he slips his card in my pocket for the dozenth time.

It's like having a protective uncle. Who fucks you.

Sometimes we don't fuck as such. He doesn't like latex, but I'm not a risk-taker by nature. So he wanks on me. I stretch out on a bed or couch or sometimes the floor, head propped up with a pillow or two, as he straddles my torso below the breasts. While I play with my nipples and his balls he jerks his shaft over my face. Afterwards, we'll find a mirror and analyse the result together – points awarded for consistency, accuracy and volume. And because he enjoys washing me, he'll let it dry a little and dab most of the damage off with a damp flannel.

The last few weeks have been difficult to organise. We never had a set meeting time, though it was usually a week-day, and usually after 10 pm. I've been busy lately. So has he. If he doesn't reach me first, he'll take another girl.

I see I've missed his call and text back. This goes on for several weeks. I'm starting to miss the glass of bubbling Pol Roger he always pours when I come in.

When I went away, he rang three times. He's getting anxious. It's like the end of a relationship: the clinginess, the unfounded suspicion.

Then, the resolution. Just a text one morning: 'I suppose we are fated to never meet again. Will miss you. X'

I'll miss him, too.

mardi, le 16 mars

N rang. 'Not seen you around in a bit. Everything all right?'

'Fine.'

'Liar.' He was correct, as usual. 'What's going on?'

I was out walking by the river in the sunshine, and it occurred to me that a year ago I was doing the same thing with someone I loved and thought I was going to marry.

'Must be in the water. I just thought about my ex today too.' This is the one who chucked him suddenly, without so much as a fare-thee-well. 'I'll come over if you like.' I just sighed heavily. 'I'll be there in ten minutes, then.'

N knocked briefly and let himself in. I was sitting on the couch frowning. 'Hey, gorgeous,' he said, rubbing my hair. 'Why don't we nip out for a bite to eat?'

'So if you could meet your ex and whomever he's with now,' N said over salad and a pint at some obnoxious gastropub, 'what would she be like?' Fat, I guessed. 'Mine, I'd like to see her with someone who's perfect – except he's impotent.'

'No, not fat. Stupid.'

'Someone who's perfect, but impotent and has a horrible set of in-laws.'

'Stupid, and smells funny.'

'Ooh, that's good. Impotent, bad in-laws and tells her she can't have a job outside the home.' He finished his pint and started on mine, which was barely depleted.

'Stupid, smells funny and has terrible taste in music.'

'Actually, he'd never be interested in someone with bad taste in the first place.'

N swallowed a mouthful of bitter. 'Impotent and bald.'

'Mine will be bald in five years' time. I believe that.'

'Impotent, bald and cheats on her. Because she knows I never would have done that to her.'

'Stupid, smells funny and terrible in bed.'

'Terrible in bed. Now we've hit the heart of it.' N smiled. 'Bald, impotent and won't fist her.'

'Really? She was that into it?'

'Oh yes,' he said. 'I never told you about the fist and the cucumber? Simultaneously?'

'Worse still, you never took pictures, did you?'

'We always said if all else failed in her career there was money to be made in film.'

'No wonder you fell for her.' I picked at the damp edge of a beer mat. 'You still miss her, don't you?'

'Too damn right. You're still in love with him, aren't you?'

'You know I am.'

'I find it strange,' he said. 'Theoretically I'm over her, but if that's so I should probably make an effort to date other women rather than avoid them altogether.'

'Ah, I know that stage,' I said. 'I'm in more of a "sabotaging perfectly good potential relationships" mode.' Not to mention being afraid the Boy might make his reappearance just as I found someone worth hanging on to.

N patted his stomach. The pub was empty of all but a few staff. 'Shall we go?' I nodded. I told him I was going straight to bed when I got home.

'After you tap this conversation into your little computer,' he corrected.

jeudi, le 18 mars

The client stood, trousers off. I sat in a chair in front of him. My shirt (white, as requested) was half-unbuttoned. 'I want to write my name in come all over you,' he said.

I smirked. 'You can't fool me, you nicked that line from *London Fields*.'

He looked at me strangely. Oh no, I thought. Better watch my mouth. 'Amis fan?' he said idly, pulling himself with one hand.

'He's not bad,' I said, reaching into the shirt to pull my breasts free of the bra.

'*Time's Arrow* was pretty tricksy though.' A glistening drop of pre-come lolled at the tip of his glans.

'Very high concept. Good book for a long train journey.' I pulled at my nipples to his appreciative nods.

It was hot and close in the room. The weather had not been so bad and I thought of asking him to turn the heating off. 'I want to smell your sweat mixing with my spunk,' he said, as if reading my thoughts.

Later, I met another client. A large hotel in Lancaster Gate. The room was small and highly decorated, which surely made it look even smaller. For the money they must be charging here, I thought it seemed a little cramped. End-of-hall room.

He was in shirt-sleeves. Short sleeves under a blazer – I hate that, it jars like light socks with shoes.

'Your nipples are hard already,' he said (black lace balconette bra and matching boy-style briefs). The window was wide open.

I draped my arms over his shoulders. 'Are you not a little cold in here?'

'I'm fine.'

'There are goose pimples all over your arms.' I smiled and walked to the ground-floor window to pull the drapes.

'Good for the metabolism.'

'Bet I can think of something better,' I said.

vendredi, le 19 mars

Think I'll stay indoors today. N came back from Belgium with a veritable metric tonne of porn to sift through, including the always-reliable *Lady Anita F (Hotter Than Hell!!!)* title and another mag with a tasty bob-haired girl doing the waterstuff all over some poor boy who no doubt deserved it. Will let you know if anything interesting, er, goes down.

dimanche, le 21 mars

I want so very little out of life, really. All a girl asks for is:

- a haircut that looks the same regardless of wind speed or direction
- to be smiled back at by people I smile at
- shoes that make you look taller, and look nice, and can be used for actual walking
- for only disabled people to park in disabled spots
- instant mastery of all things kitchen-related
- a bit of sunshine now and then
- a worldwide ban on polyphonic ringtones
- a worldwide ban on phones which give no options save a polyphonic ringtone
- a cessation of all suffering, backdated to the beginning of time.

mardi, le 23 mars

I am a cheap date.

At several hundred an hour, this is a rich claim to be making. But it is the truth. Considering the economics of sex – in which a man is prepared to invest some time, and a bit of money, towards gifts and entertainments, in order to coax a woman into bed – I am assured by clients that the cost of a call girl is on a par with the price of picking up a woman on a business trip. And she's not likely to come round and cook your rabbit later.

But I don't mean at work, where the judgement of whether my services are worth the money would doubtless involve a level of maths of which I am not capable. I am a cheap date in real life.

On paper it sounds great. Woman arranges her own transportation, buys her own pint and perhaps a few for you, and should there be a resulting relationship she is not terribly fussed about receiving gifts, holidays or other trinkets of your affection aside from the affection itself. If you go away together, she'll contribute her share; if you fail to book a restaurant on one of several major milestones she will smile and say she prefers staying in. She does not arbitrarily demand shiny things in pale blue Tiffany boxes; if she sees something she likes, she'll buy it, and if you do make an extra effort, she will of course be grateful. But does not take it for granted.

I'm a high-maintenance plot, but hire my own groundsmen, as it were.

It has taken some time to conclude this is not what men are attracted to. They enjoy the chase, don't they, the idea that a woman's value is reflected in the effort you spend to win a smile or a kiss. Even if she turns out to be rubbish in bed, by the time you have prised her iron-banded thighs apart with weekend breaks in Sardinia and a shiny carbon chip on a ring, you'll be so grateful to be there at all that it won't matter.

I reckon this means people are probably worse in bed than their ancestors – the need to win a mate with lingual talent having been bred out of the population (NB: not scientifically proven). It might also mean that women with doe eyes, slightly turned-in toes and a skill for simpering should predominate.

Film noir gave us a term for the low-maintenance cheap date type of woman, as personified by Ingrid Bergman and other cool blondes. They were, in the gruff parlance, Class Acts. A Class Act does not bombard you with whimpering phone calls to the effect of 'Why are you out with your mates watching the footie when you could be choosing sisal floor mats with me?' A Class Act does not take a split badly, or if she does, does so without so much as a peep. A Class

Act is the silhouette disappearing into the night that you will no doubt remember – but will never talk to again.

A Class Act will spend a lot of time alone, drinking spirits. A Class Act will never emerge from a local church in a shower of petals. A Class Act will never be a mummy, yummy or otherwise.

A Class Act will never have a husband who visits prostitutes.

Forget I mentioned it.

jeudi, le 25 mars

N and I had breakfast at a greasy spoon. He's not been sleeping well and it shows. Someone we know started a rumour last week that the clocks went forward before Mothering Sunday instead of this weekend, and it threw him off. He's not had a night's rest since.

He's heard things about me. Stories are getting around. Nothing earth-shattering, just a comment or two coming back round to him. Have I mentioned N appears to be the secret hub of all knowledge in London?

There's envy involved, usually the engine behind the worst, most damaging rumours. Other things. I hate this *Sturm und Drang*. Someone I slept with who asked me to keep it secret – I didn't even write about it – turned around and told, oh, about half of the city. A few personal things. That I don't mind. It's the asking for privacy, then blatantly stripping it off, that I care about. Poor etiquette in a lover.

'Maybe I should say something to him about it,' I said.

'Not a good idea,' N advised. He pointed out that this man is young and feckless, and I would be better off giving him a pat on the head than the slap he so clearly deserves. 'The onus is on him now. He's the one who's going to feel uncomfortable when he sees either of us.'

'Maybe I should start rumours of my own.'

'Keep your own counsel. Better in the long run.'

'Ah, bollocks, that reminds me . . .'

'What?'

'On his way out the door, he asked me if it was true I'd had a threesome with you and someone else.'

'What did you say?'

'Yes.'

He cringed. 'Well, I don't care, and you obviously don't, and I don't think the other girl does either. But I wonder why he was interested in a piece of trivia about my private life as he's getting out of your bed?' N scratched at his stubble. 'One too many one-night stands,' he said. 'Be careful what you say about someone else's sex life.'

I shrugged. I drank the very strong, very fresh coffee. He asked if I'd seen the car outside my house again. I have. He asked if I needed anything. I said I didn't.

'Get out if you can,' he said.

'The business, the house or the ex-boyfriend?' I asked.

'All three,' he said. 'I don't know what you're planning, but whatever it is, have a spare rabbit hole.'

The café that had been crowded when we sat down was now almost empty of people. He tipped the waitress and drove me home. His left hand rested on my knee the whole journey.

'Just be careful,' he said.

I waved him off and went upstairs.

samedi, le 27 mars

For all of the good advice I have received over the years, no one has ever opined on what may be the greatest challenge of my working life: how to deal with a non-standard-issue cock.

Penises can be strange for many reasons. They might have an unusual length-to-width ratio, or curve in a funny way, or remind you of your father's brother's penchant for turtleneck jumpers. In fact, there are probably more strange than unstrange ones. This gives the old man quite a scope for personality.

For the most part the differences can be stacked in the 'odd, but not distractingly so' or the 'odd, but not medically abnormal' bins. And when a member confounds these classifications I never know what to say.

Treat the matter lightly? As in a saucy purr of 'My, what unusual tackle you have'. Show a modicum of medical interest and ask, 'Have you ever been to a doctor about that?' Recoil in horror? Ask advice on how he would like it handled? Or would sir prefer I didn't comment at all?

I had the pleasure of meeting a customer with a most normal penis. Normal in every detectable way. It was his foreskin that was unusual. Instead of parting at the top, so the glans could nudge through, this gentleman's sheath opened at the side.

At the side. Of his penis. Halfway down the shaft. An aperture so small to wedge his cock through. Meaning that he was hooded at all times, even when aroused.

I smiled. Looked at it, looked at him. Didn't say anything. He didn't offer advice. Should I attend to the head (completely covered) or the opening (drooling with pre-come, but several inches back)? He was older than me, divorced, so obviously someone had come across this anomaly before. Was it uncomfortable when he was hard? I wondered. Would he have problems with certain positions? Would this affect the condom? Would it be insulting to ask?

I lavished attention on both the head and the opening, being careful not to curl my hand round the shaft too tightly. When we progressed to intercourse, I pinched the tip of the condom as I put it on to collect the semen, wondering if it mattered. He took me from behind, but didn't say if there was a reason above personal preference. He removed the condom himself afterwards. I never did have a proper look at the result.

mardi, le 30 mars

The client leaned over me, pulling at his member furiously. 'I'm going to come on your face,' he said. It was the sixth time in ten minutes he'd said it, growling, as if trying to convince himself.

That was all: 'I'm going to come on your face.' No instructions for me, though I played with my breasts and nipples, sucked my own fingers after touching myself, hoping that would help. All that I had known before the appointment were the details of the meeting and a request to wear a lot of make-up.

My effort didn't seem to help. He was looking at the wall, not at me. A few times his frantic hand slowed, and he dipped down to my lips. He was going soft and I sucked him hard again. He never looked down, not once. Then the masturbation would start again. And the mantra: 'I'm going to come on your face.' I writhed on the sheets and groaned.

No reaction. I bent my head forward and licked his inner thigh. Again, no reaction.

Half an hour later, he still hadn't finished. I murmured and probed, wandering fingers, gentle questions. But it seemed he wanted nothing from me, save to be the canvas he painted. It made me feel like unturned clay must, wanting to form into something, some fantasy, but not being allowed. His shoulders lumped and he fell, sweaty, into my chest. 'I'm sorry, honey, it ain't gonna happen,' he said, as if it had been my idea all along.

Avril

jeudi, le 1 avril

I've been eyeing up someone at the gym for the last few months.

This is not a habit, really. Gyms are for exercising, perhaps a bit of socialising, but the widespread idea of workouts as meat markets is gruesome by any standard. On the upside, if you do meet someone in an atmosphere of lycra-clad, endorphin-soaked madness, you can rest easy that he has seen you at your worst, covered in sweat and hair undone, and found you attractive.

On the other hand, I wouldn't want to date anyone who regularly saw me at my worst.

At the start of the year, though, one man in particular caught my eye. Shy smile, soft-looking hair, impressively muscled build. I made enquiries. Gleaned his name.

'Gay,' barked N, who is not gay himself but claims to have the most finely attuned straight-man gaydar in the south of England. It's rubbish, but I dare not say. 'Without doubt.'

'I don't think so,' I sighed, trying not to stare, as the object of our conversation worked his way around the free weights.

'Ten pence bet says he is.'

Them's, as they say, fightin' words. 'You're on.'

vendredi, le 2 avril

Conversations with clients are not exactly what one might call 'normal', but still have their rigid conventions. It's nice to know where someone is from, a general outline of what he does. Most of the men are business travellers or not frequent consumers of sex services. A little idle chatter puts both parties at ease.

There's a fine line between curiosity and nosiness, and some lines of interrogation are simply off limits. These include questions about one's parents, location of one's house (as I only do outcalls), vehicle registration number . . .

On the other hand, the fact that you are unlikely to meet again means a customer can ask the sort of questions that would get anyone else a rapid introduction to the pavement. Context is everything.

Example one: 'Do you think you'll have children?'
I like children well enough. I especially like them when they go back to their parents. Sometimes – sometimes – I am struck by the charm of a precocious *bébé* and think rearing young 'uns would be a good idea. And if someone could take charge of children between the ages of eleven and sixteen, it would sweeten the deal immensely.

Clients are perhaps the only people to whom I will give an honest answer. The ambivalence I feel towards a future family, the uncertainty whether this world is a suitable place to chain oneself to another being or beings, frankly, troubles me. As many of them are married and have children, they appreciate this. Occasionally they offer advice.

Some adore their children and family life. Some are . . . well, they're out paying for sex, aren't they?

My parents are sometimes fool enough to ask after my future plans for babymaking and receive the stock answer: 'I simply haven't met the right man.' Any paramour who dares let this query pass his lips is on a one-way trip to speed dating and singleton hell.

Example two: Questions about films, books and music.
Potential mates receive an honest answer. My taste in

126

cultural minutiae might be dodgy, but it is my own, and anyone hoping to merge his material possessions with mine will have to live with a collection of music that could best be described by the term 'selective appeal'.

In a client situation, I try to discern what his taste might be and stray not too far off the beaten mainstream. Trying to cover the finer points of free jazz while administering a soapy titwank is possibly straining the privileges of my position.

Example three: 'How many people have you been to bed with?'

No client has ever asked. Sometimes they ask how long I have been working, but whether they attempt to deduce the number of my past lovers based on the answer is unknown. Given that my working practices have been sometimes sporadic, it's unlikely they would reach an accurate total.

Non-clients always ask. If I think the man has a good sense of humour, I tell him a number that is roughly accurate. Or at least within the same order of magnitude. I don't know the real answer myself. For geeky men with extremely good senses of humour, I offer the total in scientific notation or hexadecimal. If he does not have a sense of humour, I try to change the subject or turn the question back on him.

Why does it matter? Quantity is no guarantee of quality. Frequency definitely isn't. But a low total is not indicative of personality either. Men – and women – who have been shocked by my answer were often heard to mumble, 'But you look such a *nice* girl!'

I am nice. Very nice indeed.

At the age of seventeen someone split with me because he was my third partner and this was an unacceptably high number to him. The next man, number four, claimed the number of my previous lovers was unacceptably low. There's no pleasing some people.

The last time I had a lover with more former partners (that I knew of) was at the age of nineteen.

Example four: 'We only have a quarter of an hour. May I come in your mouth?'
In the normal situation, this might meet with a grimace at best and a restraint order at worst. At work, though, typical responses range from 'Go on then!' to 'Okay, but I would rather you came on my face.'

lundi, le 5 avril

I stood by the paper towel dispenser, blotting sweat off my neck until the Ten Pence Bet came into view. He was setting up a bench-press-cum-torture device. When he turned away to slide a weight off the rack, I slid in behind him.

'Work in sets with you?' Gym-speak for asking if you can alternate on the weights. Never regarded as an overt come-on.

It was a ludicrous request, of course, I couldn't have spotted the weight he could probably lift with his little toe. 'You lifting?' he asked. Soft voice, nice.

'Maybe the bar plus twenty,' I said. Damn, I actually sound as though I know what I'm talking about.

He nodded. We went through three sets each. I stood on the opposite side of the bar as he pressed out his reps, watching the long-sleeved shirt strain at his chest. On my sets I tried hard to look cool and serious, not the giggling, feeble creature I play when N's in the gym. We finished on the bench and moved off to other sides of the gym. Play it cool, girl, I thought. Don't follow him around the room.

Half an hour later I walked through to the aerobic area. He was on a rowing machine, had been for a few minutes –

the sweat was just starting to trickle past his hairline. I sat on one a few seats away and strapped my feet in.

'Hard workout day for you, then?' he asked.

I smiled. 'Just warming down.' I rowed through five minutes, watching his reflection surreptitiously in the glass opposite us. His sweat was really starting to pour. He had taken off the long-sleeved top. I finished and walked out the door behind him, caught a glance of his back squeezing together at the end of each stroke, the droplets sliding down the crevice of his spine.

I was alone in the hall leading to the changing rooms. Wait a few minutes, I thought. He'll come out and you can say something.

Tart.

What would I say, anyway? 'Oh, to be the person who gets to lick that sweat off you,' then walk away? The door cracked. I didn't wait to see who it was. I ducked in the Ladies faster than a greased goose.

mercredi, le 7 avril

'Guess what?' N smirked.

'What?' I was in no mood for guessing games.

'I've been talking to your little friend,' he said.

'Which little friend?' N meant Ten Pence Bet. 'So what do you know?' I asked.

'He's a student.'

'Loads of people are students these days. Your point?'

'He's *eighteen*.'

Oh no, you must be joking. No one looks like that at eighteen. 'You're having me on.'

'First year at university, engineering something.'

I frowned. I thought of Ten Pence Bet, how smooth and unlined his face was. And how polite. Bells started going off in my head: good-looking men don't stay nice for long. 'Figures. There ought to be a law.' I sighed. 'They shouldn't build teenagers to adult spec. It's just not fair.'

samedi, le 10 avril

'Have fun last night?' N asked. We were at the gym.

'Okay,' I said. Yesterday was A3's birthday. I wasn't going to go because I was afraid of the Boy turning up. When I had told N this, he said I'd be silly to let that stop me. So I fretted about what to wear, flirted with the idea of not going, then went anyway.

N started warming up on the treadmill. 'Was your ex there?'

'He was.' The Boy turned up late, before the birthday party left the bar and went on to the club. I was talking to A3, we were eyeing up various people in the room and rating them on shaggability. 'Guy in the red shirt?' 'Only if drunk.' 'Him or you?' 'Both.'

Then A3, who was facing the door, caught sight of the Boy. 'Bloke in the blue-checked shirt?' he asked.

I turned round, saw who it was and shuddered involuntarily. 'Fuck off.'

'Did he say anything?' N upped his speed.

'No, he kept a good distance.' Not knowing whether or not the Boy would be there was by far the worst part of the evening. I found it difficult to keep up conversation with anyone; my eyes were scanning the room for him constantly. If I saw someone who resembled him, my mouth went dry and my words jumbled. But once I knew he was there, I relaxed.

The Boy didn't look at me, I didn't look at him. He hovered around the fringes of the large group, talking to people we knew.

N and I were both at a slow run. Sweat started to prickle my collarbone. 'Did you pull?' he asked.

'Not really,' I said. 'There was one fellow in the bar, who came up out of nowhere. He pulled my hair hard and bit me on the neck, then walked away.'

'Really? What did you do?'

'Nothing.' But my knees had gone to jelly. The stranger had held my hair for a long moment, staring at me. I stared back. He pulled harder. Our gaze didn't break. I knew all my friends were watching. Fuck them. Then the man who bit me walked back to his friends. He didn't say anything.

N ran on for a bit. 'Maybe he was doing it for a bet. So how late were you out?'

'Late late.' We went on to a club. I was talking to a friend of A3's from home, a very pretty short girl with spiky hair. I kind of fancied her and was aware that the Boy (whose voice I could hear behind me) was probably watching. We queued and went inside. The music was old-school. I couldn't stop dancing. The Boy stayed on the edge of the crowd.

N jumped off the treadmill and we went to stretch. 'And that was it? You danced for a while and went home?'

'No – at least four men tried to chat me up.'

'Get anyone's number?' N winced, as he tried to urge more length out of his hamstrings.

'Just one worth noticing. A trolley dolly from BA.'

'Male or female?'

'Male.'

The Boy stuck around for a long time, but even he was gone by 3 am. There was still a hard core of us buying round after round in honour of the birthday boy. The flight steward was more persistent than the other men who'd come up during the night, and gave me his card. I waved him goodbye as we staggered out to find the night buses.

'Weights?' N said.

'Go on, then.'

dimanche, le 11 avril

I retrieved my bag and brought out a box of condoms. He held the member in front of my face while I tore the corner of the wrapper open. I held the shaft and balanced the unrolled rubber on the tip of the cock.

'Do you have to do that?' the client asked.

'Afraid I must,' I sighed. 'Minimises the risks involved.'

'I trust you,' he said.

'That's very kind,' I said, and smiled. 'Trouble is, I don't know where this thing,' and I gestured at the instrument he brandished before me, 'has been.'

'Oh,' he said, and was quiet a moment. 'It's just that I really don't like the smell those things leave on it.'

I thought. 'I could give it a good hot water and soap scrub in the bathroom instead of using a condom,' I offered. 'Would that do?' Against my policy, but it was low risk for him and almost none for me.

He sighed in relief. It was a big fleshy black dildo – his own cock stayed well zipped up. I took the dildo over to the sink, being careful to wash all the soap off carefully so he wouldn't taste any when he sucked my juices off it later.

lundi, le 12 avril

Went to a club. Saw Angel, who was wearing a skirt that was more of a glorified belt. The girl just has unbelievable legs. The music was loud; we didn't speak, I wouldn't have known what to say to her anyway. Danced together and jumped and sang along when the DJ spun The Jam's 'That's Entertainment'. Looked at the boys who were watching us – realised none of them were old enough to know the tune. They probably weren't even born then. I smiled evilly.

I picked out one young man, a tall, thin and freckled lad, who looked like a stretched out version of the Boy. Led him back towards the toilets where we snogged, pulled up his dark green shirt, licked his nipples. 'Do you live close to here?' he asked, surprised. I shook my head no, asked if he did. He didn't. I pushed out the back exit and we fucked on the steps by the bins.

mardi, le 13 avril

It's widely circulated and well known that You Get What You Pay For. I don't agree. Some things come for free and some at a cost, but one isn't better than the other.

There are downsides to unpaid casual sex, of course. Aren't there always? By engaging in truly random, one-night attachments, you open yourself up to stalking and all manner of sexually transmitted ills. For some reason, we as a nation have collectively decided that a drunken snog in a crowded club is an acceptable overture to everlasting love. It isn't.

The men I have encountered in my working life can be characterised by a single feature – timidity. Whether it's requesting watersports or going through the back door, punters seem uncomfortable with demanding what they, as paying customers, are entitled to. If one thing can be predicted it's that the more exotic the request, the more times he will ring the manager pre-appointment to discuss it. One-night men, on the other hand, tend to just take.

Don't get me wrong. I find a client's sometime inability to express his inner desires charming. Sweet, even. But it's amusing when I ask what a man would like to do, and he replies, 'Whatever you want to do.'

You mean, go home and watch television while sipping hot chocolate in my pyjamas? I think he would feel my fee was somehow less than justified. But still better is the mumbled, 'Oh, you know, the usual.'

No, I don't know. For you the usual might be open-air rope bondage with a ring of pony girls.

Your typical club-stud, on the other hand, has a take-no-prisoners approach to his needs that I find refreshing. You're there, he's there, the DJ is playing 'Carmina Burana', which is definitely the signal to collect your coat and it's a foregone conclusion what will happen next. And to be honest, I don't pick up random men because I want a love match. Nothing less than a full cervical bruising will do, and I am rarely disappointed.

Or as N puts it, when you know you're not going to see her again anyway, why not push the boundaries?

Who else but a non-paying stranger would insist that he would only do the deed if my womanhood was partially lined with ice chips first? Who else would try – unsuccessfully – to fist me while driving (NB: not ideal in city traffic)? No client would dare, for fear I would whip out a calculator and start totting up the additional cost of this service.

There's a lot of talk in escort circles of Girlfriend Experience (GFE). That's because it's by far the most requested thing we offer. I have been cuddled to within an inch of my life by well-meaning chaps whose only previous acquaintance with me was via a website. I've sipped red wine and watched telly with single gents until the taxi beeped its horn outside. And no pick-up, to my recollection, has ever stretched out on the counterpane and told me stories of his childhood in Africa.

The last man before the boy at the club, who followed me home on a random, stayed exactly ninety minutes. We did the deed, considered doing it again, then he fretted about his ex, dressed and left. I was somewhat offended that he turned down the offer of a cup of tea. Still, I went to bed having gotten what I wanted, which was a good and forceful banging.

Clients are another species altogether. They have invited me on holiday, asked my opinion on the possibility of extra-terrestrial life, and cleaned my shoes while waxing poetic on the proportions of my profile. On the other hand, the most upholstered compliment I ever received from a pick-up was 'Coffee? A clean towel? This is great – staying at your place is like being in a hotel.'

Ah, no. I've been in plenty of hotels. And the men aren't paying for fluffy towels.

jeudi, le 15 avril

The client was a re-visit. He was in law enforcement, and the first time out he'd taken me to a semi-formal work event. From the ratio of nubile cuties to paunchy detectives, I may not have been the only paid girl there. Or perhaps the Met's PR efforts are paying off in unexpected ways. I had been seated next to my date, while one of his colleagues, a Scottish youth, looked down the front of my top.

This time the customer met me at his flat and asked a lot of questions. This can be dicey: are they just curious or potential stalkers? As they say, the truth is like the sun, its benefit is entirely dependent on our distance from it.

I have a manufactured history that is mostly, but not completely, true. Minor but plausible differences in home-town, university, degree. Other questions are more simple.

'Have you ever dominated?'

'Honey, that was how I started in the business.' When I was a student and worked briefly as a domme, it was some-thing I didn't especially enjoy and didn't want to do again. Largely because getting out of character was difficult for me. But maybe being more of a submissive in my private life led to some empathy for those who like to be dominated, because I've ended up doing it more than a few times.

'Really?' The client nodded and pursed his lips. 'Really.'

He was tall, well over six feet. Thick-framed and strong. Probably mid-forties. Bald. And single, which seems, from what I've seen, as likely in clients as not. 'I find that . . . fascinating.'

What is it about men who know seven ways to kill you with their bare hands but just want to be pussycats in the bedroom?

'Have you ever let someone take control?' I asked. He was sat in a stuffy chair, and I was curled up at his feet drinking Shiraz and stroking the back of his legs.

'I always wanted to, but—'

'Sweetie,' I said, and reached up to stroke his chin, 'don't be shy. That's what I'm here for.'

A first-time submissive is usually easy to handle and eager to please. It takes months before they start trying deviously to control the action from below. I asked if he would let me tie him up. He said yes, what with? I wasn't prepared, so I asked for a handful of ties. He led me upstairs to the bedroom and produced them.

I told him to undress. He did, as I sat cross-legged on the bed. I ordered him onto the bed. He hesitated for a moment. 'Get down, face up, legs and arms straight,' I said abruptly. He did. I pulled my skirt up and crawled over him, heels still on. Straddling his chest, I tied his hands to the bed. At the foot of the bed there was nothing handy, so I looped the ends of the ties round the wheels of the bed frame and hoped they would hold. I could feel him craning his neck, trying to get his mouth closer to my bottom. 'Lie back,' I barked. 'If I want you to touch me, you'll know it.'

It was standard SM, nothing challenging. Tease and (extremely) light torture. But I did end up with the cleanest shoes outside of a Russell & Bromley.

Coffee and N and A1 for no better reason than to dissect my love life. Again. 'So what happened to that trolley dolly?' N asked, sipping an Americano.

'Could have been something. But he called it off, by phone, this weekend,' I reported. It was annoying. Admittedly, he was probably more often in the air than in town, but this should be no barrier. In my opinion some of the best relationships involve not seeing each other.

'Did he have a reason?' N asked.

'Too busy with work. Couldn't be bothered.'

'Did he actually say that second bit?' N looked puzzled.

'No, I'm paraphrasing.' It is probably too great a leap of faith to believe a man would be so guileless as to say that he was too busy with work and for that actually to be the case.

A1 shrugged. 'Well, here's hoping he realises what he's missing.'

'Doubtful. We never got past snogging.' Three dates, lots of conversation, a torrent of email. Resulting in nothing more than a couple of awkward hugs and a bit of tongue-trying. Wary of what happened the last few times, I didn't think it right to push him too fast. But whatever his buttons were, I clearly was not pressing them.

'Really?' spluttered N. 'I would have at least slept with you first.'

'Cheers, darling,' I said, blowing him an ironic kiss.

'I have a friend,' A1 ventured. 'A bit on the short side, though—'

'Is that a euphemism? I've already seen your little friend, thanks,' I said, glancing at the crotch of his jeans.

'Ouch,' A1 said, and turned to N. 'She's never this sharp when she has a regular shag.'

N and I went out to a club he worked at a few years ago. They were playing the usual pop trash, but the doorman knew us and waved us through.

It was packed with the usual bodies. A few on the floor, shaking their money makers, more at the bar looking every-one over. A meat market but not unfriendly for it. I leaned on a white leather sofa and looked round. A familiar face in a small clutch of men: Ten Pence Bet. I elbowed N.

'Told you,' he said. Or would have said, but I couldn't hear him over the music. Mouthed. I knew what he meant. I shrugged. Being with other men is not ipso facto gay. And the bet stood, regardless.

I saw Ten Pence Bet detach from his group and spin out in the direction of the bar. Alone. Good, because I didn't think a confrontation would work in front of a crowd. I followed him. Tapped him on the shoulder.

'Yes?' He turned around, saw me, smiled.

'This is going to sound odd,' I said apologetically. 'But I win a ten pence bet if you're not gay.'

'Pardon?' The music in the club was loud; he bent his head very close to mine.

'I said I win a ten pence bet if you're not gay.'

'Who's the bet with?' he asked.

'I really mustn't say. Does it matter?'

He smiled. Thought a bit. Leaned forward and kissed me. His lips were soft, slightly moist, lingered a moment. 'You win,' he said. We walked away in opposite directions.

I found N, leaned heavily on his arm. 'I win,' I shouted in his ear. 'Do you hate me?'

'I'll prove you wrong,' he said, digging in his pockets.

'Yes, well,' I smirked. 'Until then, hand over the coin.'

dimanche, le 25 avril

We took a holiday every year when I was young. Never anywhere too exotic, and never with my father. He claimed exhaustion from his business until he retired and couldn't use the excuse any longer. By the last year of school, my best friend was one of my male cousins. We have the same colouring, the same small sharp features and freckles. People think we are twins. We still acted like children, taunting and hitting each other. But that year there had been a new undercurrent of tension: we started to watch one another cautiously for signs that one of us knew something the other didn't.

So, that year, our mothers took all the kids on holiday together. We drove to Brighton; I'd never been so far south. And with six of us in the car, it was cramped. The journey felt a lot longer than it must have been. My mother's sister, my cousin's mother, brought a bag of cassette tapes to keep us entertained. Her taste in music was nowhere as antique as Mum's. We knew all the lyrics to her tapes, and we sang loudly, car windows down. It was a sunny day. We thought the holiday would be perfect.

When we got there, the beach was horrible, wet and windy. There was nothing to do for three days. The mothers stayed in and watched telly; we kids went out looking for an amusement arcade. We spent all of our money on candy floss, penny arcades and chips.

I remember coming back to the hotel one day; the mothers were still watching television. My cousin was in the bathroom, singing, obviously unaware that everyone outside could hear him. He was singing a Madonna song, and the frankly sexual lyrics disturbed me. Without meaning to, I imagined him imitating the dancers in the video.

Then I realised only that morning I was in the shower too;

while everyone sat inside poring over the papers, I was singing The Divinyls' 'I Touch Myself'.

jeudi, le 29 avril

So I'm sixteen, or close to it. One day my cousin and I are at a swimming pool, treading water by the ladder at the deep end. He has been asking about some girls I know. I am vaguely dismayed that his taste in women is running to the obvious – tall blondes and dark-haired girls with chests everyone stares at. Plenty of the boys have received favours from these girls, but they wouldn't look at my cousin or his geeky friends twice, and he knows it.

Our friendship is becoming uneasy. Because we are related, we can and do share everything. Because of our age, attraction is possible, but obviously off-limits. When the subject of sex does come up, being shy and clever as we are, we couch it in the most neutral terms possible.

'If I wasn't your cousin, and didn't know you, I'd probably be attracted to you.'

'Me too. If I wasn't your cousin. And didn't know you.'

And we know what we mean. Then an awkward silence, usually followed by a simulated farting noise to bring things back to the mundane. These conversations foretell the sort of relationships I will have with men through university, a parade of pale, gentle boys who are too shy to admit their desire until they are drunk. A lot like the few people I dated at school, really, but with better access to alcohol. Sometimes my cousin's friends express an interest in me; he fends them off with protestations of my tomboyishness ('She would break you in half if she heard that') or maturity ('She wouldn't look twice at a child like you'). I was terribly mature. I'd even tossed a boy off in a cinema.

There are other things as well. We don't know it for a year

140

yet, but I'll be going to university and my cousin won't. His A levels were good, and he had offers, but he didn't follow through and his mother didn't press. He wants to be a Royal Marine or a mechanic. I think he's crazy. A decade later he ends up working prep in a commercial kitchen.

I pull myself up the side of the pool and scramble out in the direction of our towels, grab them both, walk back to the water.

'Hey,' he says, louder than necessary, 'you're walking differently. Does that mean you're not a virgin any more?'

'Yes,' I say, straight-faced. He starts to get out of the pool, and I throw his towel in the water. This is how he knows I care about him.

He's not sure whether I'm kidding or not, and doesn't press for details. I prepare a fake story anyway, just in case. When his mum comes to collect us, we both sit in the back of the car, and he just whispers names.

'Marc?'

'No.' Marc was in my year, and taller than the rest of the boys. He also spits when he speaks without realising it and follows me around too often.

'Justin?'

'No.' I have a crush on Justin; my cousin is the only person I've ever told. I hope he doesn't tell anyone else. Before leaving for university I will tell Justin all this in a letter, and he will never speak to me again.

He senses my discomfort. 'Eric. Has to be.'

The joke candidate. 'No way!' I say, but refrain from giving him a nipple-twister, because to do so would compromise the new air of maturity this lie has conferred.

It doesn't matter much anyway. Within a month it happens for real, with my cousin's best friend. While I flinched, I didn't make a noise. And so far as I can tell my gait was no different the day after than it was the day before.

vendredi, le 30 avril

I fly to Italy to meet friends. The plane is small and crowded, and the heavily made-up flight attendant screams at a child who keeps running up and down the aisle, even when the plane is taking off and landing. It's not clear to whom he belongs; his parents are making no effort to stop him.

The first thing I do after setting my bags down in the cool tile hallway is to check email. And there's a small surprise, a message from Dr C in San Diego, who must have gleaned my email address from A2. It's a short but affectionate note dating from two days previously. I reply with an equally short and cheerful message.

Mai

dimanche, le 2 mai

I went to the beach with a small group. There was me and one other girl; the boys sat slightly separate from us on the pebble shore as everyone stripped down and tanned on their towels.

The other girl is not a close acquaintance. A few days ago we were talking, and she asked my age.

'Twenty-five,' I said, knocking a couple of years off. She is nineteen at most.

'Wow!' she said, looking genuinely surprised. 'I never would have guessed.' I shrugged. When I was younger, everyone thought I was far older; now, the situation is reversing itself. 'You know, you don't have to tell people your age,' she said helpfully. 'You could probably say you were twenty and people would believe you.'

Only if said people were teenagers. Bless her, though.

I was reading. One boy, a blond, was listening to music and singing along. You couldn't help but smile. Some of the other boys threw a Frisbee and splashed in the shallow water.

The other girl, who was flipping through a magazine, turned towards me. 'Are my sunglasses very dark?' she asked under her breath.

'Yes, they're quite dark,' I said.

'So if I was looking somewhere, you couldn't see my eyes, right?' she asked.

'I couldn't, no.'

'Good,' she said, and turned away again, facing the boys.

Gazing, I noticed, in the direction of a particular young man. Her own boyfriend had stayed at home.

lundi, le 3 mai

The first girl I ever slept with was a friend's girlfriend.

One of my close mates at university was a shortish, thinnish, good-looking ginger boy who loved Dr Who and was a complete sex bomb with the ladies. I can't explain why. He just was, and we loved him.

We called him the Jew Boy with the Moves, because this guy could cut up your brother's bar mitzvah party dance floor like a hot knife through butter. He was all slinky hips and sultry looks and by Jove, I had an almighty crush on him. I'd never had a go, though in the first year he made his way through every single one of the women in our group. It just seemed a boundary destined never to be crossed.

Eventually he settled down with one girl. And I couldn't resent losing out because Jessica was an über-desirable petite vixen with caramel-coloured shoulders and dark blonde hair that was always in perfect curls.

One night JB and Jessica invited me and my then-boyfriend to a club. It was a place I didn't know in a part of town I didn't go to. I didn't know what to wear, and met the other three at a pub in jeans, flip flops and a thin black satin shirt, no bra. Jessica and I stood in the middle of the room while the men fetched our drinks, and I was suddenly aware that everyone was looking at us.

We sank pints and moved on to our destination, a gay club. My first. It was a mixed crowd, being a Saturday night in a medium-sized city where the staff couldn't be too picky with the door policy. There were boy couples and girl couples, gangs of students, old single boys looking hangdog at the bar and men dressed like women dressing like men's fantasies of women. I didn't know where to look. My boyfriend, alas, did – at his feet. All night.

The music was not good, but it was frantic and loud. JB and Jessica spun me out on the dance floor. They were an incredible couple to watch. Just too tiny and cool for words. Her slightly bony shoulders wriggled suggestively, her back was bare in a sleeveless, tie-on shirt. I'd been attracted to girls before, but never felt so free just to stare at one. It wasn't out of place here.

JB took me to one side. 'You know, she wants you,' he said. Was he kidding? This wee goddess? But as soon as he said it, I knew it was true, and it was like a switch had been flipped. I could imagine taking her to the toilets, tonguing her as she laughed and sat atop the cistern. I could imagine putting things in her, my fingers, the end of a beer bottle.

'She's your girlfriend,' I said, aware as the words came out how whiny and awful they sounded.

He shrugged. He said he'd take care of my boyfriend. He said he did this for her a lot – picked up girls for her.

JB drove us all home. My boyfriend lived closest, thank goodness. Then we went around Jessica's house. Her parents were away somewhere, or asleep, or didn't care, I never knew. She held my hand and we walked through her door, plain as anything. Her boyfriend waited until she waved back to him from the doorway, then drove away. Her neck was the most slender, tenderest I'd ever seen. Her lips were softer than any I'd ever kissed.

jeudi, le 6 mai

We sailed on to Croatia and I bought a paper for the first time in a fortnight. They are full of disturbing images, the sort that lead one to think about politics, war and the politics of war, and how these acts have always happened except we could never see them before. How righteous indignation and backlash sometimes seem products of ignorance because who could not have guessed this would happen? Did we really need pictures in order to know?

And you think, perhaps, there is one guarantee in life (that it ends) and one fairly safe bet as well (that it is painful) and freedom and property are illusions that can only exist in the mind. And that more clever people have already thought these thoughts and discarded them and why don't I stop this rubbish philosophising already?

I don't mean to make light of these events, but I'm hoping for a little pick-up in the terror-sex department at work when I get home. It would do me the world of good.

vendredi, le 7 mai

It's a chalk-bright afternoon and I've been walking and listening to music all day for the last few days. This helps – with headphones on, everyone assumes you can't hear them, so no one speaks to you. This is good. I don't understand the language very well. When I want to hear the sounds around me, I switch the player off but leave the headphones on. I smile a lot. People smile back. Are people happier everywhere else in the world? Sure seems so.

But I know it's not the truth. I was in a bar, talking to a man my age. He'd been through three wars before he was twenty-one.

'Why are men so horrible to each other?' I asked.

'In my experience all people are horrible. We don't know how else to be.' He smiled at my guidebook. It was a smile that said, 'Where do you want to go? You know you won't find it in there.' Not that I've used it very much anyway; I like to choose a direction and keep going. In this way I found the Jewish quarter, decimated and abandoned forever ago, like a forgotten film set. His smile, it was so understanding, so accepting, I could feel the waves of goodwill just pouring off him, mixed with a little pity for me.

That, or he may have just been trying to pick me up. We girls have an absolutely appalling reputation abroad. Was there a pamphlet distributed to men in foreign countries saying that the small islanders are simply gagging for it?

(I mean, I *am*, but you, I'm on holiday, creep. So lay off.)

samedi, le 8 mai

Holiday sex is always the best sex. I've had it everywhere – Poole, Blackpool, swimming pools.

Someone else makes the bed afterwards, empties the bin of spent condoms, even picks up your smelly towels from the floor. If the people below are kept up all night with the noises, odds are either they won't know which people were responsible, or they'll be away the next morning anyway, or you can get away with a mild blush and a sheepish giggle because you're on holiday, and only the sourest of pusses could deny anyone a vigorous bit of holiday exercise.

A1 always took me to the beach when my spirits were flagging. He never enjoyed the experience – sand gets everywhere, which is anathema to a man as fastidious as he is, and he burns easily, so most of the outing would be spent reapplying sun cream to the parts of his back he couldn't reach. One time we went away he forgot to put sunblock on his feet and they burned. For the entire week afterwards he couldn't wear socks or shoes.

But he did it for me, so I could recharge my batteries, he always said. And because he knew he'd be rewarded with an almighty screw in whatever bed and breakfast we were staying in that evening.

A2 loved the act of getting to his destination better than

the holiday itself. He would drive and drive, and we would cover the entire country in a week, making stops wherever the spirit took us. If we spent the night in the Highlands, you could almost lay money on the fact that within twenty-four hours we'd be holed up in a shabby guesthouse in Devon. We stopped and posed by abandoned buildings, funny road signs and large trees. We laid blankets in stands of trees and had sex as the mosquitoes attacked his backside. I sucked him off in bank holiday traffic going north.

A3 and I took a trip together once to look at caves. In the complete dark of underground, in the silence in the middle of the earth, he held my hand for the first time. It is difficult to think of a time before or since when I've been so thrilled.

A4 and I went on a beach holiday almost the first week we met. His housemate's girlfriend wanted cockles. We didn't buy any, but we went to three beaches looking for someone selling them. The third beach was perfect, sandy and deserted. The wind was coming up and the heat had gone from the day. The water stretched for miles and came in strong waves. A4 stripped down to his bathing shorts – I was in awe of his beauty then, and couldn't stop staring at his body. He dived into the surf and flopped around happily. I walked out to the water's edge and put a foot in. It was freezing! I jumped back.

'Are you mad?' I yelled out to his bobbing head.

'It's bracing!' he yelled back, and even at that distance I could hear his teeth chattering. I laughed and laughed. On the way home, we went past endless farms and looked at the pigs rooting in the last light of the day. A DJ on the radio was playing old songs, swing jazz, and we listened in happy silence. Sometimes to make me laugh he'd say, 'Bracing!'

But the best holiday with him, and we went on many together, was camping. We set up a large tent in the woods next to a cold water spring and stayed several days. The water was icy in the very hot summer and we bathed naked.

A giant dead tree slanted out of the water and, balancing on that, he had me over and over. It felt so wonderfully primal.

Holiday sex is the best. No one to answer to, no work, no neighbours. And if you're lucky, no phone reception. Pure sensation. It's probably what the clients at work are after.

mardi, le 11 mai

Only just awake enough to check email when I finally arrived home. A note from Dr C, who is visiting the UK soon and wants to see me. Must sleep on it, as if I had a choice.

dimanche, le 16 mai

A few days ago, I had a missed call from the agency and a text from the manager, confirming a client at half nine.

I rang her back. 'Terribly sorry, you'll have to cancel, I'm still away.'

'Ah, right, darling. You see, this man, he is so nice—'

'No – I'm actually away. Out of the country. I'm not back until late Monday.' As I had told her, in several calls and emails during the last few weeks.

'Are you certain? Because he asked specifically for you.'

Am I certain I'm not home? Yes, fairly sure of that. Unless north London has suddenly turned into a sunny seaside locale full of flowering plants. It could happen. 'I'm afraid so.'

'Can I ask him if he would be willing to book you for tomorrow instead?'

Lady, are you deaf? 'I can't do tomorrow. I'm not back until Monday.'

She sighed. For the love of . . . it's not as if the man wants to marry me. Someone else from the agency would probably do just as well. I said so, as gently as possible. 'I think perhaps you should take this job less casually,' she said tartly and hung up. Ten minutes later a text came through: 'Lost booking.'

I texted her today, but have not heard back.

mercredi, le 19 mai

There is one client with my real name and phone number. He rang to ask why I wasn't seeing anyone. Being a regular, after all, shouldn't he be the first to know if I was off the market?

'I'm not,' I said. 'Have you heard otherwise?'

He said he'd rung a couple of weeks ago and the manager said I was on holiday. Ah, yes, that's because I was, I apologised. Then I rang yesterday, he said. And she said you were away indefinitely and offered me someone else.

Had I been not-so-subtly dropped? I checked the website and the profile's still there, though rather lower in the listing than before. No matter. He offered to book with me privately for next week. I said I'd think about it.

dimanche, le 23 mai

The manager and I are still at apparent loggerheads. She hasn't rung, and I haven't tried to ring her. While I appreciate this sort of treatment may be a mainstay of all mesdames' arsenals, I don't half feel like calling her up to say, 'Pardon me, but do you know who I am?'

Must resist the urge to smack-down, though. I always wondered why the profiles on the website were occasionally shuffled to put some girls above others. Now I suppose I know.

Ahh, the (relative) freedom. No particular desire to make or keep manicure/waxing/any other appointments. Though I daresay if the sun comes out and I go into the garden in a bikini, someone may be forgiven for coming at me with a strimmer.

mardi, le 25 mai

And still no word.

'I want out,' I groaned to N. The manager's cold shoulder is beginning to wear on me. There are plenty of other outfits around, but the thought of going through another agency seems a dead end. I've even gone so far as to pull out an ancient CV and to think how it might be updated so the gaps in employment don't look Grand Canyon-wide.

'Okay, but don't leave just to sell out.' I rolled my eyes. Aren't we past the age where authenticity matters more than solvency? Everyone I know has a career, spouse, property or retirement fund. I questioned his choice of words.

'What is the definition of selling out?' he said. 'Never do anything for money that you wouldn't do for free.'

'I spend a lot of time picking at my nails. Don't think there's a chance of a career in that.'

'Don't be sarcastic,' N said. 'It never suited you.'

There is, in the end, only one place for a woman to turn in her hour of desperation. When all else has failed, when the bank accounts are running from black to red to carefully worded letters from the bank, she has to draw on every nerve she has and steel herself for the inevitable. The job pages.

I started with the administrative positions. General knowledge of computers? Check. Organisational skills? Plenty.

Self-motivated and hard-working? Sort of. Dedicated? To what – scheduling meetings and faxing letters? Being able to seal envelopes and transfer incoming calls requires dedication now?

Maybe not for me. I perused academic posts instead.

Depressing. It would seem the higher the degree, the lower the corresponding starting salary. A2 and A4 are academics, and confirm my suspicion that research grants are a convoluted plan by the powers that be to keep clever people from thinking about things like world affairs. Why pay attention to politics and other matters of import when there is a £5,000 bursary to be fighting tooth and claw over?

jeudi, le 27 mai

I am determined not to give up, in spite of the fact that papers and website suggest the London economy is based on exactly three things:

1. **Copywriting and subediting:** Been there, done that . . . actually, I haven't as such. Tried to be there and do that, and been turned down by everyone from scientific journals to *World Walrus Weekly*. The country's finer philately organs did not even honour me with a rejection letter.

2. **Temping and PAs:** Definitely been there and don't ever, ever want to do that again. Revisiting calloused fingertips from sealing billing envelopes at a stockbroker's is a fate too depressing to contemplate. The abject degradation of having to collect someone's daughter's school uniform from the dry cleaner makes scat play look a doddle.

3. **Prostitution:** Damnation.

I could stay in the business and go independent. It would mean never having to give up a third of my earnings to an agency again. On the other hand, it would mean vetting my own clients, taking calls all hours of the day and night, maintaining a portfolio, organising security and . . . oh. Too much work for me on my own. There'd barely be time for scheduling waxes, let alone any other essential maintenance operations.

samedi, le 29 mai

Letters. Applications. Download, print, fill in. Envelopes and stamps on letters to which I'll probably never receive replies. And then, late yesterday afternoon, a call from a personnel department. They want to see me for an interview. A position I would love to have.

Shortlisted. And I know the list is extremely short. My chances are good.

That's it – I'm off the game.

From the profiles on the agency website, it's apparent that a lot of the girls are not from the UK. Eastern Europe, North Africa, Asia. Britain is doing a roaring trade in importing sex workers.

I don't ask about their motivation for doing the job. It's not my business. I wasn't forced into working for the agency and hope they weren't either. If the agency was really a stable of illegal workers under the thumb of an abusive pimp, they wouldn't hire so many local girls.

Would they?

I realise that all this aside, I'm not really in a very different position to those Jordanian and Polish girls right now. Maybe they're over on student visas and in extreme debt. Somewhere along the way it was implied that the reward for working hard at school and completing a degree was a reasonable career. Now here I am wondering whether a six-month appointment colour-correcting magazine illustrations or assistant manager at a high-street retailer would be a better career move. And competing with hundreds of other graduates for the same paltry pickings.

But for now, I have shirts to iron and interview questions to worry about.

lundi, le 31 mai

I rose early to catch a train. This was a London of which I had only heard rumours: suited men and women crowding the platforms, waiting for a place in a packed carriage. Most looked slightly dazed, not quite awake; others had clearly risen early and had their schedule down to a science. I wondered whether some of the freshly made-up women had to rise at half four to look so pulled together by eight.

When I arrived, the other two interviewees were already there. We introduced ourselves, talked briefly about the social and professional connections that joined us. Then we filed into a room and, with a group of interviewers, watched each other's brief presentations. Afterwards we were called in one at a time for the interview proper.

A dark blonde, pudding-faced girl was the first candidate. When she left for her grilling, the other interviewee smiled wanly at me. 'I knew when I saw you I didn't have a chance,' he said. I had thought something similar, since although my degrees and referees were better, his experience was enviable.

'Don't be silly,' I said. 'It could be any of us.' Either, I corrected silently, since it was fairly certain the other girl didn't have a chance. Her degree was only tangentially re-lated, her graduate experience non-existent, and she had mumbled through her presentation, the content of which was not terribly impressive. The second candidate went for his interview and must have left straight after, as he didn't come back.

I entered the room for my interview already sweating. Don't walk into the table, I thought. There were three people on the other side: a tall, thin man, an elderly gentleman with glasses and a thirtyish woman with short, dark hair.

They took their questions in turns. The division of labour soon became clear: the older man asked very little and was clearly more senior. The thin man asked questions relating to personality – the usual things, such as what I thought my weaknesses were and where I saw my career in five years' time. The younger woman was left the technical questions, and these scared me the most, but I thought before starting to answer each. At some points I was aware that composing an answer left them hanging for the start of my sentences, but I thought it better to get it right than to amble aimlessly.

When the interview concluded, the three stood with me. The selection should be made fairly quickly, they said, since they wanted someone to start as soon as possible. I could expect a phone call or letter in the next few days. As I was the last candidate, they left the room as well. The elderly man and the woman turned down the hall to their offices. The tall man offered to walk me through to the lobby.

We stood quietly in the elevator together. I smiled. 'I remember you from a conference three years ago,' he said. 'Impressive presentation.'

'Thank you,' I said. Crud. Most of the presentation I'd given earlier in the day had been recycled from that one.

We walked through the quiet carpeted hallways. He started talking about his own work, something he was clearly passionate about. I like people with passion. I asked him leading questions, argued the devil's advocate while making it clear I actually agreed with him, and in the end he stood with me at a taxi queue until the cab came to take me to the station. He shook my hand warmly and closed the door for me. As the taxi pulled away, I could see him still standing at the kerb.

My heart was beating fast. That was good, I thought. Now I have someone on my side.

Juin

mardi, le 1 juin

Angel rang. It was a surprise; I had not thought I'd hear from her again.

She was crying. I was in a taxi and couldn't really hear her above the noise of the cab. I told her I was on the way to meet a friend, and she could ring me later or drop by if she wanted a chat.

She did drop by. She breezed in, looking together, but I knew it was only a matter of time until she broke down. Which she did, magnificently. Someone had just dumped her. A relationship – I had to confess ignorance that she was seeing anyone at all – had ended. By email.

I was shocked. 'No way to treat you, no matter what happened,' I cooed. I poured boiling water in a cafetière, let it steep, and poured her a beaker of steaming brew. 'So who was it?' I asked, out of mild curiosity.

'Didn't you know?' she asked, looking up, tear-stained face. 'You'll laugh.' It was First Date.

Bloody hell.

'And the worst of it, he is still carrying a torch for you.'

Bloodier hell. How do you comfort someone who has just been chucked for, among other reasons undoubtedly, a memory, and a pretty insubstantial one at that? 'I'm so sorry,' I whispered.

'You're good at things, you're talented,' she moaned. 'I just don't know, I disappoint people.'

'You can't take it personally. Someone else being disappointed in you is their problem.' Cruddy way to soothe someone, but I didn't know what to say. This woman was more acquaintance than friend, and a stressful one. But I felt for her. I've been on both sides of that equation.

jeudi, le 3 juin

An invitation came through the post a few weeks ago. I haven't replied yet for not knowing what to do.

It's a weekend in the country to celebrate a friend's engagement, and promises to be a good time, with garden parties and drunken singalongs round a bonfire. And I would be there like a shot, but for one thing. The Boy.

The odds that he was not invited are slender. With most exes, I would not mind, but I haven't heard so much as a word from him since the near-miss at that birthday party some time back, there's been no sign of the mystery car at all and I therefore have no idea whether he still pines, or hates me, or has forgotten about me altogether. And I can't decide which outcome would be the worst.

It would take only a minute to ring the bride-to-be and ask, but that would flag my concern, and if I know this couple at all, I know that other people's discomfort is their sport. So best not to say anything at all.

I could certainly use a weekend out of town, though, and it's the best option going so far.

dimanche, le 6 juin

N and A3 and I dissected the interview. N has no real idea what I studied, but is unfailingly supportive and convinced the job will be mine. A3, on the other hand, works in a similar field and is, it must be noted, grumpy at best.

'They must at least be considering you,' N said. 'I went for an interview in Newcastle once, and they rang up to reject me before I'd even got to the train to come home.'

'What were you going to Newcastle for?' I asked.

N gave me an odd look. 'Never you mind. Point is, you have to be more patient. They'll let you know in due time.'

He's probably right, but it doesn't stop me fretting. Could I have given a better presentation, I wonder, or answered their questions more professionally? Did something about my clothes or manner put them off? How did I stand up against the others? If I get the job, will I fit in, will I disappoint them? Do any fit men work there?

mercredi, le 9 juin

Possible reasons I have not yet been contacted about the interview include:

- They have decided to hire someone else, and neglected to tell me.
- They have decided to hire me, and neglected to tell me.
- They are making an offer to someone else first and waiting for a response before rejecting the other applicants.
- They are rejecting the other applicants before contacting the successful candidate (i.e. me).
- The letter has been lost in the post.
- The letter has not been lost in the post, but was delivered to the wrong house.
- I dreamed the interview.
- The letter has not been sent.
- They haven't made a decision.

I couldn't take waiting any longer. I rang the personnel department. The woman on the other end of the call was kind, although I had to give her the job reference number three times. She apologised – apparently there had been problems with the internal mail and the letters hadn't been posted, but a decision had been made. I gnawed the fingers of my left hand while she looked for the information.

'Ah, here you are. It looks as though you've got it.'

My heart leapt. I grinned. 'Really?'

'You are Louise, right?'

And just as quickly, it fell back to the pit of my stomach. 'Er, no.' The pudding-faced girl. How had they chosen her over me?

'Oh, sorry!' she tittered. 'I'm afraid you haven't been successful, then.' I thanked her and rang off.

Phone call from Dr C, who is visiting his parents and wants to drive up and visit next week. I suppose the current situation gives me some free time at least. Silver linings and all that. And I am definitely going to that engagement party. Nothing hath charms to soothe the wounded ego quite like alcohol and flirtation.

dimanche, le 13 juin

The benefits of sex with an ex:

- No chance of being shocked by what he looks like naked. That horrible mole is right where you left it.
- Not having to ask awkwardly for contact details after. If you don't have them, it's not by accident.
- He knows where your buttons are, how many there are, how long they need to be pressed and whether they should go side-to-side, up-and-down or in little circles.

And the drawbacks:

- There's probably a good reason you're not together any more, a very good reason.
- One of you will think this means the relationship is back on.
- There is absolutely no way you can tell any of your friends without coming off as the world's biggest prat. After all, they had to live with you post break-up, right?

Cripes. I'm going to commence a head/wall interface now. Back later when I have knocked some sense into myself.

lundi, le 14 juin

So, yes. Sex. With someone I honestly expected never to have sex with again.

The Boy. The effing Boy.

Still sorting it out. It's a mess. He gave me a lift back to London and now won't leave. But I would like to confirm that at least before the slightly tipsy post-coital glowing phase ended and the horrible, horrible veil of Oh-Dear-Me-Not-Again descended, it was good.

Better than good. He sat on my chest and fucked my mouth, he took me behind, above and below. I smiled and asked how he'd gotten so good with his tongue, thinking there must be some genius tart showing him the ropes now. 'I don't know,' he said. 'I just think about it a lot.' I came harder, faster and longer than usual, and for a brief moment I thought, 'If he never said anything stupid again, I could be quite happy with this.'

Sod's Law Mark 2: he will open his mouth and say something stupid within thirty seconds of thinking that. And it was raining outside so I couldn't make some excuse to vacate the flat, walk around for a bit and come back when enough time has elapsed to be certain he'd gone.

mardi, le 15 juin

There's no why to ex sex, only the how (long it will last, soon it will be over, fast can I leave). Most of my exes are friends, and most of my friends are exes, and I don't fuck them afterwards as a rule. But there are one or two who fall out of touch, usually because there was little in the relationship worth building a friendship on, and this was one.

When he left yesterday, he offered me a lift to a meeting. Thank goodness, I thought, that means he'll be on his way, hopefully never to return. Before we could go, though, he asked if I had any money on me. I didn't. Except when working, I carry less spare change than the Queen. He drove us via a cashpoint so I could make a withdrawal and pay him back for the tomatoes he had bought me. (NB: These were replacing tomatoes I already had that he had helped himself to. So I was paying for my own tomatoes twice.)

I emerged from the car shaking my head. Walked to the cashpoint. Withdrew a crisp tenner – the tomatoes hadn't cost that much, but maybe he was going to impose a surcharge on my own bog roll – and walked back to the car. Put the note in his hand, closed the door, kept on walking.

A text came through a minute later: 'Am just filling up with petrol if you still want a lift. Come back and meet me.'

I didn't reply. He rang. Did I want a lift? he asked. Yes, if you act like a normal person, I said. I described the direction I was going, said if he wanted to drive me, he could pick me up. He rang again a minute later, asked where I was.

Described the road I was on, the building I had just passed, the route I was taking. Hung up.

He sent another text: 'This is really stupid. I'm just 10 metres behind u the whole way. And as per usual, this is exactly what I knew would happen.'

A minute later, his car came up on my right. He reached across and opened the passenger side door.

'I just got your text,' I said.

'And?' he said.

'Goodbye.' I shut the door firmly and walked on. His car lingered a minute until someone beeped a horn, and he drove up to the next roundabout and disappeared. And that was it. Put on headphones. The next song was about someone walking out the door. I felt good and smiled so hard it brought tears to my eyes.

dimanche, le 20 juin

I was flopped on my bed, reading. The phone buzzed. Dr C.

'Top of the road, you said?'

Actually, I'm never quite sure which is which, but if he didn't see the number he was probably at the wrong end.

He tapped on the door a minute later. His smile was nicer than I'd remembered. He had a single bag and an old blue car. His brother's, he said. I let him in.

He dropped his bag next to the sofa. Ack, I thought. Should have put out some pillows and blankets. Wouldn't want him to think I assumed he'd be sleeping with me. We faced each other, said nothing, just smiling.

'So.'

'So. Go for a walk?'

We wandered for hours. I didn't even notice the time until the sun went behind the trees. He talked about his family, his work. He talked with his gorgeous mouth and his hands.

'Home?'

I offered to cook something for him. 'To be honest, I'm not really that hungry,' he said. I wasn't either. He brought a large bottle of liqueur out of his bag. There mustn't have been room in there for much else. We sat at my kitchen table with a bowl of ice and finished the bottle.

I was tipsy, so was he, but in a nice way, like the night we were first together. When the glasses and bottle were finally empty I took him up to my bedroom. We kissed and fondled each other through our clothes. 'Your breasts look great in this,' he said. 'May I ask you something?'

Anything, I almost said. 'What's that?'

'May I whip your breasts? Through the shirt, I mean.'

I produced a rubber multi-tailed whip for him. He started with light taps at first. I laughed. 'You can go harder than that,' I said. He did. It hurt. It wasn't the hardest anyone had ever whipped me, but it felt like the most fun. I kept laughing. He didn't say anything, but he smiled too, it seemed so ludicrous. When he finished he put the whip down and his hands under the shirt.

'The flesh is warm,' he said. Lifted the shirt. I wasn't wearing a bra. 'They're pink.' He pushed me up against the wall and had me like that. Then we fell into bed and were almost instantly unconscious.

lundi, le 21 juin

The phone woke me. I was groggy and answered without looking to see who the call was from. 'Hello?'

'Hello.' It was the Boy. I shivered. I should have hung up. Didn't. 'Where are you?' he asked.

'At home.' No point lying. No time to think. 'Where are you?'

'Outside.'

'Oh.' I gently pushed the sleeping man beside me awake. 'Um, I have a guest downstairs,' I said.

He must have heard something in my voice. 'Who is it?'

'My ex.' A frown flickered across his face. He asked what I wanted to do. 'Answer the door, I suppose.' We dressed. He went down to the kitchen. I answered the door.

The Boy stood there. Shorts and a T-shirt. His car was pulled up opposite. He was alone. The street was quiet. He asked if he could come in. I let him.

He nodded at Dr C in the kitchen. I introduced them.

Asked if anyone wanted breakfast. They said yes. I put the radio on. Everything seemed far too calm. I scrambled eggs and put bread under the grill to toast. Made light chatter with both about the weather (pleasant) and what was on the radio (rubbish) and the news (depressing). I dished up and put plates of equal size in front of them.

The Boy dug straight in, his head bowed over the plate. It was odd to see him sitting at the table.

The two of them were quiet. I couldn't sit down, just paced lightly in front of the sink nibbling a crust. The Boy finished quickly and asked to use the toilet. I said he could. He had never had to ask before.

When he was out of the room, Dr C turned to me and whispered, 'Why didn't you tell me about him?'

'Didn't think there was anything to tell,' I whispered back. 'Haven't seen him in months.'

The Boy came back in, asked if he could speak to me in my room. I said yes. We went up the stairs. I left the door open. I knew we were within earshot of the kitchen.

'I want you to be honest,' he said.

I bristled. What right did he have to ask me anything? And when had I ever not told him the truth? 'Yes?' I said.

'Are you sleeping with this man?'

'Yes.'

'He slept here last night?'

'Yes,' I said.

'I can't believe you would do this to me,' he said. I was mystified. Was I still supposed to answer to him, care what he thought of me, care what anyone thought? I asked him to go.

He was oddly calm. Usually the Boy is fidgety and talkative, but he was silent and composed. He said he could let himself out; I insisted on walking him down. Out of the door. I stepped outside after him and pulled the door shut. Dr C was still in the kitchen. Heard the lock close after me. I didn't have the key. Whatever the Boy was going to do, I wouldn't let him do it to a stranger. He would have to do it to me.

The Boy realised this. He turned, the colour back in his cheeks. 'I have to talk to him,' he said with sudden urgency.

'No,' I said, and crossed my arms.

'I have to talk to him,' the Boy said. 'He can have you, I just want him to know what . . . what he took from me.'

'He took nothing. He doesn't even know who you are. Why should he? You let me go. Twice.' The Boy asked to go inside. I refused. He asked again, several times; I refused.

I knew it was beyond his code of conduct to hit me, but I didn't depend on that and I wondered just where his breaking point would be. A few people were starting to come up and down the road in the course of normal morning business. I counted on that to save me, if I needed saving.

The Boy was clearly getting nowhere simply by asking to be let inside. 'Come on,' he whined. 'The man's big enough. He can clearly take care of himself.'

'You wouldn't touch him?' I asked.

'I wouldn't touch him.'

'Liar.' I could see his arms were crossed but his fists were clenching and unclenching over and over, turning the knuckles white, then pink, then white.

We stood. He looked at me. 'Get in your car and drive away,' I said. He stood unmoved. I repeated myself. He went. I followed him out of the garden gate. Watched him get in the car. He was slow to put the key in the ignition. I waited until he drove away. Went back to my door and knocked. Dr C let me in. We went up to my room and fucked.

mardi, le 22 juin

In the morning Dr C left. He had to drive back south. I smiled and made the bed as he packed his scant belongings. I didn't know if we'd see each other again; the bruises across my chest were already faint but may last longer than the two of us being together. I didn't know and didn't mind.

There was a car on the corner, I could see it from my window, and he knew it too. The Boy. I walked Dr C to his car and waved him off down the street, went back inside, locking the door behind me. The phone was ringing. I didn't answer.

A few minutes later it rang again. 'Hello,' I said.

'May I come in?' the Boy asked. I said no, I'd meet him outside. I locked the door behind me and slipped the keys in my pocket. Kept the mobile in my hand, just in case. He met me at the gate. Asked to come in again. I refused. Said we talked in his car or not at all.

I sat in the passenger side and half closed the door.

'I'm sorry, I know I've done so many things wrong, I'm so, so sorry,' he said. His eyes had gone red, and his shoulders turned in. I was struck with a pang of tenderness. I said nothing, though. He kept on apologising, crying. I let him. I thought of all the times when we were dating when he hadn't apologised, and it tore me up, or the few times he did and I'd hurry to reassure him it wasn't his fault.

No interrupting this time. I just let him get it off his chest.

It was hard to watch. I knew I could make the next ten minutes a lot easier for us both – maybe even the next ten days, if we were lucky – by saying I'd have him back. But I knew there would always be an argument waiting round the corner. And whatever he said, people don't just change and I had had enough.

And that's what I told him. I just whispered that I'd had enough. He sobbed but didn't keep begging.

This really is it, I thought. Was this the last chance not just for him, but for me, for ever?

'I loved you so much,' he said finally.

'I loved you too,' I said.

jeudi, le 24 juin

Just back from the gym, sweating and tired. Switched the kettle on more out of habit than a need for a hot drink.

The phone buzzed away on the kitchen counter. I looked at the screen. It was the manager.

'Darling, there is a booking for two hours . . .'

Had I misheard? 'Oh, right.' Weeks of silence and now a booking out of the blue? 'How have you been?'

'Good, darling, good. Have I just woken you up?' Just back from the gym, I said. She approved. 'Must keep in shape,' she said, and moved on quickly. 'Listen, this gentleman, he is staying at Claridge's, he has asked for you at ten o'clock.' A two-hour booking with travel and all services. At the highest hourly rate we charge.

I bit my lip. Gift horse, mouth and all that. But I'd already said I was going to meet A3 at the pub later. And I hadn't gone for a wax in ages. Cutting the pubic hedge alone would take an hour. And I was tired, and hadn't eaten. 'I'm sorry, I'm afraid I can't do it. I'm certain one of the other girls would be happy to,' I suggested softly.

'He liked your profile, wants you specifically. I can make small lies, but not a big lie like sending another girl.'

My goodness. Unheard-of honesty in a madame. Perhaps I'd just had the wrong end of the stick after all?

My voice grew stronger. 'I so wish I could, but I have other plans,' I said. I could have made it – just. The money would have been useful. But I didn't want to. A3 would be waiting, and I could imagine no better evening than letting him finish my pints and drone on about work.

'Okay, darling,' she sang. 'You are always such fun. I will speak to you soon?'

'Speak to you soon. Goodnight.'

dimanche, le 27 juin

I'm an author, the client said. Really, I said. What kind? Genre fiction, he said. He quoted a *New York Times* best-seller. Ah, I said, like Mickey Spillane. That's right, he said. I always liked that part at the end of *My Gun is Quick*, I said. Where Hammer tears the negligee off the heroine. Their single night of passion together.

I sat on his lap and he ran his hand over my thighs.

'Feels like hold-ups,' he said. (They were.)

'What do you want tonight?' I asked.

'Simple man, simple pleasures,' he said. 'I just like to come in a naked woman's mouth.'

This request may seem an expensive one, but if you think about the money and effort you might spend on a business trip, trying to court someone just to get to the possible stage of her naked and you coming in her mouth before it's time to fly home, it's not so pricey. And the result is guaranteed.

He removed my knickers and we lay on the bed. 'You remind me of someone I was once in love with,' I said. He looked doubtful. It was true – he had the high waist and ascetic limbs of a fourteenth-century tempera saint. An identical form and face to A2. I tickled the high arch of his foot and kissed the inside of his thighs.

After sucking him for a few minutes I asked what else he liked. Rimming, he said. 'Giving or receiving?' Receiving, he said. I spread his legs wider and felt between the rounded cheeks of his arse. 'Here, I think it will go better with a pillow under you.' He obliged. The pucker was tender, pink and hairless. Clean, it tasted slightly of soap. I put my lips back around his cock and tickled the hole with a damp finger. He came quickly and hard, filling my throat.

'It's only been thirty minutes,' I said. He was paying for an hour. 'I don't suppose you could manage again?'

'No, sorry,' he said. 'Too old. Too tired.'

'Shall I stay and we can chat, or leave you? Or you could turn over and I could pummel your back in a poor imitation of a massage.'

'I'd be fine if you left. I'll just go to sleep happy.'

'I'd wish you luck with the books but it sounds like you don't need it,' I said. 'Must pick up a copy.'

'Get one in paperback,' he said. 'See if you like them first.'

I dressed. The money was in a hotel envelope. 'Wasn't it Dashiell Hammett who said you don't pay a call girl to do what she does, you pay her to leave afterwards?'

'Probably,' he smiled drowsily. I closed the door softly behind me. There was only one taxi outside. I was whisked home in the light and sound of a city evening.

Septembre

dimanche, le 5 septembre

'What I want, what I really want . . . this probably sounds silly . . . is to please you.'

The client was fiftyish, dressed office-casual. Oh great, I thought, another half-hour of earnest licking from a man whose wife no doubt thinks her body stops at the waist. 'That's a gorgeous idea,' I purred.

'Tell me your fantasies,' he said, tracing the cup of my bra with his finger. 'What do you desire right now more than anything?'

I thought. 'Well, it's a good long time since I had a tit-wank,' I said.

'That doesn't sound like you'd get much pleasure,' he said.

'I do actually. There's something so . . . satisfying . . . about the feel of someone using your breasts to wank himself. Or when the come hits your face, just . . .'

'Um, that's nice. How about if I go down on you instead?' he asked, turfing me off his lap.

'Oh, okay, whatever you want,' I said.

'Oh no,' he said, slipping his face down to my inner thighs. 'It's all about what you want.'

lundi, le 6 septembre

The first thing I do is shower, wash hair, dry with clean fluffy towel. Check all shaving is shaven, all plucking plucked. Moisturise and ample deodorant: even after going through the routine so many times, I still get nervous.

I imagine there are hundreds – if not thousands – of women like me in London, doing precisely what I'm doing right now.

Hair carefully styled. Glossy but not girlish, professional but not stiff. Nice suit, just back from the cleaners. A blouse unbuttoned to the base of the neck – mustn't go flashing cleavage or people will look at you strangely. Underwear and stockings. The good shoes. Jewellery – just enough, not too much. First impressions are everything. The goal is to be asked back a second time.

Check everything in my bag. Address, phone number, toiletries. Must turn up on time, never early, never late.

I leave the flat, lock the door, and walk to the corner. Hold my hand out to attract the driver's attention. The hulking vehicle slows as it approaches. I finger the wallet in my purse anxiously. 'Morning, love,' the driver says as I flash him my bus pass. I find a seat upstairs. It's daytime and not night. No taxi waiting for me, not today.

It's a job interview I'm going to, you see, not an appointment.

mardi, le 7 septembre

I come in from an appointment with a client, strip and shower. Hanging on the back of the bathroom door is the jacket of my interview suit. It went well, I think; so well that going back to trawling the hotel circuit today was a bit of a comedown.

The man who interviewed me was round, fortyish, Chinese; very successful, very chatty. I've had clients like him.

His eyebrows shot up as he looked over my application again; as the half-hour went on, his voice grew more and more excited. Either my luck was in or I was setting myself up for yet another disappointment. I had come home and steeled myself for the follow-up. There was a call within the hour. They wanted me to come back.

Phone rings. No name and no number. Either the manager ringing to tell me about a client or a call from overseas. I pick it up, anticipating the latter.

'So how did it go in the end?' Dr C asks.

I smile involuntarily. Even the sound of his voice is enough to make me melt, and I feel my knickers going slightly sticky. 'Really well, as it happens. I have a second interview.'

'That's great. I can help you get ready on the morning.'

'It's after you've gone, unfortunately,' I say. Couldn't he possibly have asked for more than a week off work? I bite my tongue: that would sound aggressive. Besides, no matter how little time we have together I am sure the sex will be worth it – I don't usually send out to California for a take-away, but in his case I can make an exception.

I tell him that most of the interview was spent on questions about A2, how well I knew him, whether I could set up a meeting between him and the company's directors, and so on.

'He's on your CV?'

'Why shouldn't he be?'

'He's your ex-boyfriend.'

And the man who introduced me to Dr C, for which I should really send a thank-you note at the least. 'He's a character reference.' I must admit my ethics radar has been somewhat recalibrated since I started having sex for money.

Dr C laughs. 'Don't worry, if I'd thought it would improve my job prospects, I'd have done it, too. You have explicit permission to use me as a reference if need be.'

'I'd rather have explicit permission just to use you in general.' We laugh.

Sometimes I feel I've been doing this job for ever, then I remember it's only been two years. I can't help feeling I've seen all these men, had all these requests, before.

'Where do you want it . . . here or here?'

'You know where I want it,' I said in my sauciest voice.

'I want to hear you tell me.' The end of his cock was twitching, and with one of his hands on the shaft and one on his balls I could tell he was holding back until the right moment.

'I want you to come all over my face.' You know what would be nice about landing a legitimate job? Not having to wash come off my face more than once a day.

'Beg me.'

Well, whatever works for him. 'Please,' I said. Please let him give me a big tip. 'Please, come all over my face.' At that moment, he released his hands and sprayed.

Of course, it rarely ends up where you want it to. You can hardly blame the client – the moment of ejaculation is not the right time to say, 'Er, actually you're mostly just getting my hair there.' But it's a fact of life, if you want some on the face, be prepared for any result. And for your own sake keep your eyes shut – that stuff's like battery acid.

Other tips for a successful facial:

- **Eyelashes.** Waterproof mascara at a minimum; those long-lasting three-day formulations aren't bad; personally I go for the eyelash tinting option.
- **Pillow.** Adjust your head height and angle accordingly. And simply prop your head up in front of the cock, not below.
- **Smile!** It's the mental photograph he's after, and we all want to look good in a photo, don't we?

vendredi, le 10 septembre

'Looking forward to seeing your man, am I right?' N asked. We were watching telly and eating crisps.

'Can't wait,' I said. I was a bit nervous, though: Dr C had been to visit twice since we first met, and we were rapidly passing the point at which I should have told him how I pay the rent in between looking for other work.

'Damn sight better than the last one,' N said. 'You ever hear from that arsehole again?'

'Um, no,' I said and sat down, turning the television volume higher.

I felt bad about lying, but it had to be done. The Boy kept sending texts – all of which I ignored – for ages after we split. Then one night a month ago he rang. I was feeling soft and a bit lonely, and Dr C and I never asked many questions about what each other's lives were like outside seeing each other. The Boy and I hooked up. I swore it would be only the once.

Plus there are a number of reasons not to go there again:

1. His friends hate me. To be fair, most of them never even *met* me. But the ones who have definitely do not approve.
2. He's a snob. To him and his friends, girls like me are on the bottom rung of middle class and always looking for an opportunity to marry up. It's a class thing.
3. He's not the sharpest knife in the drawer. Yes, I'm a snob too.

Anyway it turned out to be only the once, as planned.

dimanche, le 12 septembre

Wake up. Panic. Run out door. Just catch bus. Tube.

Arrive at airport to learn flight is delayed by two

hours. Spend six pounds on hot chocolate and try to make it last.

Lose track of time. Feel tap on shoulder and look up and he's standing, bags in hand, by my table. Dr C smiles and I can't help but grin.

Worth the wait.

lundi, le 13 septembre

We sat on the sofa reading, my legs round Dr C's hips, his head on the hollow of my shoulder. From here it's like reading to a child, I thought, all softness and nuzzle and warmth. Though I did have to hold the book out at a strange angle in order to not block his view.

I love it that Dr C doesn't ask too many questions. What goes on in my life is seldom up for examination, and that seems fine with him. Though it is beginning to bother me: when is a good time to tell someone you have sex with other men for money? I suspect he knows there are other people and chooses not to mention it. But I'm not sure most men can make the jump from thinking their girl has an active social life to knowing she's a whore.

I've been making an effort to be as non-confrontational as possible with this relationship. When I think back on my most recent relationship, the shouting, the slammed doors, it doesn't bear much examination. We were both passionate people, yes, but the heart of the problem was the fact that he couldn't bear what I did for a living. I never want things to go like that again. I've been imagining how the conversation might go:

'You remember when I went back to your hotel with you the first time we met? I do that professionally, you know.'

'I'm glad you enjoyed the blowjob. I've had a lot of feedback on that particular move.'

'How about a little role play? I'll pretend to be a call girl, and you'll pretend not to be freaked out about it.'

Er, probably not.

He sighed and shifted in the sofa cushions. 'This is like heaven.'

'I was just thinking the same.'

samedi, le 18 septembre

A quiet day in. I asked Dr C if there was anywhere he wanted to go, maybe see some of the sights that have been built since he moved to America, like the London Eye?

'Eugh, no thank you,' he said. 'Not really my sort of thing. I left the city for a reason, you know.'

I didn't know, not particularly. Sometimes he says things – nothing specific, just a way with a phrase – that make me think he's been married once, maybe in London. But if so, it probably wasn't a good idea to ask. If he wanted to, he'd bring it up.

Met N later for a meal. Chinese. Dr C made a flourish of picking up chopsticks instead of the fork. 'No Chinese restaurant in California would even think of putting those on the table,' he smirked. Unfortunately, it was a little lost on us, as N and I are both adepts.

N and I chattered away about people we knew. Dr C turned to me and started a conversation about our mutual friend A2. Oh, yes, N knew him, too, and soon we were talking nineteen to the dozen. I noticed Dr C going quiet.

'Everything okay, darling?' I asked when N went to the toilet.

He squeezed my thigh under the table. 'Just longing to get you home,' he said. 'I'm leaving tomorrow night.'

He growled in my ear, a move that sent a shiver up my back. 'We'll make it quick,' I said, squeezing his thigh harder.

dimanche, le 19 septembre

The morning was not spent, as I'd have preferred, nibbling on smoked salmon and enjoying the weekend papers. It was spent on an alarm set for stupid o'clock in the morning and an emergency shop for things he couldn't get back in California (Marmite, and lime shower gel). But I was determined to enjoy every minute as we negotiated the bus, Tube and then train to the airport. When he suggested – repeatedly – that maybe we should have arranged a car, I didn't disagree. I waved him off (sexy embrace in front of security, check: goofy kissy faces from other side of barrier, check) and made my way home. It had been a good visit, if a little brief.

N came round, and I made supper for two. Nothing special – pasta, cream, mushrooms, asparagus. N wolfed his down, declared it the best effort yet, and for a moment it looked as if he was going to dive for mine. That or he was looking down my top. Either way it was flattering.

The phone rang. Dr C. N could tell by my smile what was up and he discreetly removed himself upstairs.

'I take it you made it home safely?' I did the maths. 'It's what, lunchtime there?'

'Yeah,' he said. He sounded tired, and no wonder. Very thoughtful to ring me first thing, though.

'How was the flight? Any good films on?'

'Um, mostly I spent the time thinking.' My heart dropped, and I knew he was calling to end it. He said he thought the distance was too far and that he was too busy to be in a relationship, anyway – man code for 'I'd like it if you were more convenient, but don't worry, I'll find someone who is.'

He said he'd been thinking this since before the visit, but he didn't want to ruin my good time.

Ruin my good time? We'd barely spent three evenings together, I wasn't the one who'd made a 12,000-mile round trip. I said nothing. No sense trying to argue about it; I'd parted ways with so many men it was practically a lifestyle choice as well as a career. As soon as he said, 'I don't want to hurt you . . .' I felt a door shut in my heart.

He paused, possibly waiting for the vitriol. Still I said nothing. 'Well, I hope we can still be friends.'

Oh, cringe. I'll say who gets to be my friend. I can play at being civilised but there is a line and he crossed it, right then. I was not going to be Cool Girl any more. 'No, thank you. I have enough friends as it is.' I hung up and turned the phone off. When I looked up N was in the doorway.

'I'm sorry,' he said.

'You're not the one who has to apologise.'

'Someone should,' he said. 'Want a hug?' And even though I thought I didn't, I really did.

mardi, le 21 septembre

Positive aspects of break-up:

- Money saved on travel expenses.
- Never having to have awkward conversation about being a call girl.
- Noticed some hairs growing out of his nose when we were on the sofa. Will not have to deal with that.

Negative aspects of break-up:

- Phone bills for calls to California not coming for another three weeks.

- Having to announce yet another failed relationship to family.
- Looking at phone so hard likely to cause blindness, if not insanity.

jeudi 23 septembre

'It's an impressive CV, all right,' the young man said. 'And your references are impeccable. My colleague was very impressed when he met you.

I smiled weakly. I hadn't had breakfast or lunch, and was constantly checking my phone. But Dr C hadn't rung. I'd turned it off before coming for the interview but was starting to regret that; surely the man sitting across from me could tell how distracted I was?

Possibly not.

I had the distinct feeling he was eyeing the line of my cleavage through my shirt, which, given that it was a high-buttoned stripey number too starchy for call-girl work, was an impressive feat.

So that's the way it's going to be, I thought. Fine, if that's what gets me through this, he can check me out. Then I can go home and cry myself to sleep. I leaned closer to the desk, pulling my arms in to emphasise my bust. Let him do the talking. And he did, for almost an hour.

'The fact is, we'd like to offer you a job,' he said eventually.

'The fact is, I'd like to take it,' I said. Fucking Dr C. When was he going to realise what a mistake he'd made and ring me? I'd better get out of here and fast.

The young man seemed taken aback with my answer. 'Ah, uh, okay. Well, when can you start?'

'When will you have me?' I raised an eyebrow. If he'd been a client this would have been the part where he pushed

186

me back on the bed. In real life this is where he stood up and offered me his hand.

'Immediately. Please call me Giles, I'll be your supervisor.'

'Splendid, Giles.' I stood and shook the offered hand. 'I'll see you tomorrow.'

vendredi, le 24 septembre

Turned up early to be shown around the offices and meet my co-workers. Everyone seems keen to ask questions, most of which I don't know how to answer. Smile and glide, I think. Stay cool. Smile and glide.

The mobile rang repeatedly in my handbag; I peeked at the number. Cripes. It was the manager. How was I going to talk to her without anyone in the office noticing?

'Just off to the loo,' I announced. Giles nodded. I scampered off to the toilet to ring the manager back.

It wasn't my lucky day. There was a queue for the toilet. The woman in front of me smiled and half shrugged, as if to say, my, isn't this terrible? She had no bloody idea. All she was doing was trying to keep from wetting herself. I was a prostitute trying to manage her appointments.

I waited until the last cubicle was free and phoned the manager back. 'Darling, hello,' she said. 'There is a lovely man who wishes to meet you Sunday—'

'Um, wait,' I cut her off. The woman in the cubicle next to me was wrestling with the toilet roll dispenser – how much could she hear? 'I've been thinking that, well, you know, perhaps it's time that I, I mean we . . . What I want to say is, er . . . I'd like to consider, you know, quitting.'

The rustling on the other side of the toilet wall stopped abruptly.

'Well, yes. My schedule outside work has been very busy lately, and I'd like to . . . consider . . . other options.'

'I'm sending only the most carefully selected men to you now,' she cooed reassuringly.

'Yes, but maybe it's time for me to stop for good.'

'If it's a matter of more money . . .'

'It's not about the money. It's more, well, it's taking a lot out of my personal life,' I whispered hotly. And what if someone here stumbled across the website? It had been hard enough to land a job; that would kill any career for certain.

The manager laughed. 'That happens to everyone.'

I froze. The woman in the next cubicle hadn't gone yet. She must be eavesdropping. 'Yes, well, I'm worried about my' – I lowered my voice – 'privacy.'

'Darling, I'm sorry, you must be losing signal.'

'My privacy!' I shouted. 'I'm concerned about my privacy!'

A snort from the next cubicle. 'You might consider not taking phone calls in the toilet,' a voice said.

'Oh, darling, if only you'd said,' the manager cooed. 'I can anonymise your photos on the website, so that no one recognises you. I'll text you the details for the weekend and we'll speak tomorrow.' She hung up.

'Great,' I said to the dead line.

dimanche, le 26 septembre

The client was younger than me. We met at a private address. He said it was his house, but I wasn't sure. How many twenty-somethings have homes over four floors of a building in central London? Probably his parents' house.

I was rushed up to the top bedroom. 'You'd better undress,' he said. I untied the wrap dress but left on the suspenders and stockings – he'd requested them specially.

He wanted oral – I gave it. He sat back in the half dark

188

and I sensed he was bored. 'Okay, enough,' he said, pulling me off his member. 'Tell me something dirty.'

I started a story about me and a girl at a club, in the toilets.

'Would you ever do a threesome?' he interrupted.

'I've done plenty,' I said. 'How about you?'

'Of course. Two strippers. I made them both come.'

It seems to me there is no need for a man to try to impress a woman he is paying for sex, but then the male of the species is an odd creature. Maybe they can't help themselves.

I rolled a condom onto him and we went at it, me sitting on him facing away – the classic Reverse Cowgirl position. An absolute lifesaver when you have to make like you're enjoying the experience, but aren't up to looking the part. I was counting down the minutes until it would be over.

Maybe I got a little carried away with the counting, because even with ball-tickling and toe-licking he was still going soft. Without any clues to go on, I didn't know what would help. Talking dirty? Squealing girlishly? Struggling a little?

No luck there. He asked me to suck him again. Oral sex after a condom is always distasteful: the shaft tastes strongly of latex and before long my lips started to swell. But the hour was winding up and I didn't think he'd take the suggestion to have a wash first very well.

The sucking had minimal effect. 'You can stop now,' he sighed. I smiled and tried to hide my relief; my lips were aching already. So what if he didn't come? 'I was nervous,' he said, 'I took a Xanax before you came over. Do you think that would have an effect on . . . ?' and he indicated his penis.

I felt guilty about judging him harshly. 'I suppose it would. I hope you didn't find me too frightening.'

'No, I think you're a nice girl. I'll call again next month.' In spite of feeling sorry for him I sincerely hoped he wouldn't. 'I think you should take the full fee anyway.'

Well, duh. If I'm going to turn up at work tomorrow on three hours' sleep it had better have been for full pay.

mercredi, le 29 septembre

The Canadian who sits behind me at work came and introduced herself today. 'Hi, I'm Erin,' she chirruped. 'How're you finding it so far?'

'Fine, thank you,' I said. She probably wants to be friends. And if there's one thing I can't take it's making friends with women.

Don't get me wrong; I have female friends, though they are admittedly outnumbered by men. But *'making friends'*, that pink-covered, sugar-coated state heavily promoted by women's magazines (Is she your Bessie Mate 4-evah? Find out on page 42!) in which two people audition each other over the course of months, years, or possibly the rest of their lives, I have no patience with.

As a result, I have few female friends and the exceptions are people of some character. Such as Angel and L.

When L and I meet it's as if we never left off. The two girls who used to pass filthy notes about their teachers written in schoolgirl French are much the same, but with wider hips and better shoes. I'm really not counting on *making friends* at work.

'Well, if you need anything, just gimme a shout,' Erin said. Given her general volume I suspect that was meant literally.

'Cheers, I will do.'

'Byeeeeee.'

Octobre

vendredi, le 1 octobre

N reinstated as a fuck buddy for the time being. Is good because: he's good in bed, has a car, and can take a hint when he's not welcome. Is bad because: wait, can't think why it would be bad.

'Hey, pretty lady. Been trying to ring you all day,' N said.

'Sorry. Dropped in and saw A1 after work. He's in a mobile black spot.'

'Fair enough. How is the big guy?'

'He's fine, said to say hi to you. Ended up waiting for him ages though, got cornered by his boss. He went to the opera with his wife last week. They went to see *Les Mamelles de Tirésias*, which the boss took a lot of pleasure in telling me meant Theresa's Tits.'

'Patronising twat.'

'No kidding. Then he was off on some lecture about breasts and how some academic boffin or other proposed that men like breasts because Neanderthals preferred their coitus from behind and the mammary glands remind one of buttocks.'

'Rubbish,' N said. 'How many arses have you ever seen with nipples on?'

samedi, le 2 octobre

How to fuck someone and still be friends:

1. **The Sex.** Must be good. Otherwise, why bother? This person is not going to raise children with you.

2. **The Companionship.** It helps if this is someone you see around socially. Puts a nice ending on all those group nights out when it looks like you aren't going to pull.

3. **The Gossip.** People will assume you're a couple. Get your stories straight and nip this in the bud.

4. **The Jealousy.** There shouldn't be any. If you suspect this is someone whose dalliances with others you might be even remotely miffed about, move on. It's not going to work.

5. **The Talk.** Must be open and frequent. Nothing sucks quite like finding your fuck buddy has secretly fallen for you.

6. **The Protection.** Never forget he has carte blanche to fool around, and so have you. Regular does not equal clean.

7. **The Foreplay.** Don't play the whole 'I'm drunk, club's shut, didn't pull, I know you're home alone' booty call shtick. Not more than half the time, anyway.

8. **The Threesomes.** With luck, there should be plenty.

9. **The Others.** If a potential amour asks if you're sleeping with your fuck buddy, don't deny it. Disclosure might send a third party running, but you were going to have to lie to someone like that to keep the peace, anyway. You don't have to be explicit. Just be honest.

10. **The Goodbyes**. You must behave like adults. Don't ring him three weeks later from Africa and say you'd marry him if he'd have you back. It's a lay, not a life.

mardi, le 5 octobre

The Canadian at work, Erin, has a friend, Mira, a moon-faced Asian girl. They talk. And talk. And talk some more. Their conversations aren't unbearable as such, just endlessly banal. It's not even a month and already I know more about celebrity breast implants than a sub-editor at *Heat*.

The other topic of conversation is Erin's fiancé back in Vancouver. As a soon-to-be-married woman of the world at twenty-four, Erin typically uses the opportunity to unfurl her wisdom on the relatively inexperienced twenty-three-year-old Mira. 'It's such a struggle being apart,' Erin moans theatrically. One key element of *making friends* with women is casting everything that happens in the most tragic light possible.

'We have to rely on the phone for everything now – I mean *everything*.' Erin lowers her voice a notch. 'Even the *sex*.'

'Wow,' Mira sighs, which encourages Erin to go on about what a *romance* it is and how this experience has confirmed for her that it's *meant to be*. I don't know if it's the accent or this girl specifically, but Erin's voice has a foghorn-like quality that cuts through everything else.

Erin's launching into an in-depth rehash of last night's phone call from her boyfriend when I put the phone down. I turn round in my chair. 'Umm, I'm very sorry, but would you two mind keeping the noise level down a wee bit?'

From the looks on their faces you would have thought I'd

slapped them each with a rotten herring. 'Yeah, oooo-kayyyy,' Erin says. 'Whatever.'

'It's a little distracting. Maybe you could talk in Mira's office.'

'Well, yeah, but you don't have to be such a bitch about it.'

I turn back to my desk, blushing madly. It's a long, long time since I've been in the company of women.

mercredi, le 6 octobre

Am keeping a bag in my desk for after-work appointments, of which I hope there will be very few. Checked the website – and the manager seems to have kept to her promise and altered my profile.

As in, the pictures are so blurred you can hardly tell the photo is human, much less a woman. I rang her.

'Um, I saw your changes,' I said. 'Are you sure this is going to work? I mean, I can't imagine anyone booking me with a photo like that.'

'Listen, sweetheart,' she said shortly. 'This is what we agreed, no? If you keep changing your mind I will have to start charging you for Webmaster time. And no one wants that, do they?'

'I'm sorry, really, I'm just . . . you know, considering whether any future career is worth . . .'

'I have to go now,' she hissed. 'We'll talk.'

mardi, le 12 octobre

Rubbish day at work. Squealing harridans behind my desk threatening to send brain into meltdown.

Phoned N at lunch for a good grumble. 'You know what you need,' he said. 'A threesome.'

Damn, he's right. 'Have you anyone in mind?'

'Have I ever! I'm thinking Friday.'

'Not sure I'll survive until then without beating one of my co-workers to death.'

'Try. It'll be worth your while, promise.'

vendredi, le 15 octobre

N is at work and we agree to meet there. She's a real cracker, he said over the phone. The only thing is, she has to be off early in the morning.

N's working the door of the club. He points me in the right direction, and yes, he's right, this one's a looker – few years older than me, tight jeans, nice figure. Huge chest. I can see what he sees in her. I introduce myself and she buys me a drink. She's obviously had a few already.

We dance. She's grinding into me, and from the corner of the room N is watching us.

He's booked a hotel. She and I head straight for the shower. N watches from the door. She's even better unclothed. Mature, but not sagging. I lather her breasts then go down on her, the warm water running down her belly.

We dry each other and head for the bed. N watches me lick her out. I'm not sure if she was really that game; she's participating, but not all that engaged in pleasing me. N arranges us on the bed side-by-side and sets to work on us, dipping his head between our thighs like a bee after honey.

But our friend has clearly had too much to drink. It's only a few hours until she has to be off, anyway. We sleep, she and N on the main bed, me on a fold-out on the side. I wake to the sound of him taking her from behind and her animal grunts. 'Want to join in?' N hisses over his shoulder.

'No, thanks,' I say and fall back asleep.

There's just enough time in the morning for a cup of tea. 'What, no breakfast in bed?' she jokes. N gives her a lift as far as the next Tube station and takes me all the way home. We spend the rest of the morning half asleep in my bed.

samedi, le 16 octobre

Was waiting for N outside an overground station. I had come from meeting a client out of town. Went back to mine for a cuppa. He leafed through my magazines. I took off my shoes and rested my legs over his lap. We started fooling around, but his touch felt strange, almost ticklish. We grappled on the sofa for a bit before he gave up. 'Not in the mood, are you?' N asked. 'That's okay.'

I felt bad. After all, I'd just come from fucking someone. But work sex feels different, it's not tied to interest or desire.

But I knew why I wasn't especially interested. It was not only the slightly disappointing threesome we'd had, nor fatigue from having just seen a client. 'You know what this month is to me?'

'I know what it is.' N put his arm around my shoulder. 'You're not over him, are you?' He didn't mean Dr C, he didn't mean the Boy. He meant the one before that. And he was right. Whenever I'm between men, my thoughts always turn back to him. I might think that this or that event has helped me move on – the shenanigans with the Boy last year, for instance – but it never has.

'I don't miss him.' N gave me a doubtful look. 'I barely remember what he was like now. I miss the idea of him.' An idea I had written off as nonsense, until I met him. The idea that there is one person you fall in love with, one right person, and you will spend the rest of your lives together. At least meeting him helped me believe 'the one' might exist.

He split with me the night I thought was going to be the first night of the rest of our lives. And unlike all my other friends, N never told me to shut up about him. Because when I met N, he was nursing similar wounds inflicted by a girl who'd dumped him just as dramatically.

'You want me to stay or go?'

'I'll feel bad for kicking you out this late.'

'Don't,' N said. He dressed and left quietly.

Later, I heard a drop through the mail slot. Bit late for the post, I thought. I went downstairs to check – a Yorkie bar. My favourite. N knows, he always does.

mardi, le 19 octobre

Manager rang early – emergency call at lunchtime. 'But I'll be at work,' I wailed.

'Do you not even take lunch?' she asked. 'In, out, done. You will hardly interrupt your busy schedule.'

'No. Absolutely not.' And yet, I thought, I probably could do it. Just. And the money would certainly come in handy.

'Darling, he's paying double. It's only a leeeetle thing. I promise it absolutely, positively won't happen again.'

I sighed. I'd argue her down another day. I had the bag tucked safely under my desk, and no one comes back from lunch on time anyway. I changed in the Ladies and stashed the bag in a maintenance closet. Was walking out the door to meet my car when I passed a co-worker.

My supervisor Giles. Shit.

His head didn't turn – must not have recognised me.

We walk down to the Italian and order without opening the menus. 'Sure you don't want anything else?' N asks. 'Go ahead. My treat.'

'Aren't you the gentleman,' I smile. 'What's the occasion?'

N looks at his hands. 'I wanted you to be first to know . . . I've met someone.'

'Wow, I . . .' How? When? Our eyes meet and he smiles. 'Have you told her about me?'

'She knows.'

'She's cool with that?'

'As long as we don't sleep together again, yes.'

'Well. I . . .' Never expected he would find someone first. 'I'm so happy for you.'

'What's wrong?'

'Nothing.'

'You're not crying, for God's sake, are you?'

'Me? Never.' I blow my nose into the heavy cloth napkin. 'It's just I'm so happy for you. You're moving on. This could be the one.'

'Statistically speaking, probably not,' N shrugs.

'I know the look in your eyes. This one's not a shag. She's different.' He doesn't deny it. 'What's her name?'

'Henrietta.'

'To you and Henrietta, then,' I say.

'No chance of a last go with you?' N asks. 'For old times'.

'I thought you said you told her we were done.'

'Can't blame a man for trying,' he smiles.

How to fuck someone and still be friends, part II.

1. It's okay to cry. As long as you happen to be watching a shamelessly romantic film at the time. Then you can tell anyone who catches you that it was Richard Curtis what did it, not the prospect of growing old alone while your friends go on to blissfully happy paired domesticity.
2. Resist urge to leap straight into a rebound relationship.
3. Do not, under any circumstances, ring your ex.
4. Find replacement activity for sex. Personally speaking, the toilet has never been so clean.

dimanche, le 24 octobre

Stumbled blearily out of the bedroom, naked, to use the toilet and was startled to see a man sitting on the sofa reading a paper. It was N. He has a set of my keys.

He'd spent Saturday night at a mate's stag do, and as my house was closer to the party than his (and presumably Henrietta's), he stumbled in sometime in the wee hours and slept in the lounge. Bless. But it gave me quite a start in the morning. To be fair, perhaps the fact that he didn't burst drunkenly into my bedroom at half three and demand to come on my face proves him to be a gentleman.

I've been to a stag do or two in my time. Never in a professional capacity, though. If there's an etiquette to being the only XX at a traditionally XY party, it's this: don't complain, don't be the first or last to go home, and don't flirt outrageously (except with the strippers).

In fact, these rules could probably be expanded to life in general.

After breakfast we went on to a friend's birthday picnic, and in the evening to another friend's birthday drinks in a pub on the Thames. I wanted to ask him a thousand questions. Who was this Henrietta? How did they meet? Did he love her? But I didn't, and he thankfully steered well clear of any mention of her.

lundi, le 25 octobre

Giles dropped by my desk after lunch to ask about some reports I'm writing. I'm mostly cutting and pasting from the Web, but I don't tell him that. He was about to leave when he turned back. 'Meant to mention, saw you going off to lunch the other day,' he said.

I stiffened. Now what? He invites me back to his office for a chat, a threat, and maybe a come-on? Can the end of my career really have come so quickly? 'Did you?' I said.

'You looked . . .' *Please don't say fuckable.* ' . . . great,' he said. I noticed Mira and Erin stop their endless chatter to eavesdrop. 'Were you meeting a friend?'

'Er, yes, just a friend. He won't be dropping by the office.'

'That's a pity,' he said, smiling. 'I'm curious what a woman like you would find attractive in a man.'

I cough. Is there any way to answer that? 'Um, yes, well.' He tapped the corner of my desk and left.

mardi, le 26 octobre

Right, I've made my mind up to get out of the sex trade for good. It's time. Not just because I checked with the bank today and am now the proud recipient of an actual salary deposit. It's been long enough. I've been turning tricks for almost two years.

There's no denying I'll miss it. Lunchtime trips to swank hotels, dinners out with the sort of men you usually only read about in the business papers, the underwear, the sex.

You might be thinking, but you had to live a double life and never got enough sleep. The most you've seen of London is the inside of a lot of hotels. What's the benefit?

I'll tell you what it is. It's getting to see the nice side of men.

The clients are not all smart, handsome and charming – in fact, few are. But sometimes, in the arms of a naked stranger, they drop the defences they've been building up since the first time Daddy told them boys don't cry and they become . . . nicer, somehow.

Like tonight. The shy fumbling, as a long-time client reached into his pocket and pulled out a tiny box. The cutest little jewel – fashioned into a bee shape, with a sparkling sapphire set in the body. Just because he thought I'd like it. I smiled, and he smiled, and that to him was worth more than the expense of my time and the price of a bauble.

That's the benefit. That, and the agency doesn't take a cut on gifts.

jeudi, le 28 octobre

A major criticism of pornography is that anyone viewing large amounts of perversion cannot help but become used to it, then jaded by it, and then (so the argument goes) so removed from the people involved that inflicting harm on random strangers seems like a good idea. In short, that Page Three girls are the thin end of a wedge leading to secret rooms in Belgian flats.

I don't buy it. I've watched loads of porn, seen about

every flavour of wank mag out there. The problem is not that exposure to large amounts of raunchy imagery encourages the viewer to objectify sex; it's that porn is by its very nature objectified. Porn is reductive. All sexual imagery is shorthand for the total experience, be it a marble nude or the sticky pages of *Hustler Taboo*. The proliferation of imagery in modern media doesn't make perverts where there were none before; it simply makes Gary Glitter's collection electronically portable.

vendredi, le 29 octobre

The phone rang. I was tired. I sort of forgot that I had promised myself not to do this again, and said yes to the manager before remembering that I was meant to say no.

'Splendid, dahling. He lives in East Molesey.' Ugh. And it wasn't even convenient.

I was kneeling over the client, pulling his cock and balls. He reached up to stroke my face. From that angle, the soft hand, chalk-white skin, dark hair – he looked like someone else. I felt like there were crossed wires in my head, making me see ghosts that weren't there. 'Your neck,' he murmured, and I wasn't sure who was saying it. His voice was papery at that volume, very like the boyfriend before the Boy – the One.

When I was young I believed that, by concentrating hard enough, anyone who was thinking about me would be able to see through my eyes for a few moments, wherever I was, and hear and feel what was happening. I wondered who might be thinking about me, and would they be seeing this? My hands on someone else's shoulders, a dark trail of hair on the lower belly that looked far too familiar?

I rested my head on his chest. One of his legs flexed, one straight, it happened again. The ghost. It must sneak in like the autumn sun slanting through the window. Hundreds of motes stirring in the slight breeze, picking up crackling bits of memory and sticking them together. I closed my eyes. At least his smell was different. That put things right.

'I'd like to see you again,' he said as I dressed. 'Call me. Not for an appointment. A real date.'

'That would be nice,' I replied, and meant it perhaps a little more than was good for me. He slipped his card into my hand with the tip. I noted the name. 'I'll ring you sometime, Malcolm.'

samedi, le 30 octobre

I'm not a superstitious person, but today my horoscope came true!

Someone from your past is trying to make contact, it read. *Your best plan is to have an open mind in the weeks ahead.*

Hey, cut me a break. It's right next to the sudoku, okay?

I went online and checked my email – a note from L, the girl I was at school with. It was nice, for once, to have an unexpected email from someone I actually cared to hear from again, instead of an ex.

dimanche, le 31 octobre

Resolved: never to pick up the phone without looking to see who's calling. Ever. Again.

It was a call I should have known would come again. It's an unwritten rule of break-ups that one of the parties involved must make ill-advised, drunken, desperate calls to the other. And no matter how it ended, who broke up with whom, it's these horrible drunk diallings that will be remembered. Whatever moral high ground the person may have had is immediately forfeited. At least that person wasn't me.

Not Dr C, though. The Boy again. Fucking horoscope.

Novembre

mardi, le 2 novembre

Flagrant violation of company policy #1: Misuse of IT resources.

God bless the internet. How on earth office workers managed to fill up their time in the years BW (Before Web) is beyond me. Have spent the post-lunch period downloading music and listening to it on headphones. The better to drown out co-workers' inanity, my dear. L and I found each other online and spent much of the afternoon in a chat, before deciding to meet for late drinks.

'You look exactly the same,' I smiled. Perhaps a little glossier and more expensively dressed, but L was the very image of herself as a schoolgirl. It was only now I realised how much she resembles Gillian Anderson. She laughed.

'Cheers dears,' she said as we touched cheeks. 'I wouldn't have recognised you. You've lost a ton of weight.'

'Work stress,' I lied.

L nodded. We curled up with our cocktails at a corner table. 'So what keeps you busy these days?'

I'd already decided not to tell her about the small matter of fucking men for money. Not that I thought she wouldn't approve, but it's a bit much to spring on someone at a reunion. 'Oh, it's terribly boring,' I said. 'I'd love to hear more about what you're up to – from law to acting? Why? And more importantly, what are the men like?'

She laughed. 'I find the professions surprisingly alike. The men are like men everywhere – hopeless.' I concurred and we giggled our way through more drinks. It's a good thing, I thought, that some things don't change.

The foot fetishists, they are tops.

I don't understand their fetish but boy can I cater to it, and they certainly seem to like me.

Despite too large a fraction of my life spent in stilettos, my feet are in surprisingly good shape. Fine-boned, high-arched, uncallused and blessed with nicely shaped toes and toenails. Of my physical features I would rate the feet rather highly.

I met S earlier than my normal appointments. Mid-afternoon at a central hotel. He had requested no stockings, and 'pretty' shoes. Non-specific. Not a shoe fetishist, then, I wagered. I wore the violet peep-toed ones.

There is always the moment of doubt on meeting a client. Will this work? Is he nice? Is this even the right person? On meeting S, he smiled, looked me in the eyes, and his gaze dropped immediately to the floor. I knew we were on, and this was definitely the man.

He poured drinks and sat on the floor by my chair. He was average height, slim, with a cut-glass accent. With one hand he slipped my right shoe off. He nodded, as you imagine a jeweller would on seeing a fine gem. 'Five,' he said, referring (one assumes) to the size of my foot and not the number of toes.

He unsheathed the other foot, turning its underside towards him, running his thumb along its length. 'Ticklish?'

'No.'

'Good.' His warm fingers pressed lightly on the top of my foot. 'Clean?'

'As per instructions,' I said. 'Why no stockings?'

'I'm not interested in your legs,' he said, nuzzling the undersides of both feet together.

Fair enough. I'm indifferent to them myself. S removed his clothes and spent the next twenty minutes on the floor, shuffling his naked body under my feet as I held my legs bent, thighs raised from the seat. He especially lingered with my feet over his face. But he was not a toe-sucker, and seemed to prefer that I keep the feet together.

'Wiggle your toes.' Finally, he brought the two feet down to his crotch, cupping them round his balls as he masturbated.

'Nails,' he said. 'Dig the nails.' I dug the nails. He came. Lifting my soles off him, I could see the pink crescents some of the nails had left in his thigh. He dressed and poured me another drink. We turned on the television and watched a gardening show.

dimanche, le 7 novembre

Conversations I'm glad are firmly in the past:

1. Mum, I'm not a virgin any more.
It happened the term before I went to university. I thought I sort of loved the boy; he wrote me (very bad) songs and compared me to heroines in (very bad) books. He was ginger. It didn't last. It wouldn't have done to go to uni a virgin, anyway. My mother cried.

2. Can you just test me for everything?
Now, instead of troubling my GP with a rundown of reasons (invented) of why I need the full complement of tests for sexually transmitted infections (and then some), I go to a clinic. You almost don't even have to ask. Blessed, blessed understanding.

3. Take me off the agency books, and I mean it this time.
It really was as simple as that. I called up the manager and didn't even say hello. Just that we were over and she could

expect a final deposit into her account on Monday. And she didn't try to talk me out of it. Suddenly, I felt lighter.

I was still feeling buoyant about leaving the agency when I came to work. The bag under the desk – no need for that any more! No need to work extra-strength condoms into my weekly budget, nor keep two separate underwear drawers, one for clients and one for everyday. I was whistling as I came in the office and didn't care much if Erin and Mira heard.

Giles was sitting in my chair. 'I've good news and bad news,' he said. 'Which do you want first?'

Was this some sort of sophisticated trap? Had my effort to extract myself from the sex trade been too slow and some-one had found pics on the website? Was I about to be fired? Ho hum, good while it lasted, then. 'Bad news, I guess.'

'I'm not going to be supervising your work any more,' he said, nodding to Erin, who was arriving. 'I've been trans-ferred so this group is being reshuffled. I'm sure whoever takes over will be pleased to have such an effective team to look after.'

Better start looking for a new job today. 'That's a shame. What's the good news?'

He grinned. 'Well, seeing as I'm not your direct supervisor any longer, we can have an affair now.'

I smiled weakly. I imagine the crash behind me was the sound of Erin's jaw hitting the floor.

mardi, le 9 novembre

Flagrant violation of company policy #2: Took breaks in excess of contractual agreement.

I can't help it. It's bloody Erin and Mira. Now they're telling anyone who'll listen that I'm sleeping my way through the management. It's like being at school all over again. To the extent that I spent the better part of an hour hiding in the toilets.

mercredi, le 10 novembre

Half one this morning, a noise at the door.

The Boy was outside with a rucksack. He smiled. 'Is there room in the bed? You look all fluffy and cute.'

'Mmmmphhfff,' I said, standing aside so he could come in.

'Is that sleepy for "Take me to bed and ravish me"?'

I am truly an idiot. I have no reason to let this man back in my life. But it is late and I need servicing. 'No, that's sleepy for "Hurry up, before I wake up properly",' I said.

jeudi, le 11 novembre

Flagrant violation of company policy #3: Had non-work-related visitor to office.

Actually, this wasn't by choice. The Boy rang at lunchtime and asked if I wanted to meet him. 'Sure,' I said. 'Where are you?' 'Look out the window,' he said.

Oh, fucksticks. He was standing on the pavement looking up, dressed in a horrible pinstripey suit and holding what appeared to be flowers. Mira and Erin hurried over to coo behind my back: 'How darling!' 'How adorable!'

'Nice suit,' I said when I finally got down to the door. 'What's the occasion?'

'No occasion,' he said.

'Bit outside your usual remit.'

'I'm trying to impress you,' he said, handing the flowers

over. I had to admit, it was a sweet gesture. But I wasn't prepared to let my guard down just because we'd had (admittedly great) sex again. We walked off to the café.

I rode the bus home, berating myself the whole way for my poor judgement. This man had made a ruin of most of the last year of my life – what was I thinking? At home, I noticed my desk looked odd: nothing was out of place per se, but it just looked as if everything had been moved and then carefully replaced so as not to arouse suspicion.

Ugh, not again. That's my payback for a moment of weakness, then – evidence that the Boy may talk nice but hasn't changed a bit. Still jealous and suspicious where he has no reason to be. Still looking for someone he can keep on a leash, and not just in the bedroom, where it's acceptable. Too tired and fed up to consider the matter further.

vendredi, le 12 novembre

The Boy rang at suppertime. I'd taken the flowers home with me; they were in an old milk bottle. He suggested another rendezvous. I rolled my eyes but couldn't help being flattered. And in spite of obviously going through my computer, he was staying mostly in line. And the sex was awesome. I'd have to keep a closer eye on him, is all. I could handle it. 'Why don't I come visit your place this weekend?' I said.

'Why? Are you trying to keep me away from your friends? Are you seeing someone there?'

Eh? What the hell? 'No, I just haven't been out of town in ages. It would be nice to have a walk on the beach or something. Feel the fresh air.' Might as well enjoy the fact that he lives by the sea, if nothing else in this perverse arrangement.

'Fffffine,' he said. 'I'll meet you at the train station.'

samedi, le 13 novembre

The Boy's room looked eerily identical to when I was last there, months and months ago. The pile of unopened post on a chair, the cards stuck on the wardrobe doors – some of them from me. A bunch of flowers, dry now, that I'd bought when he was laid off work.

I looked for signs he'd been seeing other people, and there were a few – a half-empty bottle of massage oil by the bed, a fake rose with plastic 'dew' on the petals – but it shocked me to realise how much of the mess was not just his, but ours.

dimanche, le 14 novembre

We woke early, fucked, and fell asleep again. I heard the noise of his housemates downstairs but wasn't keen to run into them. Every time his phone rang, the Boy sprang out of bed and rushed up to the top floor, claiming poor reception in his room. It was odd – we were on the same network, and as far as I could tell, my phone's reception was fine.

Finally, well past lunchtime, we went downstairs. I wandered into the kitchen, and on the counter was a letter for a Miss Susie Allen. So that was her name.

He came into the kitchen and I held up the letter. 'Friend of yours?' I asked.

He snatched it out of my hand. 'Um, yeah, just some friend of my housemate's. She's travelling and gets her post here.'

Men are such bad liars sometimes, you have to pity them.

The Boy came round unexpectedly again last night and I didn't send him away. He definitely has one thing working in his favour, and that is the sex. The man has a way with a rope, especially the third time, with my wrists and ankles bound, my back on the bed. He knelt on the bed, entered me, pulled my legs towards him so they rested with the backs of my calves on one of his shoulders. I sat up slightly – the way my hands and feet were tied it was difficult not to. When he came, still kneeling, he pulled my legs in to his body, put his hands round my wrists, and picked me up off the bed. He is a lot taller than I am and very strong. A mental image I hope to remember for a very long time.

Flagrant violation of company policy #4: Using company phones for non-work-related purposes. 'So how is the City girl?' Mum asked.

'Mum, I don't *work* in the City.' Nothing like talking to the parents to bring you straight back to the searing whininess of pubescence.

'Yes, dear.' She sounded amused. 'Will they be giving you much time off at the end of the year?'

'I get two weeks,' I said. 'I was thinking of taking the time closer to Chanukah and coming to see you and Daddy.'

'Oh honey,' she said. 'I hate to have to tell you this way, but your father and I are splitting up. So maybe your coming for Chanukah wouldn't be the best time.'

'I'll say. I'm coming up right now.'

dimanche, le 21 novembre

'I let him have the spare furniture in the extra bedrooms,' Mum says. 'He's living round the corner in a flat at the moment. Do you want me to drive you round to see him?'

No, not yet. I can just about hold it together in front of my mother, but I've always been a daddy's girl, and the thought of seeing him in some poky rental makes me want to cry. 'Maybe tomorrow,' I say. We spend the rest of the day cautiously around each other; it's the first time we've really been alone together, probably since I was a baby.

'Why did you marry Daddy?' I ask.

'He always made me feel safe,' Mum says. 'And I knew we would have clever children.'

'Flattery will get you everywhere,' I say. But I notice she hasn't said anything about passion or true love. She might as well come out and say, 'I settled down too early and this was all a mistake and I should have spent the seventies travelling Kashmir with a rucksack rather than raising children in the suburbs.' My parents married when they were still students. By the time she was my age, my mother had an eight-year-old daughter – me. 'Would you have split up sooner if you hadn't had children?'

'Don't be so glum,' Mum says. 'Your father will always have a place in my heart.' I know about having a place for someone in your heart. That's where they go when they don't have a place in your life any more.

mercredi, le 24 novembre

Flagrant violation of company policy #5: Took a sick day without ringing in until after 10 a.m.

There are risks involved in promiscuity. Some of these involve viruses and I am sorry to announce I have succumbed. I have had a stinking cold since Monday.

Still, this makes a nice change. When I was a call girl there was almost no chance of taking a sick day. I remember the first time it happened, and I asked the manager if she couldn't get the punter to reschedule. She said no, and that he didn't want anyone but me, so I had to go. 'But what if I give him my cold?' I whined. 'Who cares?' she said. Considering how conscientious we were regarding sexually transmitted infections, I thought her attitude rather ruthless. I dosed myself with as much Day Nurse as I could stand and staggered on, determined to last the two hours without giving him bird flu. It remains the only appointment in which I lied and told the client I didn't do kissing; what I didn't say was that it was because I was afraid of giving him my cold. I have no idea whether it's possible to contract influenza through blowjobs.

vendredi, le 26 novembre

Met N and A1 after work for a drink. 'Hey, sugar,' A1 said, putting his arm around my waist. 'So your Tory friend is meeting us, is he?' The first time they met, A1 and N spent the entire evening arguing politics, and ever since, N's been my 'Tory friend' to A1.

N and I were discussing the perfect mate – A1 is exempt, being married and all.

N's criteria total three:

- Ample-chested.
- High pain threshold.
- Gets on with his mum.

My list is somewhat longer:

- Tall and thin, or
- Tall and muscular, or
- Neither of these but physically appealing to me anyway, and
- Nice hands, and
- Nice voice, and
- Someone who either likes to talk or listen, and
- Ideally fits into my knickers, not habitually, just once or twice for effect, and
- Lives about two hours away – not more, not less.

The last criterion is important; I like my space. So much so that I typically live alone in quiet areas and don't appreciate a boyfriend who just 'pops round' when he wants to. See, someone who lives a moderate drive or train ride away is never round your house at all times, eating all the food, leaving mysterious stains on the carpet and getting it on with your neighbour in your bed (far preferable that he plays away with his own neighbour in his own bed). On the other hand, he's not so far that he can't be there at short notice if needed.

However, this was before I moved to London. The relationship between space and time is altered here. Hauling myself from NW5-ish to a central location might take twenty minutes, might take two hours. In any normal place it would take minutes. Once I considered seeing a man in Leyton, and the thought of the time it would take to negotiate that distance was a large part of not pursuing the affair.

Then there was the man who lived several counties away, but could drive to my house in less than two hours. He didn't survive the cut-off, either, because while he could drive to me, I could not drive to him. I have no car. Before you think me unnecessarily harsh when it comes to men, I should say in my defence that it was he who ended things with me. I'm not the only one with a two-hour rule.

dimanche, le 28 novembre

The Weekend – A Quiz

1. The weekend just gone, I went to:

a) France
b) Flitwick
c) Fulham

correct answer: a

2. I was accompanied by:

a) a committee presenting me with the Légion d'Honneur
b) paparazzi
c) the Boy

correct answer: c

3. The Boy gave me, as a gift:

a) a bunch of bright orange daisies
b) a jar of jam he made
c) a sex swing he made

correct answer: all of the above

4. I came back from holiday with

a) a Tour d'Eiffel paperweight
b) rope burns
c) Lance Armstrong

correct answer: b

'This means we're back on, right?' the Boy asked nervously. The train pulled slowly out of the station, and I silently said goodbye to the trees, the houses, the sun. According to the forecast it was raining in London.

'We're back on,' I said, and he squeezed my hand. My heart did jump, I admit. And we held hands the whole way home.

mardi, le 30 novembre

A hand waved in front of my computer screen, startling me. I looked up. Giles. I took off my headphones.

'Sorry,' I said. 'Helps me concentrate on work.'

'Can we have a chat?' he said.

'Of course.'

'Good. How about tomorrow? I'll have my secretary book something.'

For a horrified moment I thought maybe he meant a hotel room. Then I realised he meant food, and smiled. 'Great.' What the hell is he after? I wondered as he walked away.

Décembre

mercredi, le 1 décembre

'I hope you like Chinese,' Giles said, spreading a large napkin over his lap.

'Love it,' I said. Eating out in Chinese restaurants is a Jewish family tradition; by the time I left home I'd probably had more black bean sauce than HP.

'I'll be honest with you,' he said after the food arrived. 'This reshuffle is not going to go in your favour.'

'Oh,' I said and looked down at the food. It smelled of hot chilli and garlic, but I suddenly felt less than hungry. Was this my last meal? Was I really going to get the heave-ho on a Tuesday lunchtime surrounded by loud men in suits?

'I don't think it's any secret that you haven't really gelled with your team members,' he said. 'And since Erin has more experience and seniority than you, the only appropriate thing to do is to make her your supervisor.'

I stared at the steaming pile of rice between us.

'But I'll tell you something, and I'm counting on your discretion here,' he said.

This is it, I thought. The moment where he asks me to fuck him so I can keep my job.

'You're wasted in this place. I bet in a year you'll be bored and looking for something new.'

Classic man move #361: Let me down easy, make it sound like it was what I really wanted anyway.

'Come the New Year, you won't see me around any more. I've managed to secure some funding, and am striking out on my own. And I want you to be there.'

'Pardon?'

'I'm offering you a job. More pay, and hopefully more interesting than what you're doing now.'

'You mean you didn't bring me here to fire me or fuck me?'

He half coughed, half laughed into his hand. 'Flattering a thought as that is, no,' he said.

Great, now I'd put my foot in it. 'You think I'm any good?'

'I think you have potential,' he corrected. 'That's a lot more than most people in there.'

'So what do I do?'

'Put in your notice but don't tell your team,' he said.

samedi, le 4 décembre

Switched on the mobile yesterday afternoon to find three missed calls and a dozen texts. The Boy has got out of hand, and this has ballooned into what he is calling 'The Lie'.

I went out with friends, one of them was N, and I didn't immediately ring and tell him. I didn't tell him when I showered at the gym, either, or the last time I had a bowel movement. Do those count as lies as well?

Several hours later, after spending a wholly civilised evening with L, draining bottles of white and talking about our respective holidays, I did wonder why things could be so light and easy with almost everyone else in the world. When I checked the phone later, the Boy had texted a goodnight kiss. It's something he never would have done before. I waited only a few minutes before sending one back.

'How's the new place?' I asked. I was holding the phone between my shoulder and ear, simultaneously installing software on the computer.

'Great,' Daddy said with enthusiasm. 'I put a poster on the wall to brighten the place. In case I have people round.'

A little window came on the computer screen: Installation successful. I restarted, tried the password to hide the program, then unhid it. Perfect. From now on every keystroke made on my computer would be logged and stored, with no sign to the user – say, the Boy – that anything was amiss.

'Don't you worry, honey, I'll make you a deal not to date anyone younger than my daughter.'

What? Date anyone? The ink on the papers was hardly dry. 'Are you sure that's a good idea?'

'Well, it would be a little strange if you ended up with a stepmother younger than you, wouldn't it?'

'Okay, number one, no one you marry will be anything-mother, because she didn't raise me. And number two, you're dating already? Isn't there some sort of cooling-off period?'

'Honey, calm down. I'm not seeing anyone yet.'

'Cripes, Daddy, don't scare me like that.'

He laughed. 'There's such a thing as being too honest, I suppose,' he said.

'I thought you always told me the most important thing was honesty.'

'It is. But I'll give you a tip. Anyone who goes around telling anyone who'll listen about how honest he is, isn't.'

'That's a comforting thought,' I said. 'Nevertheless, when you do start dating, I expect you to be honest with me about it.'

'Well, I think we should make a deal – I won't date

anyone younger than you if you won't date anyone older than me.'

I think I have a new contender for Creepiest Conversation in History Ever. 'Agreed.' He didn't say anything about sleeping with them for money, mind. Though I suppose that meant he could see a prostitute who was younger than me. Okay, now I've made myself squirm twice in two minutes. New record.

lundi, le 6 décembre

'You sound a little down, honey,' my mother said.

'Oh, just things getting to me. Stressful at work lately.' I still hadn't decided what to make of Giles's offer.

'That's a pity. I had so hoped you'd find it less of a strain than your last job.'

Keeping in mind that supposedly my mother had no idea I was ever a call girl, I wondered what she meant by that.

'You know, when you were in that bookshop.'

'Right,' I sighed. 'The bookshop. It's just different, that's all. That job was boring more than actually stressful.' To be fair, this one was pretty boring as well.

'Changing tack slightly,' she said, by which she always means changing tack entirely, 'I received the most unexpected call the other day. From your cousin, you know.'

'Which one?' I asked. There are so many I've lost count.

'You know, J,' she said, as if it was obvious.

'How is he?' I asked. Even though we are of a similar age and grew up together, I had no idea what had happened to him after I went to university.

'He's well, and living in Central America of all places,' she said. 'Mexico, or was it Belize? Anyway, you'll be happy to know that all his problems with the law over that drug-dealing charge are long behind him and that he's really cleaned up his act. Been off the stuff for a year, he says.'

'That's great,' I said. He'd been dealing drugs? I'd had no idea; clearly I have failed to keep up.

'You should ring him up sometime,' Mum said. 'You two were always so close.'

'Were close. I wonder what we'd have in common now.' Apart from making a living on the fringes of legal society.

'He seemed to think you should go out and visit,' she said. 'I told him your work kept you very busy, though.'

Hmm. Late winter in rainy, crowded London or holiday in the sun? Maybe instead of following Giles to his new company, what I really needed was some time off to think about it. Somewhere warm would be nice. 'Actually,' I said, 'I think I may have some extensive holiday coming up.'

jeudi, le 9 décembre

Not being a call girl any more has its advantages and disadvantages:

Advantage: leg coverings. No matter how long the coat, how clingy the skirt, how reliable the stockings, you will catch a chill. The top half is usually underdressed, too (shockingly few punters request cardies).

Disadvantage: transport. Though underdressed for a cold night, one does usually get from point A to point B in a taxi while working the sex trade. Now I stand at a cold bus stop or sweat down the back of my jumper on an overheated Tube.

Advantage: selective party attendance. No longer am I required to make someone else's night sparkle. Granted, I spend a lot of time reading in the bath, but at least I don't have to feign interest in work-related conversations while my drunken client staggers into the women's loo. At times my work role was more babysitter than sexpot.

Disadvantage: spending money. Giving lavish gifts is the high point of winter, as is drinking pricey fizz. The benefit of hourly, cash-in-pocket work is being able to hit the shops on the way home.

Advantage: throwing away the fuzzy red knickers for ever. Whoever decided sexy women and Father Christmas were a logical cross should be strung up.

Disadvantage: personal grooming. Knowing fewer people are going to see me wearing less than three layers is no incentive to keep up with sit-ups, waxing or the like. Sometimes I worry the Boy will tell people my previous occupation but then relax because the state I'm in, no one would believe it.

vendredi, le 10 décembre

'You can't be seriously considering it,' the Boy said, flipping through old magazines. We'd just come from the shower, where we'd had a lovely fuck. It was like when we were a new couple, it was that good. We'd started by lathering each other, then I fingered his pucker while sucking him off, then he'd taken me up the arse. 'That would possibly count as the most irresponsible thing I've ever heard in my life.'

I shot him a look. This from someone who spent the last three years 'in between jobs'?

'Besides,' he said, 'no one really does the whole gap year thing any more. That's so ten years ago.'

'Except Susie, of course,' I said.

'Pardon?'

'Susie. Your friend who has her post delivered to your house. You said she was off travelling, right?'

'What are you implying? She's just someone I know. It's not like I'm sleeping with her. I mean, she's fat and smokes and reads *Heat*. She's just keeping a few things at my house.'

Wow, methinks the man doth protest too much. 'Well, I haven't seen my cousin in so long. We used to be very close. I hardly feel connected to anyone in the family any more.' *That's it, play the filial guilt card.* I despise myself sometimes.

samedi, le 11 décembre

The Boy was hardly out the door when I checked the key-stroke logs on the computer. I had been at work most of Friday, so he'd had a wide-open opportunity to snoop.

And he took it, that much was clear. He'd been careful to erase his history in the Web browser and had made a more-or-less good effort to replace everything on the computer desk just where it was. But he hadn't known about the key-stroke logger and I could see everything. He'd checked up on my diary, then cycled through my recent Web activity. And then – what ho? What is this? Checked his email – password easier to guess than I would have imagined. And then. His own anonymous blog, publically posted on the internet for anyone to see.

I logged on and had a look – and my heart sank. Oh, he was still seeing Susie, all right. She was away in South-east Asia visiting her dad, but they were definitely still on as far as he was concerned. He even posted some of the things she'd been sending him, comparing the way she was to the way I am.

That was the horror of it: seeing her most recent email and how banal it was. She had had food poisoning. Had he received her gift in the post yet? Looking forward to seeing him soon – maybe he could fly out in January?

Love, Kitty.

And that hurt. To find Susie calling herself by the same pet name he'd always used for me was a painful thing.

But not as much as finding out about all the other girls.

mardi, le 14 décembre

After lunch I pop by Erin's desk to 'borrow' her stapler – mine has been nicked by Jojo in Personnel. Erin's still at lunch. When I put the stapler back it moves the mouse, and her computer screen comes back to life. A chat window is open.

The employees all use a messenger program to communicate between offices – it's more convenient than phoning and, I've found, saves time when asking questions. Erin's been chatting with Giles, I see. He's almost always online.

<GilesTheMan>Hey sexy

<canadienne>Still thinking about this morning :)

<GilesTheMan>my fingers still smell of you

<canadienne>Off to lunch now . . . maybe organise a 'private meeting' later?

My face goes beet red. Not embarrassment; anger. Stupid, stupid girl, I think. And then I wonder how much of this goes on with the Boy and Susie when I'm not around.

Idiots, I think with real hatred. *Every one of them.* Erin and Giles, Susie and the Boy. What is wrong with men? Why do they need to lie, run around, and generally hurt as many people as possible in pursuit of nothing better than a screw?

I'd seen the Boy's pictures of Susie online. She was flat-chested, with short, spiky hair and glasses. The sort of girl I would have pegged as a lesbian. But in spite of the fact that I knew I was prettier, it wasn't much consolation. In fact, it made the whole affair slightly worse.

And that's what I think about this discovery: how can Erin be involved with Giles? How could someone as singularly annoying as her be hanging off the end of his cock for fun? How, in any sort of fair world, does this happen?

mercredi, le 15 décembre

Met a gentleman late, at his house.

He was an old client. I was there on business. I needed the money to offset costs for the rest of the month.

I needed to go out and relax with an old friend, someone I knew would not judge me. I needed to feel wanted without the problem of having to establish that it was just for companionship and sex, not for ever.

Was it cheating? Yes, it was cheating. I'm a fucking hypocrite. I wouldn't have rung the client, wouldn't have even thought of it, if not for that diary. The Boy thought my going to dinner with N justified a drama? He can take a fucking flying leap. What's sauce for the gander is sauce for the goose.

I needed to get the Boy off my mind for a few hours.

The client, M, is older, short but elegant. An ex-jockey who works in the City and keeps a mews house for the weekdays. Likes: white wine, white knickers and light domination. Dislikes: talking about his family, meeting before 10 pm, paying in small bills. I always left M's house with a fistful of pinks.

He didn't ask questions when I rang him. He said he was free and he'd see me at ten. He handed the cash over. We got straight down to business: brief kissing, his eyes closed, mine open; I stripped slowly, shoes first so we were on eye level. Kneeled to take him in my mouth briefly, looking up to meet his eyes. Stood up and he turned me round. He caressed my bottom and bent me over the sofa. Usually he likes me on top, but this time we didn't even make it to the bedroom. He asked if he could come on me – I said yes; he pulled the condom off and ejaculated on the small of my back.

We were lounging on the floor, half dressed, when he finally asked. He'd rung the agency a month ago; they sent another girl in my place. 'So why all of a sudden, out of the blue like this?'

I shrugged and drained my wineglass. He refilled it. 'No good reason,' I said.

He nodded. The details weren't important. If there was something in my voice, or in my eyes, he let it go. And then the oddest thing. He started telling me about his family – here was a picture of his wife; and about his daughter, an artist. He had saved clippings from the paper where her work was mentioned; here was a black-and-white photo, of a curly-haired Jewish woman. His daughter. Who was older than me.

At the end of the appointment I went up for a shower. Next to the bath was a hairbrush, and wound through it long, dark hair. Just like his wife's hair. Like his daughter's. Or it could have been another call girl's.

'Love is patient, love is kind,' I said to the wet tiles. I wondered, if I were a wife, how much I would want to know. How much I would be able to forgive.

I can barely stand to look but I manage somehow to obsessively read all of the Boy's past emails and his weblog entries. The list of objectionable women in the Boy's life runs roughly thus:

1. **Sierra Hohum**. Bland, blonde medic. Extremely jolly-hockeysticks. As far as I can tell, he simply idolises her, but she hasn't slept with him. I met the girl several times and was never particularly impressed.

2. **Susie**. The dark horse. Clearly their relationship is ongoing while she is away in Thailand. He constantly refers to her as 'a bit thick' and clearly finds her smoking unattractive.

3. **Georgie**. Like Sierra Hohum, but fan of sci-fi. And will deign to fuck him, judging from email she sent asking whether he avoided catching anything while she had thrush, since her boyfriend seemed to be having odd symptoms. Why are men always suckers for a posh accent, pear shape and pashmina?

4. **Lena**. Frizz-haired stick insect I caught him in bed with over a year ago. 'She was just sleeping next to me in her underwear,' he claimed. His email begging her to give him another chance tells another story. She clearly wised up and moved on.

5. **Jo**. Large, frumpish first girlfriend ten years his senior who would drop everything – job, boyfriend, identity as an autonomous human being – to be back with him.

6. **Me**. I hate myself for even letting him back in the door.

I should definitely get away. Ring J in the morning. Tell him I'm coming, and I'm bringing a bikini, and I mean business.

lundi, le 20 décembre

Giles and I met again for lunch. This time I chose the venue: a small Polish restaurant I know well. I waved to the waitress and ordered us both *barzcz* and the huntsman's stew.

'So what have you brought me out here for, then?' he asked, as a smile of amusement flickered across his face.

'I'm sorry to do this to you, but I don't think I'll be able to join you in the New Year.'

'You've decided not to leave your job?'

The waitress plopped two bowls of soup in front of us. 'No, I've just reconsidered my priorities,' I said. 'I'm going to do some travelling, really think about whether this is what I want to be.'

He sipped the soup and smiled. I don't think he liked it.

'It'll be a pity to lose you,' he said. 'You have abilities that will be difficult to replace. Frankly, I'm surprised the company haven't made you a better offer to stay on.'

'There's been no offer,' I said. Jojo in Personnel had accepted my resignation with the same aplomb I delivered it and no one had said a word about it since.

He quit the soup after three spoonfuls. 'I do hope you decide to come back,' he said. 'For purely selfish reasons. You'd be an asset to any firm lucky enough to get you.'

'I would have thought you found the talents of some of my other co-workers a little more compelling,' I said, raising an eyebrow. 'Erin, for instance.'

He smoothed the napkin on his lap. 'Be that as it may,' he said, 'there are some people I find I can . . . collaborate with . . . on an occasional basis. That isn't the same as respecting their professional talents.'

Good on you, I thought. At least you haven't denied it. But I wonder why he bothers with a workplace affair? If he was a friend, I would recommend he spend his time on call girls instead. Who knows, maybe he already does.

vendredi, le 24 décembre

'What's up,' my cousin J says, as if we'd never stopped talking.

The line sounds clear, as if he's just round the corner.

I smile. Has it really been so long? Almost half our lives? It has. He says he is well and certainly sounds it.

'So are you coming out or what?' he asks. There's no pressure there. He's so laid back. I can't help but envy the obvious calm in his voice, and tell him so.

'Serenity, girl,' he says. 'It's the journey, not the destination.'

Well, whatever. I start unloading about work, about the Boy, and he interrupts me. 'Just come and crash at mine for a while and get some sun. You don't have to decide nothing.'

Oh, but I already have.

samedi, le 25 décembre

Some things never change. A4's mother will always roast a turkey at Christmas, even though no one in the family except A4 eats it. I have a single slice of the breast, but to be honest, I don't much like it, either. Everyone else has chicken.

A4's sister-in-law will always scowl at me until I produce my usual gift for her, handmade rum truffles and a mix CD.

A4's brother will grumble if anyone gives him a combination Christmas and birthday card. His birthday's on Boxing Day, but don't you dare buy him a single gift for both occasions.

A4's auntie will nag us both about why we're still single, and why don't we just get back together already?

A4's mum will drink too much and insist on everyone singing carols, and when they refuse, will sulk and take unflattering photos of the family as they pass out on the sofa.

I wish my family never changed.

dimanche, le 26 décembre

When I get up, A4 is in his appointed spot, by the television. News is on, not unusual. What's strange is his stillness. I look closer – a giant wave, a tsunami, has wiped out most of South-East Asia.

'Jesus,' A4 says. Being of staunchly Catholic stock, it's odd to hear him utter even this mild blasphemy. 'You don't know anyone out there, do you?'

Apart from Susie? No.

lundi, le 27 décembre

Took the early coach back – no trains. Was tempted to fall asleep, but instead watched mist lifting off the fields. Rail lines along the road joined and parted again, malevolent silver, like mercury. The closer we came to London, the more snow was on the ground. And finally in London it turned to oily slush. Winter wonderland. Wondered how long it would be before I saw it again.

'I'm going to miss the hell out of you,' N said.

'Same here,' I said. 'And how's it going with you and . . . ?'

'Henrietta,' he said. 'I don't know. We'll see.'

'Something wrong?' I'd been so wrapped up in my own drama I had no idea what was going on with N and his girl.

'No, not really,' he said. 'Just get the feeling she might be bored and preparing to move on.'

'She'd be a fool,' I said, putting my hand on his.

'Well, like I always say, there are two kinds of women in the world, stayers and goers. She's a goer. If she doesn't think I'm The One, it's just a matter of time before she's out the door, and probably sooner rather than later.'

'I'm sorry,' I said. He shrugged. 'Which am I, if you don't mind my asking?'

'Oh, you're a stayer,' he said. 'But you spend a lot of time trying to convince yourself otherwise.'

mardi, le 28 décembre

The Boy rang to say he was coming to visit, and invited me home with him for New Year.

I checked the Boy's email. Susie wrote to say she will be coming back because of the tsunami, and she'll arrive in London on the 30th. I can see that he replied, and wonder why he decided not to spend the holiday with her instead.

We meet A1 and his wife for dinner. Our respective mates are told to secure a table while A1 and I go to find a cashpoint, as the restaurant he chose doesn't accept cards.

'I didn't expect to see him with you again,' A1 said.

'To tell the truth I didn't expect to be with him again,' I said. 'But here we are.'

'Is it going better this time?'

'Not really,' I said. 'But I'm going to stick with it. Find out for once what lies on the other side of the first crisis. See what all the long-term couples are on about.'

When we got home the Boy seemed a little tired, but I mounted him on the sofa and fucked him hard. I tasted the beer on his breath and myself on his cock. And all I could think the whole time was: *Is this better than Susie? Can she make you come like this?* I'd never fucked with so much resentment, not even when a prostitute.

jeudi, le 30 décembre

The Boy was out in the garden with his brothers and I was inside, on the computer, chatting to A4.

<luvlyjubly>How is it with the family?

<belle_online>Almost bearable.

<luvlyjubly>Is it a nice house?

<belle_online>As far as these places go. They've stuck me in another wing.

The Boy's parents had kept his room just as it was when he left for uni, with bunk bed, a stuffed elephant and old water-colours he did at school on the wall. He still received post there. I idly picked up a short cardboard cylinder on the desk.

<belle_online>Anything special planned for new year?

<luvlyjubly>Same as last year, going to P and R's for drinks.

The postmark and stamps on the tube were odd – where on earth had that been posted from? I opened the tube and extracted a rolled piece of card. It was calligraphy of some sort, drawn in wide brushstrokes. The characters were not Chinese, something else. I looked closely at the smaller writing along the bottom in English. The Boy's name. And Susie's. And a love heart. My stomach turned.

<luvlyjubly>How about you?

<belle_online>I think we're going to the fireworks with his brothers and parents. Though considering his dad, that implies an all-night-brandy-drinking sesh afterward.

I looked again at the postmark. She must have sent this as a Christmas gift, before she knew she was coming back. I put it back in the tube and went off to listen to music. Billie Holiday. The down-turning strings, the voice cracking, always just behind the beat. Unbearable, given the circumstances, but somehow nothing else would do.

Janvier

vendredi, le 7 janvier

There is very little to signify my last day at work: handing in the identity card that opens the outer door and the key for the door to the office, packing my belongings in a box: a few pens, a half-used notepad and a reference book. There's nothing of interest on my computer, but I upload my work files to the company server and reformat the disk anyway. At lunch someone takes my chair away; it's been bagsied by a pregnant woman in Billing.

'Are you gonna need this?' Erin bangs her fist on the top of a filing cabinet at the end of my desk. I shake my head.

This is the last time I'll hear Erin's voice.

This is the last time I'll walk out this door.

'Helloooooo? You fergot yer mouse pad!'

'Keep it,' I say. *Okay, that was the last time. With luck.*

dimanche, le 9 janvier

The Boy met me at home just as I was taping the last of the boxes shut. Anything that was left had either been in the flat to start with, was going to a charity shop or was being squeezed into my luggage for the plane.

'I presume you'll need me to take these in for a few months?'

'No, I've already made arrangements,' I said. A4 was hiring a car and after I'd gone would be coming round to check the post, drop off my keys with the estate agent and take my things to his.

'Oh, you should have said,' he said. His face dropped. I suppose he'd assumed I would be asking him for last-minute favours; it never occurred to him that I could be more organised than that. And there were plenty of good reasons not to keep my belongings at his. For one thing, I knew the cupboard under the stairs in his house was already full of boxes of Susie's crap and that, due to the tsunami, she was coming back earlier than expected. For another, I knew he couldn't be trusted not to go through my stuff.

'Not to worry, he offered,' I said, referring to A4. 'Anyway, I want to spend the time with you rather than spend it moving boxes.' And if we happen to split up soon, at least I won't have to collect my boxes from your house.

lundi, le 10 janvier

The Boy and I planned to go out but we had to change tack. The hurry of packing had left me a little worn, and I was feeling fragile and on the edge of getting a cold. He doesn't take not getting his way very well, but even he understands that not to make a show of sympathy is a bad idea. 'Is there anything I can do to make you feel better?'

Sex for starters, I thought. I smiled weakly. 'The muscles in my legs are aching. You could massage them.'

I pouted and indicated the massage oil. He poured some into his hands, rubbing them together so it would warm. He then applied himself to my left thigh, slowly at first.

'You can go harder,' I said.

By the time he was massaging my right calf, my foot resting on his shoulder, he was stiffening. When he reached the toes of that foot he was hard. He shifted so he was coming out of his shorts, put my other leg on his shoulder, and scooted up the bed until he entered me.

'You go on top,' he said.

'I haven't the energy,' I protested. Plus, I loved the way his cock felt inside me at this angle. He reached down and grabbed my breasts roughly, harder than he ever had, hard enough to leave marks. I love that. I ground myself into him and felt his shorts – still on him, pushed to one side – sodden with my juices. He came, then coaxed me to orgasm before taking me the same way again.

We drank the red I was saving for something nice, and ate crisps, spreading crumbs all over the floor. His hands danced under my white dressing gown. We fucked again, him leaning me up against the sofa, then over the boxes in the hallway.

No sense getting too much sleep the night before I leave.

mardi, le 11 janvier

'What can I do to bring you back?' the Boy murmured into my hair. Pedestrian traffic to the ticket hall parted around us.

'Stay faithful,' I said. There was no reply and we held each other quietly for a moment in the noisy airport; after all, what could either of us say? He believed nothing he did should ever be questioned. I believed he'd be in someone else's arms within an hour of my departure. I knew from the website that Susie had come back from Thailand and was disappointed he hadn't collected her from the airport.

We played the goodbyes just as they should be done, with long kisses and clinging at the point of separation, and yes, once past the whisky stands of the duty-free and the purgatorial waiting area, I allowed myself to cry. But not for that long. Sometime tomorrow me and my bikini will be in another country where it's sunny and warm.

mercredi, le 12 janvier

The drive from the airport is a long one. In the dark I have no sense of where I am now, only that it's warm and the air is heavy, smelling of the sea.

Air travel is a sort of miracle, isn't it? Just this morning I was freezing cold in London. Now, even stripped down to a T-shirt and trousers, I feel too hot. I can't stop my head swivelling as we drive from the airport into town, trying to decipher the bright signs, the unfamiliar road markings, the voices on the driver's radio.

I'm the last person to be dropped off. The van drives away from the dark bungalow. J had said the key would be under the mat, but when I check, it isn't. Great.

'*Buenas noches,*' a low voice comes out of the trees.

'Hello? Is anyone there?' I can't see anyone, but the bushes rustle ominously.

'Good evening, are you cousin?' A small man shaped like an inverted triangle steps into the garden and points at his chest. 'Tomás.'

'Hello, Tomás,' I say, setting the bags down and reaching out to shake his hand. He doesn't offer it.

'I have key,' he says. 'Your cousin thought maybe safer.'

'That's great.'

'You speak Spanish?' he asks, with a little hope in his voice.

'I'm afraid not.' He nods as if this is the expected answer. I feel a bit of a twat. 'But I'd love to learn.'

Tomás beams. 'Tomorrow maybe I come by?' He opens his right hand and gives me the key.

jeudi, le 13 janvier

It's late when J finally turns up. Or rather, it's early: by my reckoning it was somewhere between half three and the dawn chorus. Not that there really is such a thing here – with insects singing all night you hardly notice when the birds join in.

I stumbled out of the bedroom. 'Oh, wow, here you are,' J said, as if I'd just come back unexpectedly from a trip out of town. He was a lot taller than the last time I'd seen him, and a lot more tanned. His eyes looked tired and a little crinkly. 'I didn't wake you, did I?' He leans in for a rough hug. His shoulder is huge and freckled and smells of soap.

'Don't worry about it,' I said. 'You all right?'

'Wicked,' J said. 'How's the crib?'

'The crib is fine,' I smile. 'Did you have a nice night?'

'Yeah, good, actually. A mate of mine just bought a DVD player so I went round and we watched scary movies.' In person his voice sounds a lot less affected, a lot less street; but I also notice it's diverged significantly from mine; it sounds quasi-Jamaican, sing-songy.

'If you go to bed now you'll have bad dreams,' I taunt.

'Good thing I'm not going to bed, then,' J said. 'How about some coffee?'

vendredi, le 14 janvier

'Rule number one,' J says, 'is that nothing around here works. I have a mobile, so when the landline's down – and it usually is – you're welcome to it if you need.'

'Ta,' I said. Actually, I made it online for a brief time before the connection inexplicably failed. But it wasn't the country's dodgy infrastructure that was getting my goat. It was the Boy, who according to his recently updated weblog had gone straight from seeing me off at the airport to Susie's bed. And he was upset.

Not because I left: because Susie had evidently gone off him sometime between leaving for a year out and seeing an entire island washed away. She was refusing to have sex with him. If I hadn't cried I would have laughed, or something like that.

I leaned over and switched off the monitor. 'That shit's a waste of time,' J said. 'You want to go to the beach? Drive somewhere? You need to go shopping?'

I asked him what we had to eat and he shrugged. 'I'm no cook. Come on, let's go get you something.'

We walked round the corner to a grocer. I blinked against the strong tropical light, eyes watering. J took off his sleek sunglasses and put them on my face, which helped.

'Rule number two,' J said. 'Let's get this done and dusted first – no alcohol in the house. I don't go out to the bars, so if you want to go, ask Tomás to take you. Some of them are not nice places for women on their own.'

'Okay,' I said.

'And if you have prescription drugs, put them out of sight,' he continues. 'It's a daily struggle for me to stay clean, so I need to know you're on my side.'

'Of course I am.'

The grocer was an old man, fat, and spoke to us in English.

'That's nice,' I murmured to J. 'But shouldn't we be at least trying to speak Spanish to him?'

J laughed. 'He doesn't speak any more Spanish than you or me. Almost half the people here don't. He's Greek. Rule number three: most people here are tourists. Even the locals.' I selected a few strangely large citrus fruits, a can of beans, bread and a weird, star-shaped fruit. J carried our bags home.

samedi, le 15 janvier

J left me a bicycle and a note with instructions to find my way around. I didn't learn to ride a pushbike until I was a teenager, and it was J who taught me.

All the houses are small bungalows with improbably lush gardens. There are a lot of shops, I notice, and a lot of payphones. And an oddly high concentration of dentists.

I need a hat. After half an hour the back of my neck is prickling hotly. I've never burned easily; on the other hand, a Yorkshire summer consists of about a net hour of direct light every year. And while an occasional trip to the sunbed was de rigueur for a call girl, I hardly went often enough to build up a base tan. Happily, this is the tourist section, and as far as straw hats go, I am spoiled for choice.

dimanche, le 16 janvier

We leave the doors open when someone's home, because it's hot. Tomás lets himself in. The screen door shuts loudly behind him, a hollow aluminium clatter. I jump up from the computer, where I've been agonising over the Boy's weblog again – should I post an arch, suggestive comment, or otherwise let him know I know?

'Oh, hi!' I say. 'I thought you were coming around days ago.' Tomás shrugs. Punctuality clearly isn't a priority. 'You going to teach me Spanish today?'

He laughs. 'You think you can learn in one day?'

'Probably not,' I smile. He helps himself to a fizzy drink – it's frighteningly green and, I guess from the label, supposed to taste of lemon. 'Today,' Tomás says, flicking on the television and sitting on J's sofa, 'only watch Spanish television.'

'Okay,' I say. 'Anything in particular?'

'I came over to watch the sports. You mind sports?'

'I don't mind,' I say. Lesson one consists of catching up with the football. Which is pronounced 'futbol'. This may take longer than I hoped.

mardi, le 18 janvier

Phone message in the morning from the Boy on the landline. I do the maths: he rang about 4 am UK time. I ring back.

He doesn't ask about the flight, or how I'm settling in. Probably just as well; apart from 'long' and 'fine', I haven't much to say. He natters on about friends or something – it all seems so far away now.

'When is a good time to ring you?' he asks.

'Mid-afternoon, I suppose,' I say.

'Good, I'll ring you tomorrow. I really do miss you and love you, you know.' I put the phone down. Why the renewed enthusiasm? I wonder. Susie must be serious about the embargo on fucking. I have to admit, the thought makes me smile – I know he won't like going without sex for long. And knowing what a reserve of girls he has standing by, he won't have to.

mercredi, le 19 janvier

Tomás invited me round for a meal just after sunset. He's in the kitchen chopping and slicing with the speed of a pro. 'Are you a chef?' I ask. He shakes his head. He preps and waits tables in his brother's restaurant on the beach.

He goes through the names of the vegetables – *zanahorias* (carrots), *cebollas* (onions), *hongos* (mushrooms). I ask him for a piece of paper, so I can write them down, but he says no. 'You want to speak Spanish,' he says, 'you learn by doing.'

I nod. He offers me a beer, which given the lack of alcohol at J's, seems like a flood after a drought. I have just one, thinking it might not be a great idea to go home smelling of beer.

Tomás produces a lot of food and though I have no idea what most of it is, I eat loads and it's all tasty. So he's cooking as well as teaching me a bit of Spanish – wonder what's in it for him? A girl could get used to this sort of treatment.

'Is it okay?' he asks. I nod, and ask him how to say something is tasty.

'*Este está sabroso*,' he says slowly. I repeat it. Is this a date? I wonder. He's not my type. On the other hand, the language barrier means only essential conversation is exchanged – a relief after the non-stop wittering of the Boy. And his gentle openness is very different from the clients I used to see, who usually kept their guard up as long as they possibly could. He's not at all like I imagined Latino men, not conceited or chauvinistic, which is awfully sexy.

lundi, le 24 janvier

I love J, I fucking love my cousin. How did I manage so long without him in my life? He is so the man, for reasons including, but not limited to:

- His taste in music fucking rocks. That is to say, he owns all the CDs I never quite got round to buying. Granted, these were probably all purchased with drug money, but I don't think that makes it ethically wrong to borrow them.
- He uses my face creams. One day I came home and he was

watching the football, face slathered in a pore-tightening clay-and-sea-mineral mask. Okay, so he was probably using twenty quid's worth of product without my permission. On the other hand, he's not asking me for rent. It seems a fair exchange.

- He loves scary movies. I love scary movies! At last! Someone I can watch them with!
- J is an unashamed consumer of junk food. I have always felt that one of the privileges of being an adult is the ability to eat chocolate for breakfast. J lives the dream.
- J makes faces at me whenever the Boy calls. Inevitably I start giggling. 'What's going on?' the Boy asks, worried. 'Oh, nothing,' I say. 'Just thought of something funny.'
- He completely understands when I don't want to return the Boy's calls for a few days.
- J loves hugs. In fact, his sense of personal space is distinctly un-British. Maybe that's something you pick up in prison.

mardi, le 25 janvier

Over at Tomás's for supper with J and some random girl. I just hope she's not a screamer; the walls at home are thin.

The sky is still light long after the sun goes, and it goes down far later than it does during the British winter. I love the twilight, the open windows and ceiling fans, the sound of insects in the half-night. The food is excellent. J brought over a few things, and I admire the gusto with which he eats everything from crab to sausage. He never asks what is in anything and never appears squeamish. I love that. I like the food, too, but am a bit more cautious.

Growing up, we rarely ate anything explicitly non-kosher, so things like lobster and pork were relatively unusual to me as an adult. I can't get over the ingrained response that there's something wrong with this kind of food. It tastes great, but unlike with sex, I can't quite let myself go all the way.

Missed call from the Boy when we come home. I check the clock and figure it's too late to ring back. I bid J and his lady goodnight and toddle off to bed.

She is a screamer.

samedi, le 29 janvier

Tomás's brother owns the restaurant he works in, which is good because Tomás usually has something extra sent out for us that doesn't make it to the bill. I've already learned the Spanish for 'You don't have to pay' (*No tiene que pagar*). Is bad because Tomás's brother is hot. Distractingly so. Enough to turn a girl's mind away from her nominal boyfriend.

It makes me feel a touch of sympathy for Tomás, who is lovely and kind but never in a million years would I find him physically attractive. To grow up in the shadow of someone who is . . . well, let's not mince words here, godlike, must be frustrating.

Of course, Tomás does have one up so far: for all the smouldering looks the brother and I have exchanged, he does not speak or understand very much English. I may have to put a little more work into my study. Although asking Tomás what the Spanish is for 'Your brother is so fucking fit' might not be a good idea.

lundi, le 31 janvier

Odd conversation with the Boy. Something has clearly unsettled him – Susie, I'll bet, or some other bit of brainless fluff – and all he does is ask me, over and over, if I care about him (yes, or, if I'm being honest, sometimes) and if I'm sure (as far as I'm willing to tell him, yes). I ask if he's okay. He just says 'Good, because if anything ever happens – if anyone ever rings you about something weird – I just want to know . . .'

Well, whatever. But it puts an odd thought into my head. What will happen if and when the Boy and I split up for good? He was relatively low key about our last break-up: of course he went and told anyone who'd listen what a rotten human being I am, but at least he didn't tell everyone about my former profession. But I shudder to think what might happen if he did.

It frightens me so much that I'm a shaking wreck when J comes home. 'I want to ask you to make me a promise,' I say to him. 'If anyone ever rings here, anyone you don't know I know, don't tell them I'm here.'

'Are you in trouble?' J says, taking my elbow and leading me to the sofa.

And I suddenly realise how ludicrous this is, worrying about such stupid things to someone who's been an addict, been a drugs dealer, been to prison. To someone who literally hit rock bottom, my problems are small beer.

'I'm sorry,' I said. 'It's nothing that level of serious. I'm not ready to tell you yet.' It's not because I think he would judge me. He's been honest about his past and expects nothing in return; I'm just picking the moment. I talk around the subject, drop oblique hints, and decide to leave it for another day.

J smiles. 'You don't have to tell me anything,' he says. 'You're my cousin. Whatever happens, I got your back.'

Février

samedi, le 5 février

The tourist boat outing was my birthday present to J. Twice-daily tours out in the Gulf, no guarantee of seeing dolphins but a possibility. The sort of thing you only do when someone else buys the trip for you, so I did.

The sky was blue, bright and heavy. The rows of grey fold-down seats were empty. There was a woman standing near the rail, looking down, watching the bow cut through the water. She smiled at me. J was busy taking photos with his hands; neither of us had a camera. 'Man, I should have brought a camera!' Then a few minutes later: 'Damn!'

The woman was wearing a flimsy dress and an open coat. I knew that dress from Topshop last year, knew she had to be British, too. She said her name was Vic.

'Aren't you hot in that?' I asked.

'Not really,' she said. I reflexively looked at her chest. Large breasts. She caught me and laughed. I smiled and shrugged. She wasn't embarrassed.

Vic stepped off with us at the end of the two hours and we three walked together as far as the turnstiles. She mentioned her hotel name and room number, and I thought she was friendly. J wanted to go for a meal where Tomás worked, so we did, and I promptly forgot her.

mercredi, le 9 février

Ugh. Ugh, ugh, ugh. They say knowledge is power but I'm not convinced. Discovered an email the Boy sent to Susie today, after an apparent attempt at reconciliation:

Oh, little lass, hope the smell of me on your pillow convinces you to open your heart and your loins again. [Loins?? Cripes.] *When are you coming to visit? Cannot forget the memory of you greedily ridding me* [sic]. *You will have to help me get fit again, in any way you choose.*

Went for a run on the beach. On the way back could see my footprints from the way out, the depth and vigour of them, each a well waiting to be filled with unspoken hatred.

samedi, le 12 février

J and Tomás went night fishing together. I said I wasn't feeling up to it but really I had sort of had it with practising my broken Spanish for an evening. I was bored and restless and decided to go to one of the hated tourist bars instead. I perched on a stool and wondered when my going-out uniform of tight jeans and silky top started to look too conservative. Everyone around me was pouring out of Day-Glo bikinis.

Vic, the lady from the boat, was there. I didn't recognise her at first; the hair was different, worn up. She smiled and talked to the man next to her. She had a wedding ring, he didn't. Friend? Lover? Husband? I lay across two empty seats, head on one hand. Vic looked at me and smiled. We started chatting. The man looked dejected – not her husband, then. Nothing to worry about, she giggled at him, just catching up on girl talk.

'I thought I recognised you.'

'You never rang.'

'Would it help if I said you looked fantastic?'

'Maybe.'

'And your handbag is great, too.'

Once upon a time I swore I would never sleep with a married person, but time and a job as a call girl changed that. After tonight I was feeling turned on and mildly malicious. The Boy's words to Susie running a circuit in my head: *cannot forget the memory of you greedily ridding me*. Well, great, thanks to that email I'll never forget it, either.

I was tired of reading about the Boy's conquests. Tired of his ringing up every night hinting about my helping with the air fare. I never asked him to come.

I was feeling no sympathy for men, no quarter for their pathetic teenaged fantasies and clunky seduction techniques. The obvious befuddlement on the man's face when Vic made it clear she'd rather be talking to me than having his awkward, sweaty palm travelling up her skirt – priceless. Sorry, mate, I grinned at myself. You're not even going to get a look in here. She's coming home with me.

I cornered the DJ and made a few requests. He played one, but that was enough. It was my dance. The song wasn't even half over before she found me and grabbed my shoulder.

'I was looking for you.'

'You found me.'

'You like to dance?'

'Fucking love to.'

I pushed her against the wall and kissed her neck. She laughed and grabbed my hips. We walked hand in hand to the next room and started kissing outside the ladies' toilet. Her breath tasted of smoke and Guinness.

We danced together. Kissing, grabbing, and generally making a scene. Her top was low-cut, showing impressive cleavage. I ran a finger along her neck, down into that crevasse. She had a tiny tattoo on one shoulder. Vic was narrowly built under those curves, and my arms went all the way round her. Below that her hips flared out, ample and fine. She was laughing, falling over and certainly drunk. I wondered what she was after, and thought about what I knew: two children, a mortgage, a husband who was only in it for the kids now. Decided it was probably what I would have done, if I was her, if it was my holiday.

'You aren't scared, are you?'

'Women don't scare me.'

'I didn't think so. Just making certain.'

I closed the door softly, but knew from the absence of lights that J was still out. 'A shower?' I asked. 'I know I need one.' My clothes were a heap on the floor before she even had her shoes off. The bathroom was small with large mirrors.

Vic came in a few minutes later. She was naked and glorious. 'Mind if I join you?' Of course I didn't. I asked if she wanted a cooler shower – I like it very hot. She said she was fine. There was a squeezy bottle of shower gel, I squirted some out, and soaped her.

She looked better with her clothes off. She wouldn't stop kissing me. I held her face and it was small, fine-jawed; I wondered if it felt strange to her, having a woman's face so close to her own. My tongue felt every inch of her face, neck, shoulders. Her ears were tiny and soft. Closer now, in the light, I could see the tattoo on her shoulder was a lily. I licked down to her chest. She had the kind of nipples that stand right up, the kind perfect for nibbling.

Water and steam filled the room quickly. On my knees I soaped her torso, those unbelievable breasts, so heavy they slid out of my hands. The tiny scar inside her hip, the gently purple-grey stretch marks. Her legs were long and thin. I was jealous and aroused at the same time. She had natural pubic hair, though, and it spread through her inner thighs.

Vic pulled my hair, but I stayed down. Spread her legs and felt her with a finger. Her labia were dark and prominent, she was starting to swell and flush. I washed her carefully. Just touching, just exploring. Bent down so low I could see her reflection alone in the mirror. Her face was a picture, a mixture of surprise, curiosity and pleasure.

'Look at me.'

'I am.'

'What colour are my eyes?'

'They're perfect.'

We dried each other and went to bed. She was small and girlish, and looked years younger without the make-up. I always feel conscious of looking like a teenager even now. I knelt between her legs and she raised her hips towards me, a question in her eyes. She was willing and ready, but what now? She said it was her first time with a woman.

Between her legs, I had a strange drunken flash, a sort of gynaecological moment. I was about to screw someone's mother. Hadn't done that before, not to my knowledge. A new milestone. Then the moment passed, and I was in that hairy thicket, and her hands were at my hair again, but leading me down instead of up.

What can I say? This isn't a sex education course. You know what's down there and what to do. Or maybe you don't, and are looking for pointers. Afraid I can't give you many. Sorry, but it's just that I was born with the equipment and have been test-driving my own for some time now. Clitoral stimulation, oral pleasure? Not even the introduction. I can make a woman come with my pinky, the back of her knee and a well-timed exhale. You'd be carpet-bombing her pussy for days with no result.

If it makes you feel any better, I truly do believe that men should be allowed to give other men blowjobs on a strictly friends basis. After all, how could a woman really know how a man wants it?

'Don't you ever leave me.' The things we girls say when we're drunk.

I smiled. 'I'm right here.'

'What about tomorrow?'

'We'll see about tomorrow when it comes.'

She was happy to kiss me; she seemed fascinated by my breasts, far smaller than hers. She asked me to show her how I masturbated and looked at my cunt for ages. 'I want to see how you look when you come,' she said, and I laughed.

We held each other for a long time, though it was late and we were both tired. Her legs were wrapped round my left one; my right hand was buried in her thick hair. She smelled dark and warm like mushrooms. The moisture between her legs was dripping down the back of my thigh.

Eventually we went to sleep, spooning together in the bed. It was warmer in the room than she liked, so the covers were off. When morning came, I got up to shower and boiled the kettle. When I came back she was still half asleep.

'Coffee or tea?' I asked.

'Is there real milk?'

'Yes.'

'I'll have tea, please.'

Sitting on the edge of the sofa, I watched her drink the hot tea in tiny sips. She reached over and put the television on. Cartoons and news. I was worried about her turning up at the hotel and the children waiting for her. Watching their mum stagger in hungover, hair in all directions, would probably scar them for life. Then again, it was a holiday.

'Any plans today?'

'I'm going to stay in and order up scrambled eggs, salmon and champagne. We only came here for the kids' sake, after all. I need some holiday as well and getting sand in my hair is not my idea of a good time.'

'Travelling the world with room service, though. Sounds like a good reason to have children.'

'It's only once a year. Usually it's me up in the dark, pouring Coco Pops down their throats.'

'That sounds pretty good, too. Would you like a taxi?'

'I'll take the bus, thank you.'

'I'll walk you to the stop.'

dimanche, le 20 février

J, Tomás and I were flopped on the sofa on the lanai. Now, how cool is that? Outdoor rooms complete with power supplies and, here at least, a television. You couldn't do that in Britain. We were eating pizza and watching a schlocky horror movie. The sort of film where blood spurts with the energy of a thousand suns.

The phone rang. J went to answer it, came back outside and flipped the receiver towards me. 'For you,' he said. It could only be the Boy. Ugh. I hadn't told him about Vic and didn't think I was going to – it felt good to have a secret.

'Hello, little kitty,' he said. I hate that name now. 'I have some great news.'

'What's that?' I said, as yet another nubile teenage girl was beheaded by the chainsaw-wielding antihero. I wondered vaguely whether Susie had responded yet to the Boy's sad little email begging her to have sex with him.

'I'm coming to visit next month!'

Question answered, I suppose.

mercredi, le 23 février

'So should I book a flight via Canada or via the US?'

'I have no idea,' I said. I was outside on the sofa, bare feet, watching ants make a steady trail from the definitely-out-doors of the back garden to the semi-outdoors of the lanai.

'Does one take longer to get through customs than the other?' the Boy asked.

'No idea,' I said. 'America, probably.' In fact they'd gone through my luggage when it was in transit here, which I discovered only on opening a suitcase on the third day to discover a friendly note from the Department of Homeland Security inside letting me know that, for the sake of public safety, they'd had a good paw through my knickers.

'Oh, kitty, I am so looking forward to seeing you,' he said.

'Please don't.'

'Pardon?'

'I hate it when people recycle pet names.'

He was quiet. I could all but hear the wheels turning. What the . . . ? Does that mean . . . ? But in the end he must have decided that questioning me might lead to an argument, because he didn't follow it up. But he did find a reason to be off the phone pretty quickly.

dimanche, le 27 février

Food and drink are not my strong points. Yes, I enjoy them as much as (and sometimes more than) the next person, but am not particularly knowledgeable about which beverage goes with what meal or the difference between sardines and pilchards. Come to think of it, does anyone really know?

But I am, slowly and with Tomás's help, trying to improve my cooking skills. And I must admit, learning under such a talented and patient cook is a bonus. We've already tried out dozens of things for me to cook when the Boy is here that I can't wait to try.

lundi, le 28 février

I see the Boy paid his bloaty ex a visit. Clearly hoping to get a little ego fluff before coming to see me.

Fucktard. I went out and laid a gorgeous woman and you dry-hump a beached whale. The thought didn't make me feel particularly better.

Mars

mercredi, le 2 mars

<TheBoy>I don't know what to pack. Do I need a suit?

<belle_online>No, just a lot of shirts and shorts. Swimming trunks. Don't forget suncream. You'll burn in a nanosecond.

<TheBoy>what about insurance?

<belle_online>pardon?

<TheBoy>travel insurance

<belle_online>I wouldn't bother but it's up to you.

How tiresome! I know this is the first time the Boy's been abroad without his family for purposes other than skiing (and, by extension, having gluhwein-fuelled sessions with brainless totty), so he needs plenty of hand-holding. On the other hand I also know this holiday is taking the place of the one he didn't have in Thailand with Susie, so I'm not as excited about the prospect as he imagines.

dimanche, le 6 mars

The Boy's plane is late. I tried to check the status online before leaving but the connection was down. Gives me time to wander around, not that there's much to the airport.

When the plane unloads I scan the crowd: there he is. He looks drawn, but that's not surprising. Including flight changes the journey took sixteen hours. He jogs slowly towards me and picks me up. We kiss. He smells different.

'Wow, it's hot,' he says. We haven't even left the airport yet, which is air-conditioned. And it's only March. I smile.

'Bring sunscreen?' I ask.

'No, I brought after-sun instead.' I knew he wouldn't, so I bought sunscreen anyway. Factor 30. Will have to sneak it into his food or something.

mardi, le 8 mars

I'd forgotten what it's like to be part of a couple. All those annoying habits that can be kept at arm's length over a transatlantic telephone line are suddenly right up in my face. Such as:

- **The snoring**. Really, why do men do this while women don't? Although, considering how few women I've shared regular sleeping arrangements with, perhaps I'm generalising.
- **The inability to make decisions**. 'Would you like me to cook something, or shall we go out?' And he just sits there, mouth agape for several seconds, before saying he'll do whatever I want to. Well, if I wanted something in particular, I wouldn't have asked, would I?
- **The man stuff**. You know when a man comes onto another man's territory, how they have to be competitive? The Boy actually offered J an arm-wrestle within twelve hours of being here. Luckily J laughed it off.
- **The ignored advice**. I told him to bring suncream. He didn't. I offered him mine. He didn't use it. He got burned within an hour.

• **The fucking phone.** I came up behind him to ask a question and saw him tapping 'Hiya lass, arrived safely, miss you!' into the hated thing. 'Who are you texting?' I smiled. 'Uh, m-m-my brother,' he stammered.

mercredi, le 9 mars

The Boy's sunburn is not improving. Note to manufacturers: after-sun is all a bit of a scam, innit?

The choices in such a situation are: he wears clothes that cover the burn, and complains endlessly about the pain of fabric against skin, or he doesn't, and risks more burn. And I don't want to go into the sexual contortions necessary to avoid rubbing the burn – because while I like it a little rough in the bedroom, and the Boy loves dishing it out, he most emphatically cannot take it. You'd think he was being flayed alive from the sound of it.

At least it's payback to J for my putting up with the screaming lady.

jeudi, le 10 mars

'You're not taking him on the bus,' J laughed.

'What?' I said. 'It's the easiest way to get around, and it's cheap.'

'It's cheap for a reason,' J said. 'Those people are crazy.'

'If you don't think we should take the bus while he's here,' I said sweetly to J, 'the least you can do is loan him your pushbike.'

Calling J's glorious machine a pushbike is an understatement along the line of calling Harvey Nick's a corner shop. It's a titanium-framed beauty, and clearly cost thousands.

'No. Fucking. Way.'

'Pweese?' I put on a baby voice and batted my eyelashes, just like I'd seen the Screamer do to him once.

'Fine, okay, whatever,' J grumbled. 'But don't you two go and do anything stupid!'

vendredi, le 11 mars

I knew of a river, starting from springs inland, that ran as far as the sea. It was supposed to be a great place for swimming and canoeing. I reckoned if we set off early enough, we could cycle there, hire canoes and paddle down it.

'What should we do?' the Boy asked, about the bikes. 'Chain them to something?'

'It's that or take them in the canoes,' I said. The Boy considered this seriously. 'Of course we chain them up.'

The Boy disappeared to find a good place to hide the cycles while I paid a bored-looking woman for canoe rental. I went down to the edge of the springs. The water was glass-clear and smooth.

Hmm, he's taking his time, I thought. I pulled the canoes down to the edge of the water, went back up for our bags of food and water. Retrieved the paddles and sat on the ground. Still no Boy. I bet he's ringing some girl. It put me in a black mood to think of him whispering sweet nothings to some slag while I was all but turning cartwheels to keep him entertained.

By the time he came back – some twenty minutes – I was not in the mood for our outing any more. 'Oh, why do you always have to be this way?' he said, trying to put an arm round my waist. Why do I always have to? Is he actively trying to make me angry? I turned away. 'I just wanted to ring my family before the battery runs down. I didn't know the charger wouldn't work here.'

The sooner that battery goes dead the better.

samedi, le 12 mars

The Boy loves food. Correction: the Boy loves large amounts of food, and he's not picky. In fact, he has probably the worst palate of anyone I've ever met. Nothing is salted enough, and a slow-simmered white wine sauce, in his opinion, holds nothing against a jar of shop-bought Bolognese. At least he's easy to please, and once you have the bulk equation cracked, it's smooth sailing. Also it saves money as Michelin stars are mostly lost on him.

Unfortunately the Boy doesn't like the local food. In spite of his brawny appearance, he is the sort of man who goes into a curry house and asks for extra-mild korma. Luckily the tourist restaurants cater for less robust palates. Well, I think, if you can't take the chilli here, I can't imagine what you would have eaten with Susie in Thailand.

dimanche, le 13 mars

Which part of 'That feels good' – in the sexual context, of course – is so difficult to understand?

When I was paid to sleep with people, being told 'That feels good' was a signal that I was on the right track and, if lucky, could expect a generous tip or a repeat customer. Therefore, when someone told me that something felt good, the last thing I would have done was stop doing it.

But now that my services are available to one person only and on a strictly voluntary basis, it seems 'That feels good' means the opposite of what I thought it did. Because as soon as I say something feels good . . . the Boy promptly stops.

I've tried several times to remedy the problem. First I stopped saying anything at all, but that led to the assumption that I wasn't enjoying anything. So I moved on to the subtler approach: squirming and groaning with pleasure, for instance, instead of vocalising my approval. He thought I was being ticklish and stopped. So no gain there.

And while some people like a bit of direction – harder, there, more, now – it can be a touch deflating when your partner comes over all Orson Welles on you with 'Do the windmill thing with your tongue again, but more slowly, and not pinching at the same time, please, and for goodness sake don't breathe on me unless it's a dry breath and not a damp one. Starting when I tap you on the shoulder, okay?'

Or maybe – gulp – he's become so accustomed to other women that he can't remember what feels good to me. The weirdly fussy way he's been handling my nipples might support this. I don't like softly-softly when it comes to breasts; I like rough handling that leaves evil-looking marks and probably comes within Geneva Convention definitions of torture.

The thought drives me round the bend: I've kept multiple lovers at the same time, and in the line of work had to deal with the unrelenting newness of many clients, night after night. It's not so hard to figure out what a stranger wants, whether he likes blowjobs shallow or deep, with light teeth or without; whether the cheeky finger up the backside is a welcome intervention or not. You get used to adapting to the signals, and by the end of the hour should be fucking him just the way he wants to be fucked. If not, you haven't done your job. So to a so-called partner, reading your signals should be second nature, right?

Maybe we've been apart too long.

I'm a woman. As such, I am privileged to enjoy certain prerogatives. One of them is to have arbitrary rules of conversation that are indecipherable to men. There are lines, and then there is between the lines, and that's where I prefer to conduct things at times. I know it's not fair, but then men get to pee standing up.

The commandments go roughly thus:

1. I am the woman, the one in charge of the conversation. Thou shalt not have any subject changes unapproved by me.
2. Thou shalt remember the first ten minutes of the morning and keep them holy. The period before my first cup of tea is not suitable for chat.
3. Thou shalt not use sporting analogies too often.
4. Thou shalt not interrupt *The Simpsons*, even if it is dubbed into Spanish and the only thing I clearly understand is Mr Burns saying, '*Excelente.*'
5. Thou shalt not covet another woman's rack unless I have mentioned it first.
6. Thou shalt not refer to PMT, even if I am clearly experiencing it.
7. Thou shalt not pronounce the word 'controversy' with undue stress on the second vowel. Do you know how annoying that is to everyone else?
8. Thou shalt not use the word 'hypocrisy' in conversation. In writing thou shalt not spell the word 'hippocracy'. That would be a government run by horses. There are online dictionaries, and thou shalt make use of them.
9. Thou shalt not expect conversation when I am reading, even if it's only the paper or the back of a packet of rice.
10. Thou shalt not talk to me through the toilet door. Ever. That's just wrong.

lundi, le 21 mars

The Boy's mobile must really be dead now because I haven't seen him using it and he's been asking for access to the computer. I sigh, warn him about the intermittent service, and leave him to it. I return a few minutes later to get a bit of newspaper from the room.

He reaches across instantly and turns off the monitor. I look at him. 'Why did you do that?'

'Umm, umm,' he says. There really is no explanation, is there? He was either snooping around in my things or writing an email to another girl. Twat. When will men realise that if you play it cool, you can get away with a lot more?

mardi, le 22 mars

Note to self: don't go through a man's wallet. Ever.

I couldn't help it. Especially after the computer thing. The Boy was outside, talking to J, and his wallet was splayed open on the table. Just a quick peek, I thought. I suppose I shouldn't have been surprised, but I found a condom inside.

And extra-large? Is he kidding? I've seen the literal length and breadth of men's cocks in my time and there are few that can't be contained in the average-sized Durex. There's a good case for smaller condoms for smaller men, but extra-large?

He came back in, without J, and I threw it at him. 'What's wrong?' he said.

'Condoms in your wallet?'

'What? This? It means nothing. That's f-f-f-f-or . . .' I could see him straining to think of something plausible. 'You know, in case we're trapped somewhere and need to carry water.'

'Really? I would have thought the spermicide might adversely affect the taste,' I said bitterly.

'Oh, why can't you stop this?'

'Stop this? You have a fucking condom in your fucking wallet. You are fucking writing secret fucking emails to God knows who. You're the one who needs to fucking stop.'

'Enough with the language,' he said, and turned away smugly. Ooh, I hate that. My use of expletives is a greater error than finding condoms in his personal effects? Fine, then, I won't talk.

Ten minutes of silence truly unnerves him. He decides to try a softer approach. 'Please, I forgot it was in there. It's probably been in my wallet for years. Please believe me.'

'The date on it would indicate otherwise.' I'm a past master at keeping tabs on condom expiry dates. This one came out of a packet purchased last year.

'If I was cheating on you – which I would never do – you must know that I'm not the sort of person who uses condoms, anyway.'

Oh, I know that all right, and it chills me to the bone. The privileged classes incubating chlamydia between themselves like it was some sort of private club. If I wasn't already in the habit of being screened for diseases at regular intervals – considering my past, you can never be too careful – this would have sent me straight to the clinic. 'That. Is not. A comforting. Thought,' I said between clenched teeth. 'You don't use condoms? Could you imagine if I told you the same thing? That makes you lower than a streetwalker in my opinion. And that's a considerable insult to streetwalkers.'

'I'm not the one who took money for sex,' he said, with real bite in his voice.

'Really? Then perhaps you should have done, because the number of girls you've been running around with, it might have been a very lucrative sideline.' He started to open his mouth. 'Don't deny it – I've read your email.'

There, I've said it. I haven't admitted to the diary, but I've said it. He isn't certain whether that means I read his email yesterday, or in general. He says nothing.

I straighten my shoulders and wipe the tears from my cheeks. 'I don't care where you go, but get out of my sight for the next few hours.'

'You're chucking me out? I'm in a strange country!'

'I care? Get out,' I said. 'Don't come back before supper.'

mercredi, le 23 mars

In fact, the Boy didn't come back until well after supper. I was in bed, reading; he slipped in next to me. We said nothing for the longest time. I thought if we did I might cry.

'Please, I'm so sorry. I don't know what would happen if I lost you.' I notice he didn't apologise for any wrongdoing in particular, but it's enough. It's more than he would usually offer. Eventually we kissed and made it up, very gently so as not to wake J.

In the morning I was still sad and distant. The Boy was much more subdued than usual. Tomás invited us over for lunch, and we went, the Boy occasionally reaching over to stroke my fingers while me and Tomás chattered in half Spanish, half English.

Suddenly the Boy grasped my hand. 'Is that his cat?' he whispered loudly.

'It is.'

'That has to be the fattest tabby I've ever seen.'

Tomás noticed we were talking about the animal and brought her over.

'Cripes,' the Boy said. 'That's no cat, that's a land seal.' He laughed and I suddenly felt much better.

We're walking on the beach at night, me with shoes in one hand, hanging onto his arm for support. We're both a bit tipsy. We've just had a huge seafood meal at Tomás's brother's restaurant and are feeling a bit jolly.

'How about a roll in the hay – roll in the sand,' he says.

'Have you ever had sand in the crack of your arse?'

'Not yet.'

'How about here instead,' I say and drag him under the pier. We do it standing up. At least, he's standing; my legs are wrapped round his hips and my back is rubbing against what might be, I think, a barnacle. Or broken glass. Whatever. I don't care.

He comes loudly. We rearrange our clothes and walk on. 'Laaaaaaaand seeeeeal,' he sings, going deep, his big chest booming with the sound. It disappears into the road of waves. He turns back toward the pier and tries a falsetto. 'Laaaaaaaaand seeeeeeal!'

'Are you for real?' I say, but it's sing-songy, and we laugh.

'Come have a feeeeeeel . . .' He pirouettes in the foam at the edge of the water. 'Of my beautiful land seeeeeeal!'

I fall over laughing. He instantly pounces and starts kissing my neck. I can't stop laughing; I'm spluttering now, it's actually hard to breathe. 'You're making me squeal,' I gasp.

He raises himself on his arms. The curls of his hair move slightly in the wind. 'I haven't heard you laugh so hard in such a long time,' he says.

'Marry me, and we'll have a litter of pups,' I say and pull him back down.

'If I didn't know you were lying to please me, I'd say yes.'

vendredi, le 25 mars

I wonder why women have the reputation of being the more demanding of the two sexes. From my standpoint, men are the fussiest little fusspots on the face of the earth.

Yes, we ladies go in for hair-based rituals, obsessive shoe collection and bag hoarding. But when it comes to the meatier subjects, men are just big girl's blouses.

Example: pain. Ask a woman for a list of the most physically painful experiences and you'll get an answer like childbirth and pubic waxing, in that order. Men, on the other hand, find shaving cuts an ordeal. Shaving cuts. A wee blade getting a touch too close to the skin.

Male egos require constant stroking. Every task is an achievement, every success epic. That is why women cook, but men are chefs: we make cheese on toast, they produce *pain de fromage*.

The Boy claims the domestic high ground because I once burned a powdered custard. Hold me back, Heston Blumenthal. And I bristle at the feeling I have during this visit, that by shacking up with me for three weeks he's auditioning me as a cohabitee. Frankly, I could give a monkey's for playing housewife.

And then today he turned an all-white wash of mine shocking pink in J's washer. So much for being a paragon of the home arts. Obviously, he being a man and therefore having a man-sized ego, we will never bring it up again.

samedi, le 26 mars

I'm torn. I'm ready for the Boy to leave, but worried as well. There's so much we haven't had the time to do while he was here. We stay up far later than usual, having sex and talking

– not about anything serious. We're both aware that the luxury of having the other around all the time is about to end.

And the sex is changing. When he came here it was quick, fast and urgent; we'd both been looking forward to it. Now it's taking longer, we're going more slowly, it's less about instant satisfaction and more about building up . . . I don't know what, really. Nice memories to take home. Something like that. He holds me for ages afterwards. Is this because he wants to have something to remember me by because he doesn't expect to see me again?

'When are you coming home?' he says as I put the light out.

'I don't know,' I say. I don't miss England, to be honest. I miss my friends, I miss my family, I even sometimes miss him but I don't miss home. 'Soon.'

dimanche, le 27 mars

His luggage has expanded; he's taking back a dead horse-shoe crab in a shoebox. 'Do you really think they'll let you take that into the country?' I ask.

'Worth a try,' he says. And I send him home with sun-screen – for next time, I say.

The flight leaves on time, everything goes smoothly. It's still morning, and I am stood in an airport, alone.

Sunny day. Think I'll go to the beach.

lundi, le 28 mars

J's not a man of many words. Or rather, J's not a man of many serious words. He just looks at me and cocks an eyebrow. So much has happened the last few weeks and we've had no time to sit around and chat. I feel I have some explaining to do.

'I know, I know,' I say by way of apology. 'You don't have to tell me.'

'You're going to have to pick his pubes out of the soap yourself, okay? I ain't going near that shit.'

mercredi, le 30 mars

I lay on a wooden bench by the beach reading. A man came up to me – fifties, local, smart suit and sunglasses, probably a business owner – and looked at the cover of the book (Seneca, *On the Shortness of Life*).

'Very interesting,' he said in English. 'Are you comfortable here? Enjoying yourself?'

To be very honest, I was half thinking about falling asleep but feared sunburn. 'Yes,' I said.

He smiled and extended his hand in a friendly manner. 'Please continue,' he said, and walked away.

Avril

mardi, le 5 avril

According to his weblog archives, the Boy makes fun of me for not liking jewellery and flowers, which defies explanation in my book.

Clarification: I don't want jewellery and flowers from a lover. As treats I buy for myself, fine; as gifts from friends, acceptable. But something about the obligatory roses on a birthday or bracelet on an anniversary leaves me cold. Now, gifts from clients, that was another matter.

There's a particularly filthy image A2 emailed me. It's a parody of those horrible print ads for jewellery. It shows a woman in silhouette, lips clamped round what you can only assume is her partner's love machine. Below, the picture of a particularly large diamond, and the slogan: '*Diamonds. Now she'll pretty much have to.*'

Yes, I admit I sniggered more than may be ladylike. But it's also a depressing thought. Are men still resorting to buying expensive baubles to ensure their ladyfriends perform a service which – may I be frank here? – should be more or less expected in any normal sexual relationship?

Or are women who actually enjoy sex in the minority, and I somehow missed the memo on requiring a down payment for play? If so, it makes me wonder why some women are so quick to criticise prostitutes, when it appears their main motivation for sleeping with their lovers is collecting gaudy jewellery. Methinks the ladies do protest too much.

Closer examination of the weblog archive reveals that Susie was exactly opposite to me in this regard. She demanded holidays abroad, expensive meals, the lot. Greedy cow.

A2 rang to see how I was getting on, and I lamented this fault. 'I should have at least insisted on trinkets and tributes with most of my boyfriends. They must have thought I was a cheap date.'

A2 never bought me any regrettable rings during our time together. His gifts tended more to the hard-bound variety. Though he did once part with the better part of a grand to procure a handbag I adored, and, what's more, did this without my ever hinting for it. 'But getting earrings wouldn't improve your relationship,' he said, quite reasonably.

'True, but at least I'd have something to show for it.'

Well, I have a handbag, anyway.

vendredi, le 8 avril

'Yeah, this town is small beans. Thing is, right, I'm in the army so there's nothing I find shocking.'

'Really,' I said. This was the worst sort: people who could not be blown off through lack of conversation. He'd already told me how long he'd been living here, about some girl he was having sex with but who doesn't return his calls now, and extended an invitation to his house, bought with retirement payoff from the paras – with detailed directions of its location. Undoubtedly he had a backlog of stories and was prepared to tell them all.

'Anyway,' he said, 'I've seen it all, me. There's nothing you could say that I haven't been through. Go on and ask. Kosovo, whatever. Drugs. Criminal underworld, like. Been there, done that, like they say, ha ha ha.'

'Is that so,' I said. 'How about I prove you wrong and then you fuck right off?'

The obscenity startled him, but then it always does. People don't expect words like that out of the mouth of someone who looks like me. He regained composure instantly. 'Go ahead, try me.'

I don't like one-upmanship. On the other hand, it was time to roll in the heavy artillery. I waved him closer, so only he could hear what I was about to say. He grinned the grin of the Cheshire Cat, already prepared to say that anything I'd done had been done by him, first, and better.

'I once shat on a man's chest. For money.'

I stood up and left.

dimanche, le 10 avril

Email from the Boy is sparse and his nightly phone calls are a bit stilted – he thinks J is eavesdropping. He's right, but it's not out of malice. It's a small house and the walls are thin. Last night I had to listen to J reaming another girl, so I think subjecting my cousin to a few pallid phone conversations is hardly squirm-making.

I suggest more emails and find a few erotic stories on the Web to send to the Boy. Maybe the email isn't working properly because I haven't heard back.

OK, email is definitely working. Maybe he hasn't had time to read them yet. Or he is trying to find something good to reciprocate with.

He has read them. Hasn't said anything. Scratch the stories.

jeudi, le 14 avril

Another important difference between me, Susie and all the other girls of the Boy's harem: I don't want marriage and children.

If I'm meant to feel maternal instincts, shouldn't they have kicked in by now? J and I recently visited neighbours and their newborn. I was relieved to get out without anyone asking whether I'd like to hold the baby. Because there is no way to say no politely.

You may be thinking I'll change my mind. Or that I'm a selfish modern woman, too self-absorbed to care for anything above herself. You may be right.

I was a wanted child. My parents planned for me, longed for me. They survived disappointments and heartbreaks to have me. Whatever became of their relationship later, I grew up knowing I was special, wanted. I'd never wish to bring someone into the world less sure of it than that.

So the Boy and I were discussing this stunted maternal drive the other day. I get silly over things like lizards, and sometimes – if they don't poo – kittens, but very rarely react to human children. 'You're just a broody thing,' I accused him.

'No, don't be silly, I don't want children soon,' he said. 'I don't think I could take the thought of going without sex for that long, not just yet.'

Er, no sex while pregnant? Cripes, some women will try anything to get out of it. The only reason I can see to cut back your sexual practices when starting a family is the fear that your children might walk in on you, and then you'd have to sit them down for a chat and explain the facts of life, perhaps a bit earlier than you had expected.

'Actually, I think it's pretty safe,' I said. 'And anyway there are always alternatives to vaginal sex.' The third-trimester anal, for instance. 'It's the time right after birth that's probably sex-free.'

I backtracked quickly. 'Of course, I don't want to think about it yet,' I said. 'Not quite ready to accept peeing involuntarily when I laugh.' He seemed to find this very funny.

Brief phone call to Mum. By her choice, not mine – she's got a new man and he's keeping her busy. Before she rings off, though, she offers the extremely disturbing advice that I should put off getting married as long as possible.

Er, did she even notice which daughter she was talking to? I've been staunchly anti-marriage since about the age of eighteen. Months.

Marriage is a fantastic institution for one and a half people to enter into. I would marry if only the right person came along, really I would. But all the men on my list of ideal husband material (as opposed to just fanciable) are imaginary, dead, gay or some combination of these.

- Ian Curtis (dead)
- Morrissey (gay)
- Johnny Cash (dead)
- Joe Orton (gay and dead)
- Gromit (as in Wallace and) (imaginary)
- D. Boon (dead and gay)
- Inigo Montoya (imaginary)
- J.T. Leroy (imaginary and gay)
- Quentin Crisp (gay and dead)
- Virginia Woolf's Orlando (imaginary)

So you see the problem.

samedi, le 23 avril

J has noticed that I've not been out much since the Boy left, and has taken me to see Tomás at work – I've already had

291

everything on the menu but it really is all very good, and it's lovely to see friendly faces.

Tomás's brother brings our meals, and comes round again to collect our plates – it's slow in the restaurant tonight so he's given most staff the night off. He waves off any payment and sits down with us afterwards.

J kicks me under the table. I give him daggers. What, are we fifteen?

'I think our gentleman companion here fancies you,' J says in his most exaggerated English, hoping Francisco won't work out what he's saying.

Evidently he doesn't, because he talks on. Now he and J are comparing tattoos – J has one of a screaming skull emitting smaller, flaming skulls from its eyes, which he swears he does not remember getting, though I reckon from the size and complexity of it, it must have taken some six hours to have done. Francisco pulls aside the shoulder of his shirt to show a delicate fairy etched there. I can smell his skin.

'Does she have a name?' I ask, my finger lightly tracing the wings.

'Raquel,' he says.

'That's lovely.'

'The same as my daughter,' he says.

Oh.

dimanche, le 24 avril

The Boy keeps saying how happy he's been since coming here and he can't wait to visit again. I send him a photo he took on our holiday. My top was a little tighter than I remember and I look very busty indeed.

<TheBoy>WHORE!

<Belle_online>Pardon me?

<TheBoy>I spelled that wrong, didn't I?

<Belle_online>As far as I know there is only one spelling.

<TheBoy>I meant the noise you do when someone looks great.

<Belle_online>Did you mean PHWOAR?

<TheBoy> Yes, that's it.

But the conversation never really recovers. Maybe he wasn't exaggerating about his spelling after all.

mardi, le 26 avril

The heart is a lonely and extremely self-sabotaging hunter. We've gone back to the phone since the misspelling episode. But with less editorial power over what he communicates to me, I notice that the Boy has contracted a bad case of mentionitis. At least four times in the last two days he's made reference to 'someone I know who works in the medical field' and 'a doctor friend of mine'. And I go back on my promise to stay off the diary, and have a peek – he's spending time with Dr Blowjob again, Georgie. So this is how much the holiday meant to him. Fuck all. I regret sending the sexy photos.

mercredi, le 27 avril

It's late. I'm cycling down the beach. The stars are more numerous here than at home – even with the streetlights I see entire constellations that you would never pick out in London. And I could never tire of the smell of the sea, or the sound of palm fronds in the wind.

When I pass the restaurant, I see Tomás outside and stop. Francisco is there, straddling a giant Harley-Davidson. Tomás must have left his car, because he's climbing on to ride pillion. 'Nice bike,' I say, unsure whether there are different words for pushbike and motorcycle.

There probably are, because they both laugh. 'So is yours,' Francisco says.

'I didn't know you liked those,' I say, choosing to avoid the noun in question.

'The restaurant is a second wife,' Francisco says. 'I call this my girlfriend.'

'It's gorgeous.'

'You should come for a ride,' he says, looking me in the eyes. He's a good-looking man, and damn but does he know it. I think I soaked myself on the spot.

'Maybe,' I said, mounting my rather less high-tech model. 'Race you home?'

They laughed again, and I waved the two brothers off into the clear, warm night.

jeudi, le 28 avril

The Boy rings as per usual. We're just chatting, when I ask if he has any plans for the weekend. He says he's going to a music gig.

That's nice, I say. Who is it? He mentions one of my

favourite bands. Wow, now I'm jealous, I say. Who are you going with?

'Uh, uh, uh.' Oh God, the stammer. I know he's about to tell me a lie. 'Mates from work.'

'Really? Who?'

'Um, Andy and C-c-c-c-c-hris had an extra ticket.'

I let it drop. But as soon as he's off the phone I check his email. Two new: one confirmation email for payment for the tickets from the venue, and one from Georgie.

Really looking forward to it! she wrote. *I'm up for anything, just as long as it isn't death metal!* Yeah, I'll bet you're fucking up for anything.

vendredi, le 29 avril

So he's asked her out to a gig. I shouldn't be so upset, nor particularly surprised, except he's taking her to see one of my favourite acts.

Okay, I'm really upset because of her *death metal* comment. How lame exactly is this girl? On a scale of zero to Leo Sayer I'd say about point eight Leo Sayer. People that limp shouldn't be let into concerts. This is the sort of woman who turns up her wee nose at the masculinity of rock because it's all a bit sweaty.

As long as it's not death metal? Heaven forfend something might be jarring or challenging. Or loud. I bet on closer questioning she would also reject 'gangsta rap' and 'angry female singers'. It's the musical equivalent of 'I love books, as long as they're not hard' or 'I love movies, as long as they're not subtitled'. It's people like her who keep Dido in royalties. It's not just death metal they hate; it's anything that can't be played low in the background at a dinner party.

My only consolation is that a rival so pathetically vanilla probably carries that quality through all aspects of her life.

Straight suck and fuck, and a roast chicken every Sunday. Which, on consideration, is exactly what the Boy wants from a woman – in spite of his protestations otherwise. I've been thrown over for a snivelling, pasty nonentity too many times to believe men actually want anything else.

Wasn't it Jerry Hall who said that men need a whore in the bedroom and a maid in the kitchen? It's not true. The kitchen part is correct. But they seem to keep their whores elsewhere. I suddenly want to find and kick this girl very, very hard. Repeatedly. And I want Will Oldham to write a song about it.

samedi, le 30 avril

An email from Georgie, sent from her work: *Cheers for last night! I think I have tinnitus. We'll have to do that again sometime but maybe something a little more mainstream?* She blathers on a bit longer, but it isn't anything you couldn't get from a random Victoria Coren generator.

My stomach lurches and gurgles. I have to stop doing this. I make a promise not to read his diaries and email again.

Mai

dimanche, le 1 mai

There are facts and there is the truth, and they do not necessarily converge. I was keenly reminded of this after yet another phone call with the Boy. The Boy has a little problem with the truth. But only when it involves him. So I was grumbling about fidelity again today – so what? Just last week he was taking another girl out on the town. And then today, in an email, she called him sexy and made it clear that if they aren't sleeping together yet, it's not far off.

He can't admit to guilt directly, but does snipe back with, 'Someone with your background really should watch where she pitches stones.'

Being female and Jewish, I'm down with the concept of guilt. There is no past faux pas too small for me to chew over daily. If someone points out my faults, not only will I instantly acknowledge them, but I will flagellate myself with the knowledge for at least a decade. I slept with men for money: this does not sit easily on my soul.

The Boy takes full advantage. If I lose my rag over anything he's done, he has only to say, 'Well, considering what you were like last year' to send me off into a miasma of guilt and apologies. When I hang up, I'm angry. He still hasn't owned up to taking Georgie to the gig, and it's a slap in the face as hard as finding out that he called me and Susie 'kitty'. Damn it, I'm the one he should be going to gigs with. I'm the one who likes music. She's just simpering arm candy.

Never let it be said that my powers of investigation – or rather, the internet's – are below par: I track down Georgie's number and phone her in the UK. As soon as she answers I know it's a mistake. She sounds haughty, the way I would have sounded if one of them had rung me. 'You said you're his girlfriend?'

'Yes.'

'How long have you known each other?' I give her an answer which, in Hollywood circles, would be equivalent to something like three reincarnations with the same mate. 'I've never heard of you.'

'I'm not surprised.'

'He and I only slept together once, ages ago,' she said. Not that I believed her.

I know she's going to ring him and pass on exactly what happened.

When he rings later, he is angry. 'What do you think you're doing?' he yells. 'What sort of a bunny boiler are you?'

The phrase stops me dead. Bunny boiler? Sorry, but what? He thought, and then deployed, the term 'bunny boiler'? He actually dared invoke *Fatal Attraction*, a misogynistic cliché so cheesy it makes Camembert blush?

And *I'm* the bunny boiler? He's the one who was once removed from my house by the police. He's the one who stalked N after we split up. He's the one who went through my rubbish. He's the one who read my diary first. Who tells me he will love me for ever, then turns round and fucks some glorified nurse on the side. We have three words for that where I come from, and they are 'pot', 'kettle' and 'black'.

lundi, le 2 mai

I leave the phone off. Tomás comes by in the afternoon for language study. He's picked up a second job at a hotel, so it looks as if our meetings will become even more irregular.

He fumbles, smiling, in his bag and brings out a pine-apple. '*Ananas*,' he says. With a pocket knife he fillets the fruit expertly and offers me a slice. We pore over vocabulary lists together, munching the pineapple.

We quit early. Now I have enough Spanish for conversations, I ask him how his work is going, how his brother is.

'Some days are better than others,' Tomás says. Then, apropos of nothing, 'You are very beautiful.'

I don't know what he means by that, what is implied if you say something like that in Spanish. Is he . . . does he fancy me? Or is it just a statement? 'I think you are nice,' I say. 'But I have a boyfriend,' and for no reason I start to cry. How different would life be if relationships were as simple as that? The man thinks you are beautiful. You think he is nice. You fall in love, have babies and grow old together.

'*Estás preocupada por algo?*' Tomás asks. Are you worried about anything? His thick-fingered hand rests lightly on my shoulder.

I shake my head.

'So why are you sad?'

'My boyfriend . . . My boyfriend is . . .' *Mi novio es . . .* I gesture for the dictionary to look up the word. Tomás passes it to me. Finding the right word takes a few minutes. *My boyfriend is a liar*? *My boyfriend is a cheat*? *My boyfriend is a pretentious shite*? 'My boyfriend is a big idiot.'

'It happens to everyone,' Tomás says. '*Debes tratar de resolverlo.*' You should try to resolve it.

mardi, le 3 mai

I click through to the pictures from the Boy's website. A Sunday walk in the country and lunch at a pub he took me to once, years ago, when he still cared about trying to impress me. Lambs, a stone cottage, a national park. Peacocks and a walled garden. And her.

So this is Georgie, eh? Nothing I couldn't have predicted.

301

Short legs, round face. Sunglasses holding her brownish hair back in a way that looks natural on her sort and ludicrous on everyone else. Wearing one of the Boy's rugby shirts.

You meet them everywhere, from the enclosures at Ascot to dining-ins at the officers' mess. The mouse-haired posh girls, heavy bosoms sagging in bias-cut satin dresses, each one hanging on the arm of a fit, godlike man who in a true meritocracy would not be plighting his troth to good old Wellsey, the dim, horsey daughter of a merchant banker.

There's nothing someone like me can do to compete. These girls wear their expensive lifestyle the way it should be worn: carelessly. I can't do that. I put shoe trees in my pumps and am on a first-name basis with the dry cleaner. I'm a try-hard. Nothing in my life has ever been careless.

But what they don't know is that I may look tame but I am really feral. That's why we become the mistresses. The call girls. And I would rather be bought for the cost of three hundred an hour, keeping my spare time my own, than for a token heirloom ring. I'm a man's woman. Someone who can down gin by the half-pint and shoot a decent frame of snooker. The sort of girl you have an affair with, not the sort you marry.

I fucking hate them.

Except, and this is the jam in the works . . . I still love him. It's not just wounded pride that makes it hurt. It's the rich, aching desire of wishing he was here. I know I could do better, find a real man, find my equal. That isn't the point. It's him I want.

jeudi, le 5 mai

'Don't do it,' J says, watching me dial. 'When you come to your senses, you'll never want that man again.'

'The heart has its reasons, right?' I say. I haven't eaten in days and can think of nothing else. I can't hold out any longer, I want to hear the Boy's voice.

J grabs the phone and hangs up before it connects. 'Fucking hell! You're my cousin, and I love you, but you're crackers.'

'I love him,' I say.

'That's not love. That's addiction. I know. I was the same way, only with drugs.'

The phone rings. It can only be the Boy, calling back. J shakes his head. 'Then you have to do for me what your family did for you,' I say. 'Let me make my own mistakes.' It's a low blow, but it is the truth, and he knows it.

'Fine,' he says. 'But if that stupid fucker comes back here, he's not staying with me.'

samedi, le 7 mai

Twice a day. That's how often, twice a day. We phone each other, but we're both still angry and distant. We don't have anything to say. Sometimes he draws enough energy to start a tirade at me, and when he does I put the phone down and quietly walk off. Sometimes I can be gone for ten minutes and when I come back he's still going at it.

'You ruined my life, did I ever tell you that? I've lost every opportunity I ever had because . . .'

I walk off again. Because when he's finished, he'll say he loves me, say he hopes I stay safe. I don't say anything back. I remember what J told me, before I came here, those months ago: *You don't have to make a decision.* Eventually the Boy will yell himself out and then we'll see where we are.

303

mardi, le 10 mai

'Darling, I'm on my way,' a voice said down the not-particularly-clear line.

'Pardon?'

'I'm on my way! I'll be staying virtually a hundred yards from your door from next week.'

'That's lovely. Who are you?'

'L, you silly goose,' she said.

'Omigod! Sorry, the connection is terrible,' I said, sitting up in bed. The fact that it was also half four didn't help.

'No worries, darling. I'll e you the details. Get back to bed before I wake you up properly.'

dimanche, le 22 mai

Do I know what today is? J asks. I don't. Go ahead, have a guess. I know it's not his birthday. Some obscure local holiday? No. Full moon? No, J says, it's a year since. A year since what? A year since I went clean. Why didn't you say? I'll take you out. No, J says, I'll take you out. A year since I realised I almost lost my family. Where to? I ask. Where else? J asks. Tomás and Francisco's, of course.

Francisco has brought his Harley to work today. It gleams darkly outside the restaurant like a giant insect, poised to leap. 'Hell of a motor,' J says. 'Ever ridden one of those?' I say no. J says I should give it a go. Then pats his pocket. 'Fucksticks, I forgot my wallet. I'll just pop home and get it.'

He gets up from the table, has a word with Francisco, then leaves in his car. When Francisco comes over to the table I realise: J has paid the bill, he's not coming back to fetch me, he's told Francisco to give me a lift home.

Francisco's mouth is screwed down. 'This is difficult,' he says under his breath. 'My brother is here.'

'I'm sorry,' I say, hoping he knows it was J's idea, not mine. I could walk home, I think. But then the bars and restaurants will all be letting out about now, and the narrow streets will be full of drunken British thugs, and I will at the very least feel uncomfortable. 'You don't have to, I'll walk,' I offer.

Francisco waves his hand dismissively. 'Wait outside,' he says. 'I'll be ten minutes.'

The motorbike speeds away from the restaurant and my hands are tight round Francisco's waist. We take the long route, the way along the beach. The long curve of yellow streetlamps is reflected on the calm water. My hair whips wildly around my face and his, and he urges the motorcycle faster, faster than I think must be safe.

We stop in front of my house. 'I like you,' Francisco says, unzipping his leather jacket.

I don't know how to reply. I don't know what weight the words carry in Spanish, what my response may or may not imply. 'I like you, too,' I say.

And then suddenly he pushes me against the wall, making my elbows raw, and he is kissing me. He grinds his hips into mine and pushes me off the ground with the force. His tongue is quick and certain, and mine replies in kind. Then, just as quickly, it's over. We stand a few feet apart.

'*Tiene una esposa*,' I say. It's not a question, it's a statement: you have a wife.

He looks at me, holds his hands out at his sides and shrugs. It's a classically male gesture, a so what? Implying that it doesn't matter to him and it shouldn't matter to me. I am being disingenuous, I know this, but he doesn't. He doesn't know the number of husbands I've had, the number of fathers.

And I know that, for all the outward show, the Catholic piety of people here goes about as deep as my Jewishness. An identification – not a system of belief. I wouldn't be the first girl he's had on the side. My refusal would give him no more than a moment's pause. Anglo girls are ten a penny.

I say goodnight and enter the house. The lights are off, but I know J is there, know he heard everything.

lundi, le 23 mai

'Cardinal rule,' L says, turning over to tan her front. Her skin is fair and freckly, but she's managing well thus far. 'Don't bring up the wife and child unless he does first.'

'You sound like you've been involved with married men before,' I say.

L harrumphs but doesn't answer. She's staying at a rented *cabaña*. 'The long and short of it is this: if a man wants to be single, he'll be single. If he wants to cheat, he'll cheat. No sense throwing his lies back in his face.'

'Noted,' I say, rubbing more suncream into my shoulders.

L laughs. 'My entire life's a time out,' she says. 'The actress who never acted, the lawyer who has yet to practise law.'

'It's a hell of a way to live.'

'It's a tough life, but someone has to do it,' she says.

mardi, le 24 mai

I cycled down the beach, oblivious of the crowds and noise around me. Before I knew it I was at Francisco's restaurant, so I went in.

Tomás didn't seem to be around. I chose a small corner table. Francisco came over and offered a menu, but having had everything on it three times over, I told him to bring me whatever he thought I would like and a carafe of wine. He smiled: this pleased him. I saw the restaurant was very busy for midweek but he waited on my table himself.

After the first glass of wine I went to the toilet. When I was washing my hands the door rattled. '*Es ocupado*,' I said back.

'*No, es Francisco*,' he hissed from the other side. I let him in.

Without even locking the door he pushed me against the sink and started kissing me. One hand pulled me up onto the edge of the sink and the other fiddled with my left nipple through my shirt. He was definitely someone who had moves and knew what to do with them, I decided.

'Saturday night,' he said. It was a command, not a question, but to be honest I like a man who says – not asks – what to do. 'I'll see you after work.'

He left the toilet and I waited a minute before emerging. It was all I could do not to fall over on the way back to the table. He brought out my courses as if nothing had happened; I settled the bill and walked home. What to do with this? I wondered. A married man. But I'll bet he's great in bed. And no good reason to deny myself . . .

The Boy rang shortly after I returned. Idly I wondered what – or who – was keeping him up so late.

'You seem to have a far more active social life by yourself than you ever do with me,' he said.

If that's what he thinks, good. 'That's because you never took me anywhere and never introduced me to your friends.'

He went quiet. It was, after all, the truth: introducing me to more people than strictly necessary would have put a serious damper on his extracurricular activities.

mercredi, le 25 mai

'Let me see if I understand,' J says. He's taken me out for ice-cream and a tan. No, really – it turns out his favourite place to go is a combination tanning salon and ice-cream parlour.

Genius. 'He says he wants to marry you, but has he ever actually asked you to marry him?'

'Not as such, no.'

'And he let you leave the country and come here,' J says, swirling his spoon around in the remains of a knickerbocker glory. 'But if he'd given up the other girls and asked you to stay in England, you would have done?'

'That's about the size of it, yes.'

'So what do you have to feel guilty about?'

'Everything I did wrong.'

'Everybody makes mistakes,' J says. 'You make the best decision you can at the time. Sometimes it's wrong. So what?'

I look in the bottom of my empty bowl. I all but licked it clean. I fucking love ice-cream, could eat it in place of almost everything else in the world.

'No ring, no contract,' J says and punches me on the shoulder. 'Come on, stop shitting on yourself. You're much better than that. And what's a kiss? Nothing worth feeling this bad about.'

I smile and let him pay.

vendredi, le 27 mai

Pre-cheating preparation checklist:

- Condoms, procured. Although on closer inspection of the bag from the shop, I notice the same surname as Francisco and Tomás's. Ah, crumbs, it was probably his father.
- Clothing, chosen. Tight jeans, cool short-sleeved black silk blouse, fetching jewellery. Nice knickers. Nicer bra.
- Hairy bits, shaved.
- Good hair day, as planned for as possible. Skipped washing today and hoping for favourable weather conditions tomorrow. It is a fickle beast.

- Conscience, suppressed. This largely achieved through listening to lots of music at full volume, the better to drown out any doubts.

samedi, le 28 mai

It doesn't happen. I'm primed and ready and it doesn't happen, and not because I don't want it to. I really, really do. But dressed and made up, sitting nervously on the end of my bed, waiting until what I think might be closing time on a busy weekend night, it gives me a lot of time to think.

I shouldn't be doing this, think of his family.

Since when have you ever worried about a man's family?

Okay, think of the Boy.

Yeah, think of the Boy – there's one reason why you shouldn't say no.

Finally I ring the restaurant. Tomás answers, surprised and happy to hear my voice. I hesitate and ask for his brother and he goes silent. I ask again for Francisco. It takes a moment, and he comes to the phone, sounding tired but sexy.

'I'm sorry, I can't see you tonight,' I say. No explanation.

Not just because I don't know the Spanish for it. I don't think he would particularly want, or need, my excuses.

'Yes, I see,' he says. 'It's very busy here, I must get back to work. Goodnight.'

'Goodnight.' And that's it, I've blown my one chance with him, I know. The unopened packet of condoms sits on the end of my bed, next to my handbag.

lundi, le 30 mai

The Boy rings. We're still at arm's length. I make round-about apologies, not placing blame on anyone: *I'm sorry you're still angry. I'm sorry that what I did upset you.* I usually hate half-hearted apologies, the kind of thing a politician would say to look good without actually admitting guilt. I shouldn't even be talking to him, but I want this relationship to last, and know from experience that forgiveness trumps anger every time. Ninety per cent of me is unconvinced that I'm the one who should be on bended knee. But the remaining, louder, 10 per cent really wants a cuddle. And sex.

Unlike him, I am not convinced that a secret summer romance would cheer me. So I email him a few new photos. The beach, the fruit stand, the house. And one photo of myself post-beach, naked, in the bathroom mirror. Suddenly we're on speaking terms again. Such is the power of tan lines.

mardi, le 31 mai

Someone knocks at the door. I go to answer, it's Tomás. 'You don't have to knock,' I smile. 'Come in, please.'

He stands on the step looking at me. His face is blank, I think perhaps he's angry. 'I hope you will not continue seeing my brother,' Tomás says, formally.

I sigh. Of course. Surely he's stood by and watched Francisco fooling around before. Possibly not with a neighbour, but still . . .

'I'm not interested in your brother,' I say. 'He is married and has children.'

Tomás nods soberly. 'He has.'

'Please don't stop talking to me because of this,' I say. '*Tú eres mi amigo.*'

He smiles. 'You are my friend, too,' he says, in English. I smile and invite him in.

Juin

dimanche, le 5 juin

I suppose Georgie must have tired of toying with my boy-friend, because today he's rung three times. It's annoying that men are so transparent, but I can't say it's not nice. And when I went on the computer for a chat he was there. My only complaint is that he seems more keen to exchange social pleasantries than to talk about sex. Does this mean he's forgotten? What if I go back and he's gone off me altogether?

lundi, le 6 juin

Some juxtapositions are too awkward to be explained away. The Boy's invited me to a wedding on the day I'm due to return home as soon as he finds out when I'm due to fly: absolutely transparent. It irks me to be second choice; but then, having worked as a call girl, I should be used to it.

mercredi, le 8 juin

It's awkward making contact after so long. I feel a little excited and a lot guilty.

The familiar voice answers. 'Hello, gorgeous,' N says.
'How did you know it was me?'
'No number came up. Who else could it be?'

'An Indian call centre?' N laughs. 'I'm sorry I haven't been better about contacting you. I am a bit of a shit.'

'No worries. I'll beat you about the face and neck later. So when are you coming home? I miss the hell out of you.'

God, I miss him, too. 'Soon,' I say. 'Next month.'

'Can't wait to get my hands on you,' N growled.

'What about the girlfriend?'

'She dumped me right after St Valentine's Day.'

'Nooooooo.'

'Yes,' he says. 'If I'd known, I would have been rid of her before Christmas and spent the time with you instead.'

'You're too sweet.'

'All part of the service, ma'am.'

jeudi, le 9 juin

I went back to the Boy's blog. I wanted to know whether there was anything I'd missed, either good or bad. He hadn't updated it in a couple of weeks. I scrolled back through the archives, looking again at the evidence of his affair with Susie, at the lies he'd told everyone, the ways he'd hurt me.

Except, it didn't look quite like that this time. Yes, he'd fooled around; and every one of those girls he'd compared with me. Over and over he'd written how he'd wished that we were together.

He didn't rabbit on about making a life with Susie, he didn't indulge in maudlin recollections of previous good times with the others. It was me he thought of when he was alone; me he said he wanted a future with.

And hidden in a long entry I'd only skimmed before: 'Now I know that she needed me most when she first moved to London and was struggling to find a job, and I wasn't there.' I'd started working as a call girl because I'd had difficulty finding a job. He didn't openly wonder whether I might not have chosen sex work if he'd been around more. But it was interesting to see he'd considered this.

I was upset, but not in a bad way. I decided to quit while I was ahead and make a real effort to stop reading his blog for good.

samedi, le 11 juin

I can't get sex off my mind – the replacement activities (sitting on the beach, walking with J) are not sufficiently distracting to keep me from thinking about it for long.

The funny thing about being starved of sex is that you remember things you might otherwise have forgotten: a particular night, or a lover whose name has long since slipped your mind. I've spent more than a few hours recalling:

- The man at uni who had dated all the girls in our circle of friends but me. We finally did it, the night after graduation. Anal. We never spoke again until five years later when he emailed me out of the blue (he's married now).
- The man who loved asphyxiating me, and since I didn't know any better, I didn't refuse him. Until, that is, the time I became unconscious, and remained so for several minutes, according to him. I don't remember it. But I never let anyone throttle me again.
- The time I had sex in a hotel room (not with a client), and the man used the clips of a trouser hanger to pull on my nipples – quite clever improvisation, that; it comes with a built-in handle, and we took it away when we'd finished – while I masturbated to orgasm. Afterwards, we watched Eurotrashy soft porn on the television.

Tomás has given me a phone card, and I ring Daddy.

'Hello, honey, how are you?' he asks. I tell him I'm planning to come home next month. 'That's great news,' he says. 'There's someone I'd very much like you to meet.'

Good thing he can't see my face, because it just turned in on itself. He's about to ring off, when I can't resist asking.

'Daddy, did you and Mum ever really love each other?'

'I loved your mother very much,' he says softly. 'Still do.'

'You two are always so vague when you talk about each other, and now you're both seeing other people and . . . I don't know, I don't want to come home to two new families.'

'Honey, it's hard being alone,' he says. Oh yes? I think. Tell me a-fucking-bout it.

'Do you even remember how you felt when you met? How can you just walk away after all you two have been through?'

'Sweetie, there are many things you don't understand.'

'Well, I'm almost thirty. Don't you think it's time I did?'

He sighs. I can hear in his voice a note of defeat that was never there when my parents were together. I wonder who this woman is; she's probably young, and knowing how soft-hearted my father is, she's probably a mess. He deserves so much better. 'Things between me and your mother have always been complicated, right from the start.'

'But you met as kids. You've known each other for ever.'

'Yes, we did,' he says. 'And then I didn't see her for years, until me and her brother were at university together and she came to visit. She was still at school then.'

I knew my parents had married early, when they were both still students. 'Well, what could possibly have been difficult when you were both so young?'

'I never told you this, honey, but she was pregnant when

she came to visit. Her brother couldn't take her to have a termination, so I went with her instead. That was it. We were together after that.'

Oh.

'I have to go,' Daddy said. 'I'll ring you soon.'

And that was it, he was gone.

I walked home slowly. Why did they never tell me? I thought we knew everything about each other. Scratch that – almost everything. Honesty was always held to be so important at home.

And yet . . . I could imagine the strain on a young couple. He loves her, she's pregnant by someone else, someone who won't even do what is needful, and he has to take care of the mess left afterwards. The mess another man has put her into. Over time, they might get over it. Or they might bury it, it might fester and poison everything. I know that I don't want to know exactly why they split; knowing this is enough.

I turn round and go back to the phone, ring the Boy, and tell him I love him.

mardi, le 21 juin

Just heard from A1. His father, who'd been hovering at the edge of death for years, has passed away. I didn't know what to say.

A1's father was legendary. He was a big guy, big laugh. He was a Jew, kiddo, but not a reedy, neurotic Woody Allen type. The elder A1 wheeled, dealed and chewed scenery with the best of them. He gave me a lift from one end of the country to the other once, and here I was, a frightened teenager who was sleeping with his too-old-for-me son, and you wouldn't have known it. Mr A1 chattered and joked the entire way down and gave my mother the eye when we arrived at our destination.

317

Mr A1 had a talent for inappropriate jokes, most of which I found the opportunity to recycle years later when I was entertaining men on an hourly basis. He had known the charms of call girls, too – one of his favourite anecdotes concerned a prostitute.

It was when he was in the army, and he and some friends threw their spare money together to get a girl for an hour. There wasn't enough time for every lad to have a few minutes with her on his own, so they took her into a men's toilet and watched as each in turn did the deed.

When it came Mr A1's turn, he just wanted oral relief. She went down in front of his friends and provided it. Then, with his come still in her mouth, she said – and here he would imitate her voice, her mouth full of his seed, a sort of half-gurgle – 'For another pound I'll swallow it.'

'It's yours now, love,' Mr A1 said. 'Do whatever you like.'

If I was ever meant to have a father-in-law, surely this was the man. When A1 and I split up, I was sad, not just for the end of that relationship, but for losing his family.

mercredi, le 22 juin

This, in case I ever have to tell my children or grandchildren, is how it happened. I'm cruising around on a bicycle, long skirt tucked between my knees, huge sunglasses, enjoying the sunshine. A man waves at me. He's wearing white linen trousers and a blue T-shirt, he's cute. I wave back. He tilts his head and I stop to talk. What's the worst that can happen? He mentions maybe lunch? I know a place. We have a lot in common – we're from the same area, have similar experiences, laugh at the same things. Soon we're finishing each other's sentences.

He looks at his hands, sad. 'What's wrong?' I ask. 'I wish I could go with this,' he says. But he has a girlfriend, she's coming to visit next month. I have a boyfriend.

His name is David, I'm meant to be leaving in about a fortnight, and I am so fucked.

jeudi, le 23 juin

Spotted A4 online.

<belle_online>ugh

<luvly_jubly>what's wrong?

<belle_online>stoopid slow connection, looking for a flat. Don't suppose you know anywhere going?

<luvly_jubly>actually I'm moving back north

<belle_online>noooooo!

<belle_online>what about work?

<luvly_jubly>this is for work. A2's starting a northern office in Macclesfield. You can move into my place

<belle_online>you're joking!

<luvly_jubly>all your things are here already anyway, would save my back

<belle_online>true

<luvly_jubly>and you already have a key

<belle_online>true

<luvly_jubly>and it would save you having to stay some-where looking for a place

<belle_online>enough already, you've convinced me! You will probably live to regret this

<luvly_jubly>probably

vendredi, le 24 juin

'I'm a mess, I'm an idiot when it comes to men,' I say to L. 'I used to have a clue, you know? I used to be cool. Now I'm like some stupid chick-lit woman, and I've no idea why.'

'What on earth makes you say a thing like that?' she said.

'Well, why am I with my boyfriend when we so clearly drive each other mad? Why do I meet a great guy just when the timing couldn't be worse? How did I manage to lose a great guy like A4? Will I ever do anything right?'

L reapplied lotion to her thighs. A swimsuited young man brought our drinks over on a tray, and she smiled at him winningly. 'Don't be silly,' she said. 'You do what you have to do.'

'The question is, do I really have to do this? Act like a completely stupid girl just because I don't want to be alone?'

'It's not stupid,' she finally said. 'You've glimpsed the future, and while it's nice to be running around with a cute little body like yours now, someday you'll have to choose whether you are willing to compromise when it comes to relationships or prefer to become the intensely lonely fossil who, on finishing the eighth double Scotch of the evening, blankly stares into the middle distance, considering the irrevocable march towards death.'

Yikes. 'Sounds like you've thought about that a lot.'

She shrugged. 'It's what made me a good law student. And will guarantee that I reach the age of sixty with a houseful of furs and antiques rather than children.'

samedi, le 25 juin

The Boy rings to say that, because of family obligations, he won't be able to ring me over the weekend. This has the ring of untruth but I bite my tongue. Fuck it, let what happens happen. Things could all be different in a week, anyway.

dimanche, le 26 juin

David and I go to his house. He has local beer in the fridge and lets me choose the music. It's a nice house, I say, is he renting? No. Owns. He's moved here permanently, to start a business. His girlfriend didn't join him. He got the dog.

The dog is called Fritz, and hasn't taken his eyes off me since I came in. I scratch his belly and pet his ears.

'I can tell you're a sensual person,' David says.

'How's that?'

'By the way you touch his ears.' Fritz suddenly licks my face. 'Don't do that Fritz, I haven't even kissed her yet!'

I don't fall for someone often, and feel like fate is mocking me. He's funny. Smart. Has his own business. And is, of course, not quite single. His on-again, off-again partner, who lives as far from here as mine does, is visiting after I go. At least he's straight with me. He owns up to her existence. It's a bittersweet flirtation. In a parallel universe we're probably carrying on a scorching love affair without even a pang of guilt. But in this one, we're both Jewish.

'What do you want to do?' I ask.

'You know what I want to do.'

'I don't. You haven't even kissed me yet.'

'I'd like to take you on the floor and spend the next three hours fucking.'

'Really?' I say.

'Really,' he says.

My breath is heavy and uneven. 'Oh.'

Before we part I step towards him – a move which, in other circumstances, would signal the big romantic clinch; in this case neither of us can bring ourselves to cross that line. I can smell him, feel the warmth of his skin. But we don't even kiss. I stay up all night wondering what the Boy's up to and thinking what an idiot I am.

lundi, le 27 juin

I find out why my boyfriend is incommunicado. It's all in the online photo album, isn't it. I so despise indiscretion.

He is at home seeing his family, all right. Seeing his family – and taking along his ex-girlfriend Jo, who has been nursing a crush on him ever since they split. I'm hardly blameless, what with going off and falling for someone else, but still . . .

mardi, le 28 juin

'So you read her email and saw the photos,' L said. 'What's this one like?'

'I shudder to recollect. Plain and dumpy.' And weirdly convinced, as so many large girls are, that head-to-toe black is a slimming look – well, not when you're standing against a pale background, it's not. And you're almost always stand-ing against a pale background.

'You reckon he's shtupping her?'

'No,' I say. 'It's the lie more than anything. If she's just a friend, sure he can spend time with just a friend. I spend loads of time with other men. I don't know why he feels he has to hide it; I don't hide my male friends from him.'

L came out of the dressing room, wearing a pink bikini. 'I know, doesn't go with the hair. But I'm so buying this.'

Truly stunning piece of logic. 'You should have had all currency instruments confiscated on entering the country.' Keeping up with L is costing me, too – nothing wildly extravagant, mind, just the endless rounds of drinks, shop-ping, and so on. But I can't claim I'm not enjoying it.

L retreated behind the faux-bamboo door to change into street clothes. 'Has it occurred to you that he's worried about your male friends? That he finds them threatening?'

'But that's the point – I make them obvious, so he knows they're not a threat.'

L peered over the door, sunglasses holding back her hair. 'You know what I think? You should forget about the lad here and the one at home and marry that one you're always talking about. The one with the flat.' A4. 'You guys are so still in love and you know it.'

'It's been six years,' I said. 'Anyway, he split with me. So it's up to him to declare his intentions. I'm not going begging.'

'What the hell kind of a rule is that?'

'Standard operating procedure, surely?'

L gave me a look. 'Never heard such nonsense in my life.'

Juillet

mardi, le 5 juillet

It's that time of year again, isn't it? Somewhere between early spring (the wedding season) and late summer (the everyone copping off on holiday season). The exes-writing-letters season.

My previous amours are divided into two camps, those who stay friends and those who disappear. Every year around this time a few of the disappeared make themselves known again with the casual 'Oh, I just thought I'd drop you a note' email. It's not my policy to respond, though it is interesting to see who sends them.

The surprise this year? All the exes are writing to let me know they're married. Do they expect gifts or something?

On a hunch I go and check the Boy's email. Yep, the fever has struck him, too: two sent letters.

To Susie he writes a bunch of sappy crap:

Hello, a bit out of the blue I suppose. If ever you are sitting round yours on a sunny day or warm evening with nothing to do, please call me, lass. I would love to take you out to a country pub on the moors and treat you just once. Or even just to the cinema?! I do know that you have completely moved on, but I would really like to very much. We spent most of our time together hundreds of miles apart, and now ironically we are not together but only 500 metres apart! It's all very frustrating but beautifully ironic. Sigh. Take care, lass, and thank you for all the happy memories.

Actually, it was thousands of miles apart, not hundreds, but then he's never been especially good at maths. And to the stick insect Lena, who I caught him in bed with the first time we were dating, some really quite unbelievable statements:

I know I really ruined my chances with you and I want you to know that your man is very lucky. You are by far one of the sexiest, cleverest and all-round stunning girls I have ever met, lass. If you ever change your mind, I live in hope.

Now maybe I live on a deluded island of self-belief here, but I own a mirror. I've seen this girl. I've met her. I know that I'm prettier, smarter and certainly a better all-rounder than she is. If that's what he finds valuable, if that's what he thinks stunning, why do I bother?

jeudi, le 7 juillet

Tomás came over first thing and woke me up. That was how I found out about the attacks in London. We woke J and his girlfriend, put the television on the news and sat for hours, stunned. The news here shows more blood, more screaming; throws more suspicion and rumours around than the news at home would dare do. I thought about ringing home but knew there was no chance of the lines being free.

After several hours, names of the victims started to come through. The first name I saw made my heart stop. It was my mother's.

It wasn't her, it couldn't be, I knew that. J squeezed my shoulder – we didn't say it out loud so the others wouldn't worry, but I knew we were thinking the same thing. Mum isn't dead. I knew she was nowhere near London today but seeing her name shook me, just the same.

I have never felt so far from home in my entire life.

vendredi, le 8 juillet

Mum's fine. But I'm still shaken. I don't want to fly home, I don't want to be standing at the airport, on the Tube platform, eyeing everyone else and wondering, just as they all will be, Who's armed here? Who might be carrying a bomb? If it was a month earlier, maybe I wouldn't go back. But my ticket is booked. I've rung the airline just to be certain; surely everyone is trying to fly home today. My seat is booked, my reservation will be honoured. There's little I can do.

The night before I am due to leave, David comes along to say goodbye. In thirty-six hours' time I will be in the arms of my boyfriend and he will be in the arms of his girlfriend. Meanwhile, everything back in London seems complete chaos. It's difficult to make any conversation that doesn't revolve around those subjects. So we talk about sex. The things we like, don't like, and would do if there wasn't this damned business about being committed to other people. I'm almost painfully turned on.

'You're very cute, you know that?'

Take me, please, here, now. On the suitcases.

'Thank you. So are you.'

Have I ever wanted to touch someone this badly in my life? Apparently there's a phenomenon known colloquially as terror sex, where people after a traumatic event on the scale of what just happened in London have extraordinary sex. I know it exists. Two weeks after the World Trade Center was attacked, I met A2 in the US and had what I still remember as my biggest orgasm ever.

'Out of curiosity, do you have any condoms?'

'Yes,' I say. 'I should take them back and demand a refund. I don't know what sort of spell the chemist put on these, but I haven't had sex since buying them.'

'That is a waste.'

But we can't do it. We don't. Neither of us is brave enough to move from the realm of the desired to the realm of the definite, where we may be disappointed, or never see each other again, or never want to be parted. I see him in his underwear, he sees me out of my bra ('How did such a small girl get such boobies?' he says), and painful though it is, we stop. Our reward will be in heaven, except I don't believe in heaven. There is no reward.

samedi, le 9 juillet

'Don't you fucking cry,' J says, crushing me to his shoulder. Over my head I hear him sniffling. He holds me at arm's length, looks at my face. 'You're gonna be okay, right?'

Tomás hands me an envelope. He's made a card, drawn a picture of our houses next to each other. Inside, in Spanish, a wish for safe travel and luck; a photocopy of something by Mother Teresa he's always had taped to the top of his bathroom mirror. That's when I really start bawling.

'I'll call, I promise.' J puts a finger to my lips. 'Shut up,' he says. 'You live your life, we'll live ours, everything will be fine. I'll see you,' he says, as if I'm going round the corner, not thousands of miles away.

dimanche, le 10 juillet

The Boy is standing just the other side of the arrivals barrier, between crowds of families and drivers holding signs with names on. He looks different from the person I remember – tired, maybe, a bit dumpy and unshaven.

Then again, it is six in the morning and I hardly look

catwalk-ready. There's an odd, faraway look in his eyes, as if I don't quite match his memory, either.

He drives us to Wiltshire, where he's booked a room at an adorable B&B for the night. We fall straight into bed, with the alarm set for four hours' time; when it rings we rise, shower, have a quick fuck, then dress for the wedding. I'm wearing a peacock silk halter dress, loaned from L, with gold sandals; he looks nice in his dinner jacket.

I touch his chin. 'Now now, let's have a good time.'

And the wedding is good, in its own way. There is much drinking of Pimm's and walking around gardens and making conversation with aged aunties. After the meal, we dance to 'God Only Knows' and I realise it's the first time we've ever danced slow together. There's a dark-haired man who's been making eyes at me the entire time, but I ignore him. Only . . . ? Do I recognise him? From *work*?

Ah, shite. Everyone always talked about what to do if something like this happened but I never honestly thought I'd run into an ex-client outside the confines of a hotel room.

The bride has thoughtfully booked a club in town for the younger guests after the formal affair breaks up. At the club the Boy is in his element – he's been drinking all day and needs little excuse to dance like a loon. Everyone laughs at his antics, and for once I don't mind. They all know he's here with me and I'm sort of proud.

The Boy lurches off to the toilet and his place is quickly taken by the man who's been looking at me.

I'm drunk enough to cut to the chase. 'Your name wouldn't happen to be Malcolm, would it?' I say, and smile in a friendly way.

'Jonty.'

Ah, I was wrong about spotting an ex-client, then. It happens. 'Oh, okay. My mistake, then.'

'Wouldn't it be a good thing if I was this . . . Malcolm?'

'Probably a bit of yes and a bit of no. Slightly more yes than no, if I was here on my own.'

'Then that really is a pity.'

The Boy had come back from the toilet and was watching us dance, arms folded in that particular way I despise. Jonty handed me over, but not before leaning close to my ear and saying, 'I would recognise you anywhere.'

And that was that, until we left. Jonty came up behind me and, hands on my hips, turned me round and planted a not-so-innocent kiss on me. Not over the line, but just under it. 'So what are you doing with him?' he asked, indicating my man. 'He's such a Boy Scout.'

Maybe so, relatively speaking. 'I like Boy Scouts,' I said. Saves me from myself sometimes.

mardi, le 12 juillet

Things you should never do on your first day of work:

1. Wear fishnets. Particularly if you're the only woman in the office. But my only other pair of stockings had a ladder.
2. Spend the entire day on the phone, giving your boyfriend directions to the new house so he can start moving in.
3. Squeal and kiss your boss on seeing him. 'Ohmigod! Giles! It's been too long!' Wait five minutes, at least. Especially if he has potential clients with him, meeting 'the core team'.
4. When the person overseeing your introduction to the new computing system asks if you have any questions, do not make it 'Where's the nearest place to buy chocolate?'
5. Have argument on phone in front of entire office with said boyfriend, who is clearly feeble of mind if he does not understand left, then left, then through two mini-roundabouts, then right and it's on the right.
6. Have a hangover, though to be honest I'm not certain,

given all of the above, that anyone particularly noticed. Apart from Giles, who just left a bottle of water and two Nurofen on the corner of my desk.

mercredi, le 13 juillet

I couldn't help it, I had to look. Even though I'd promised myself I wouldn't.

The site was just like I remembered. I clicked through the pages until I found what I was looking for. I narrowed my eyes. *Fucking typical*, I thought. *I should have known. After all these months nothing's changed.* My profile was still up on the agency website.

I looked closer . . . Those weren't my photos! I read the description again, the summary I had sweated over. *Friendly and petite Northerner, enjoys long conversations and longer nights in . . .* That was definitely the profile I'd written. And that was certainly my working name. But those photos were definitely not me.

Someone else was playing me now, had taken on my persona. I had to smile and shake my head. What else had I expected? Maybe one or two old clients got confused, ordered up someone they thought was me . . . but the business has a short memory. I'm sure they've all but forgotten me now.

samedi, le 16 juillet

The Boy arrived home early, but I had come home earlier and was already cooking. I served up the meal.

'House rules,' I said as we finished eating. 'I'm doing all the cooking, so you're doing all the washing up.'

'Okay.'

'No more leaving the house to make your phone calls.'

'Yes.'

'I don't care how many days your job keeps you away, you're paying half the rent and bills. And I'm not having your name on the lease.'

'Okay.'

'And you're to ring me from work every day. And if I get even the faintest whiff of funny business, you know you're out on your arse, right?'

'I know.'

He cleared the table. It was easier than I had thought. Was there something else I should demand? I wondered.

He came past my chair and kissed the top of my head. 'I hate when you go all quiet,' he said softly. 'It's worse than you yelling.'

mardi, le 19 juillet

I went round to the estate agent's with the banker's draft for the deposit so I could officially take over A4's lease. The Boy picked me up afterwards, it was near his work. 'Ugh, that was the biggest amount of money I hope to part with for a while,' I said. 'But at least it's all over with.'

'Poor you,' he said. 'You're short of pennies?'

'Not short, as such. The holiday was a little more expensive than I'd planned.'

'Really? How much was it?'

Ooh, I should have seen that one coming. Probably going to go straight to his diary and call me an extravagant cow or something. 'About eight thousand,' I said, knocking a few grand off the total. I'd had plenty to spare, but there are always a few things you don't anticipate.

He frowned and we drove on in silence. Of course, to one

of his posh totties, eight thousand would be lipstick money. But us underclass, we're not allowed to spend. Hmm, didn't someone write a song like that once?

'What's wrong now?' I said.

'That's half the cost of a wedding. You could have spent that money marrying me.'

I almost laughed. Was he kidding? He hopped into someone else's bed literally an hour after I left Britain and spent the summer getting blowjobs from junior doctors.

'Well, I don't mean to be blunt, but if you'd wanted to marry me you would have asked.'

'But I do want to marry you, I tell you that all the time.'

'Funnily enough, you only ever say it when we're arguing. Now let's drop the subject.' To my credit, I said all this at a normal volume. To his credit he did not mention it again.

mercredi, le 20 juillet

'Looking good,' Giles said as I came into the building.

'Careful, you, or people will start to think we're up to something.'

'A man can live in hope,' he said. 'Listen, we need you to meet the Japanese clients this afternoon – is it enough warning? I'm afraid you're the only person we have capable of explaining the conversion algorithms adequately.'

Some days I don't wonder what would have happened if I'd stayed a call girl.

jeudi, le 21 juillet

He licked my tan lines, hardly faded since returning. 'What right do you have,' he murmured, 'to be firmer and sexier than any teenager?'

I wrapped a towel round myself and led him down the back steps into the garden. 'Against the far wall,' I whispered. 'The neighbours are out.'

He spread the towel gently on the ground instead. 'Quickly,' I hissed. 'Before the insects find you.' But he didn't listen, slowly running his tongue around until everywhere that had been covered by a bikini last month was soaking wet.

vendredi, le 22 juillet

Met N for a meal at our favourite Italian, just the two of us. N's looking good: leaner and more tanned than when we last saw each other. He tells me about his recent women: a German postgraduate who loves pain, the lady we had the threesome with. And he's made friends with the man running his local sex shop, who is now passing on to N all the videos he can't hire out legally.

'You really do have the most amazing luck,' I say. It's ages since I've seen any quality porn, and N promises to pass some on, particularly one involving a heavy rope bondage session and a spiked glove. He swears up and down the woman looks like an older version of me.

I've been a bad friend and I know it: ignoring him for months, taking him for granted. I know in my heart of hearts that regardless of how the Boy feels about him, he'll always be my friend, and no man should ever change that.

dimanche, le 24 juillet

My life as a call girl revolved round the phone. If I didn't answer a call straight away, the work might have gone to someone else, which meant that for almost a year I was umbilically attached to the mobile.

Now all that has changed. I can go days without checking voice mail, and it's an incredible luxury. The phone goes dead and it's not a life-or-death problem.

Fate has a funny way of making you see yourself as others see you because there's hardly a minute when my boyfriend isn't on his phone. Worse still, he has one of these sexy little camera/email/does-everything-but-your-washing-up models. We've been sailing in a gale and he's on the phone. He's forever texting at the dinner table. Now I see how unbearably annoying it must have been for my friends.

I'm obsessed with schemes for getting rid of the thing. When it's raining, I keep hoping it will turn up waterlogged. If he's washing up and takes a call, I fantasise about giving him a bump and plop! It drops straight into the sink.

What better way to guarantee I will never have to do the laundry again than by not-so-accidentally leaving his phone in a trouser pocket? The idea has possibilities.

mercredi, le 27 juillet

We went to one of the Boy's work dos, as a couple, together. I played it down but was secretly thrilled. He kept looking over at me uneasily whenever we were parted – I wasn't saying something I shouldn't, was I? But he had nothing to worry about. For one thing, I was caught in conversation with one of the most boring women in the world.

M was a tall girl and heavy, dressed in flat London black with flat London hair, and was telling me she despised the concept of the one-night stand. This, I realised, was the flip side to fifteen-year-old tramps giving blowjobs at bus shelters. The thirty-something single city woman who has convinced herself that only true love is worth waiting for.

I don't understand. M and thousands of women like her deciding that not only do they prefer time alone to a bad relationship but that if there's no relationship, there's no sex. So the teenagers are banging mindlessly, while the very women who are not only cresting their sexual peaks but also have the discretional income and storage space for a host of boytoys and their accessories choose instead to spend their time in the company of BBC Three and a vibrator.

I mean, sex does not equal relationship. If the man is sexy, but not the one, no one said you have to give him your keys. I was stunned that a woman would so happily suppress her needs. I'd love to dine at a Michelin three-star establishment every night, but in the meantime I still have to eat. And if the restaurant isn't so hot, honey, I don't go back.

And London is a lonely place. Sometimes human contact for its own sake is nice.

I gritted my teeth. 'And if Mr Right just happened to walk through the door tonight . . . ?'

'That's different,' she said. 'Not that I'd take him home on the first night, either.' Obviously. Because you'd rather the love of your life thought you frigid than you thought yourself a slut. Because your approach to the sexual double-standard is to accept that men can have stringless fun but you must martyr yourself on every loser attractive enough to dampen your knickers.

We're our own worst enemies.

samedi, le 30 juillet

Unmarried couples living together. A modern perversion and leading cause of the sky-high divorce trend, if the right-leaning papers are to be believed. I can sympathise. There is nothing so unnatural to the human state of being as being tied to one person in domestic cohabitation indefinitely.

Looking at one naked body for the rest of your life, it simply isn't right.

Which is why I had such a thrill when a package came through the door today – unmarked, brown paper wrapping.

Glorious porn. Bouncing tits, shining cocks, come by the bucketful. If I can't arrange a threesome yet, at least a girl can window-shop.

dimanche, le 31 juillet

The Boy woke up in a mood. He rolled out of bed early, monopolised the toilet for half an hour. I could hear him tearing through all my bags in the cupboard – what the hell? If he came across that box of condoms, I could only imagine what he'd think. He pounded downstairs without so much as a 'Good morning'.

My stomach turned over. We weren't going to start down this route again, were we? I know these things take time, but I had hoped that most of the past was firmly where it belonged – behind us – and we could begin to be together, like a real boyfriend and girlfriend.

I toyed with my phone. The number had been pro-grammed into it for ages. In case everything went tits-up and I really needed some collateral. I brought the contact list up – there it was, under S. Susie. I dialled the number.

My heart was beating fast and hard. The phone on the other end rang and rang. No answer. I hung up, no message. It was then I heard the front door slam.

'Thank God for that,' I heard the Boy say in the hallway.

'Are you okay, dear?' I could hear the false note in my voice.

'I don't know whether it was something I ate,' he said, coming through to the sitting room. 'But I've had the runs something terrible all morning.'

'Oh, honey,' I sighed. 'Why didn't you say?'

'It's a bit embarrassing. Besides, I went through the cupboard in the bathroom and couldn't find anything for it.' He shook a small paper bag from the corner chemist. 'Just in the nick of time,' he said.

I couldn't have agreed more.

dimanche, le 31 juillet (later)

The phone rang. I clocked the number: Susie. My heart started beating violently. Let it go to voicemail or answer? I answered the phone.

A sharp Southern voice, a bit of a lisp. 'Hiya, this is Susie. Did you ring?'

'Pardon?'

'I had a call from this number this morning. This is Susie. Were you trying to reach me?' Not a hint of the haughty, playing-at-posh woman that Georgie had been. Just some girl. I looked around – no sign of the Boy. Must be upstairs reading, thank goodness.

I hesitated. After all this time, I could finally settle a score, make her know that I was the real girlfriend, had been all along. Then I remembered all the trouble phoning Georgie had caused. And even if Susie didn't hang up on me and straight away dial the Boy, who would no doubt tell her a pack of lies, what right did I have? I knew they were over. Maybe she even had good memories of him. Maybe the thought of him still make her unhappy. She wouldn't tell me anything I didn't already know. A few more details, but whom would that help?

'It was a misdial. I wrote down a wrong number. Sorry about that.'

'Oh, okay,' she said. She sounded so young.

'Well, bye, then,' I said. And hung up.

Five years on:

What's changed, and what hasn't?

So what's different now?

Wow, I can't believe it's been over five years since I started blogging . . . since I decided that going on the game, and writing about it in public, was not necessarily professional suicide!

Looking back now, there is so much that is different, and yet somehow still the same. I think the French have a saying about that. What I really enjoy when I look back over these episodes, though, is knowing how it all turns out in the end. Even while cringing at some of the obvious mistakes I made.

First off, as you roll your eyes through my on-again, off-again relationship with the Boy, know that I am in total agreement. What on earth was I thinking? The natural state of a hooker is single, unencumbered. It makes sense both from the emotional management and the logistical points of view: your pussy needs downtime, and there is much to be said for your day off being off in every sense of the word.

It's only going to be a minor spoiler to let you know, but look away now if you don't want to find out: we've split up now.

Shock of the century, right? I hurt a person I thought I loved, repeatedly, and always in the same ways; I let him do the same to me. Why? Because even though we weren't perfect, that's what I thought love was: struggle and effort. I'd never believed there was any such thing as a soul mate. What I didn't know yet was that you can pour in loads of effort in an attempt to get it to 'feel right', but that's the wrong way round. It should be that when it feels right, you put in the effort.

After a time it seemed that not only was performance a significant aspect of my job, but also that I was acting through my personal life, as well. Pretending things were okay, manageable, even great between us – when they blatantly were not – was exhausting. Eventually (but far past when I should have done), I had to let it go.

Want to know what I really miss, though? His dad. And the cat.

What's the same?

In spite of now being in a happy and stable relationship with a man I adore, I still don't believe in a soul mate. A2's now long-time girlfriend snorts when she even hears the term. 'Soul mates? Damage mates, more like.' And she's right. Virtually everyone I know has had a relationship where they mistook someone with complementary damage to theirs for someone with complementary assets. And oh my, the trouble that causes.

Word to the wise: love at first sight is a danger zone too. When you go loopy for someone without even knowing if they are suitable or not . . . I ain't saying it's impossible. I'm just saying leave off mingling your living arrangements/current accounts/gametes for a few months first.

Because if love was really about finding the one person who was 'made for you', the one being created for your passion and pleasure on this earth, isn't actually discovering where they're hiding out something of a statistical im-probability? What if you're out trawling the pubs and clubs of Fulham and your true love died in a trench in Ypres 90 years ago? Or how about if they were in fact accidentally incarnated as a soup spoon? You might discover each other and go live the rest of your lives in wedded bliss in a cutlery drawer. Or you might just throw him in the dishwasher and die alone.

But even so I'm an ickle bit less cynical than I was before. Might have something to do with being happy. Sometimes, you find love. Sometimes, love finds you. Mine found me in the Casual Relationships section of the Gumtree website. Oh yes.

Hotels: A new international standard?

Now that I have been on both sides of the fence – having gone from being a hotel-based service provider to a user of hotel services (though not the sort I used to provide, ahem), I feel qualified to comment on the state of hotels worldwide.

But you probably don't need me to tell you they suck bollocks.

Seriously, what is so difficult to understand? The needs of the vast majority of hotel guests are easy to predict, yet rarely catered to adequately. Powers That Be have decided that instead of a sensible set of amenities in every room, what we need is a sewing kit, a Bible, and a remote control that is both larger, and more difficult to operate, than a lunar lander. (Although if you are partial to the odd religious-guilt-tinged BDSM scene involving readings from Ecclesiastes, needles in tender places, and don't mind the possibility of accidentally changing the channel while using the remote as an improvised paddle, you have struck gold. The rest of us are shit out of luck.)

So what I propose is no less than a bill of human rights as regards hotel rooms. Any operation falling below this international standard is guilt of gross inhumanity and should be subject to trial in Brussels. I have no doubt the UN will back me up on this.

345

After much consideration and debate, here are the ten principles:

1. **Guaranteed in-room hot drink making facilities.** This is not simply about being British and needing constant unimpeded access to a cuppa (though of course that is also true). This is about the basic biological fact that all people are sub-human from the point of waking until the moment of ingesting their first hot beverage. Tea, coffee, Horlicks, gluhwein – I'm not fussy. But it needs to be hot, liquid, and most important of all, FREE.

2. **Decent shower pressure.** A hotel without good hot showers is like a man with a hairy back: everything might appear outwardly fine at first, and usually by the time you've discovered the truth, you're wet, naked, and past the point of no return. Oh, and a decent dressing gown is an integral part of the bathing experience, so let's throw in one of those too, eh?

3. **An iron.** I mean really, if you require an explanation as to why, we have nothing more to discuss here. You're probably the kind of person who still takes laundry to your mum's for her to sort out.

4. **A minibar tariff based in reality.** I know it's a money-spinner, but let's try to exercise some restraint, please. It's past midnight, room service is down to their three-item overnight menu, and there is nowhere open in a five-mile radius that doesn't feature salmonella prominently on the menu. It shouldn't cost the Lithuainian GDP for a Toblerone the size of my clit.

5. **Housekeepers who knock** *before* entering, not *while* entering. Self-explanatory really.

6. Swift, stress-free checkout. Approximately 50 minutes of the hour it takes to be released from the clutches of Marriott is spent waiting for the reception staff to print off your broadsheet-sized bill and locate a suitable envelope, but as they do this approximately 600 times every day, you might imagine there are ways to make the process a touch swifter. Fucking sort it out, man.

7. A complimentary morning paper that isn't the *Financial Times*, *Frankfurter Allgemeine*, or *USA Today*. As all sensible people will avoid the first on principle and the other two on account of not understanding the language they are written in.

8. Soundproof walls. Rarely have I been awakened by the amorous exertions of guests in the next room, which can only mean they are being kept up all night by mine. Apologies, but it isn't my fault, you understand.

9. Hair dryers. For reasons I am at a complete loss to comprehend, there appears to be an inverse relationship between the cost of a night's stay and the availability of a hairdryer. Perhaps they are considered vulgar among a certain set? In any case, walking through a five-star foyer is precisely the last place I want to be seen looking like a refugee from the humidity work camps.

10. A full breakfast worth the name. If staying at a hotel in England and your breakfast does not include grilled tomatoes, FAIL. Same goes for Scotland and lorne sausage, Norway and brown cheese, and America and fluffy pancakes. If I'm paying upwards of 25 Euros for the privilege of accessing your steam table buffet, then it had damn well better offer something passably edible. And stocking juice glasses that hold more than a cumshot's worth of liquid wouldn't go amiss either.

It amazes me how much has changed, and how quickly, in the online world. When I started blogging it felt as if all the bloggers in the UK knew each other (apart from me, of course) and were a tight-knit, in-crowdy bunch. Thankfully that clubbiness quickly ended, and the variety of voices and stories out there is amazing. Here are some other trends I've observed:

Going Up

Journalists getting it right, mostly. At least they no longer feel obliged to explain what a 'blog' is every time they write about one. Though they do still occasionally use the word 'blogsite', which a) doesn't actually exist and b) is plain silly.

Expensive books of ironic photos. Really, these are specifically designed to appeal only to the 28–38 age-range. It's as if the Internet never happened, and we all need a copy of those amusing cat pictures in dead tree form.

Jacket blurbs by people you've never heard of. Just to tacitly acknowledge that nobody really cares about those anyway. It's all about the content, innit.

E-books. And the insufferable gits named Julian who can't stop talking about them. Yeah, and I bet you bought a Laserdisc player back in the day, too. Thanks very much, but I'm happy to wait for the prices (and formats) to settle down. Anyone else remember Betamax?!?

Anti-hooker lit. Because not having sex is the new having sex, or so they say. Which is what you *would* say if you weren't getting any, isn't it? Oh, I'm kidding. I'm sure you're a lovely girl, really. Really.

Going down

Hot pink paperback covers. Finally, you can walk into a bookshop and it doesn't look like an explosion in the Barbie factory. I like my infantile fluff to at least look passably respectable when reading on the Tube, dig?

Misery memoirs. I imagine it's because the supply of sepia-tinted waifs has been completely exhausted, or something. Phew. I was beginning to think touching up your kinfolk had somehow crossed the Atlantic.

Grand literary feuds. Norman Mailer's passing was truly the end of an era in more ways than one. A new generation with decreased attention span means no one can spare 20 years hating on Salman Rushdie any more.

Full-price books. If it's not at least on a 3 for 2 offer, you're shopping in the wrong place. You would feel a bit of a tit for paying the cover price for that new Tony Parsons, amirite? And while we're at it, paid-for content on websites is shortly to be shown the door. Great for readers, but who knows where it will lead to? I for one am excited.

Coffee shops in bookstores. The incompetence of coffee shop staff with the eccentricity of bookshop staff rolled into one! The toilets are locked, the baristas are on perpetual smoke breaks, they're out of sugar free vanilla syrup again, and it's impossible to hold that giant mug and read at the same time. What was the point exactly?

Where are they now?

It's a funny thing – I still remember the first email from a blog reader asking what happened to one of my friends. It hadn't occurred to me that people were just as interested in their stories as I was! Thinking back on where we all were then, and what has happened in the interim, has proved interesting – who could have predicted that . . .

A1 is: Settled in perpetual domestic bliss with the woman of his dreams (read: trapped in suburbia with a mumsy divorcee). Still hoeing the old row, drinking hard and offending many, but with the insouciance – and immunity – of the truly handsome. Refuses to sperminate his missus, which is a cause of neverending tension. Oh, and she has a cat she makes clothes for and feeds like it's a teenager on steroids. Superb.

A2 is: Settled in perpetual domestic bliss in sunny Spain with his primary partner, her toyboy, and the occasional sleepover from his two other girlfriends in a gorgeous house with twenty acres and three cats. Or as I like to call it, Living the Dream. Apart from the cats. At least he doesn't dress them up.

A3 is: Settled in perpetual domestic bliss with his girlfriend who lives on the Continent and visits for a weekend every other month. Really, the mechanics of how and why this appears to work for him completely escape me. Also why he is so stubbornly faithful to her. Or as I like to call it, In Denial About Being Functionally Single.

A4 is: Settled in perpetual domestic bliss with his widescreen LCD telly and broadband connection. Appears to believe that the perfect woman will rock up and knock on his door one day. While not impossible, the fact that he lives in a flat behind a six-foot locked gate makes this increasingly unlikely.

N is: Settled in perpetual domestic hell with a woman who can't make up her mind. One week, they're on the brink of engagement, the next, she's dumped him again and high-tailed it back to the shires, citing as her reason . . . oh, I don't know, some pseudo-therapist mumbo-jumbo. Never let it be said he doesn't cut a vast swathe through the lady-folk during the times he's officially single, but still, I want to slap that woman – hard, and not in a sexy way – for playing him for a fool.

The Boy is: Living about as far from me as it is possible to do in this country. This isn't by accident, but design – the last time I moved, I changed my phone number and left no forwarding address. Sadly, that wasn't enough to halt the barrage of contact, and I was forced to ring his father to have a word with the venerable elder fellow. Far more effective, and less embarrassing, than ringing the police.

A word to the boys: so you're weighing up seeing a pro . . .

So, you're thinking about being a client – or perhaps, you already are one. All you need is the money, the equipment, and an internet connection, right? Well, maybe. But if you want to be remembered as a good client – as opposed to a 'usual' one, or even an 'OMG girls, AVOID, AVOID, AVOID', then you could do worse than to consider a few 'Dos' and 'Don'ts' of the other side of the game.

Funnily enough, it's a little like dating. We women might seem mysterious creatures to your eyes, but in fact we are simply responding to the cues you put out. Be an ideal client, and odds are, your experience of paid lovin' may well be better than you anticipated. Step over the line, abuse, and otherwise disrespect the women? You're on the fast train to Creepsville, bud.

DO be on time if you're an incall (coming to see her), and ready on time if you're an outcall (she comes to see you). Because in case it wasn't already clear, why yes, you will be charged extra if you're late or just need to hop in the shower when she gets there.

DON'T change the date and time of an appointment unless it is a genuine emergency. Flakiness on meeting times is a seriously hackle-raising red flag for a lot of girls, and you don't want her apprehensive before she even gets in the door, right?

DO offer her a drink if it's an outcall. Seeing as you've already spent a few hundred to have a visitor, a little extra wine should be nothing. And it's only polite.

DON'T be surprised if she turns it down, asks for water instead, or takes one sip and leaves the rest untouched. It's not a comment on either you or the drink, it's the desire to stay focused, in control, and aware of her surroundings. Trust me, you'll have a better time if she's sober.

DO mention if it's the first time you've done something. If it's your first anal, for example, letting the girl know this can help her help you get the most of the experience. Don't just aim blindly and start jabbing away.

DON'T talk about other hookers you've done things with. That is creepy and weird and while of extreme interest to the 'collector' type of client, of little or no interest to anyone else. Sorry, guys – save it for the call girl review websites, or your mates.

DO have some condoms to hand, especially if you have a preference for type or brand. She will have some as well, but it never hurts to be prepared – not to mention reassures her you're not going to be one of those irritating blokes who is always pushing to go bareback!

DON'T ask for her to go bareback 'just this time', or offer more money for that. Come on – you already know she sleeps with other men. Loads of other men, in fact. Why would you even consider this a good idea?

DO say something. It's hard to talk to a stranger, and she will be doing her best to help you out, but keeping still and silent is unnerving for us – almost as much as talking too much, in fact.

DON'T ask her real name, about her real life, or – yes, people do this – if she has a boyfriend. For one thing, that crosses a line, especially if you're not a repeat client of hers. And odds are she won't tell you the truth anyway.

DO tip if you want to see her, or anyone from her agency, again. Yes, I realise from the first-time client's point of view hookers are like easyJet – loads of hidden extra charges. But keep in mind that she hands over a lot of dosh to the agency (or has high overheads if she's independent). Also, girls talk. A cool guy who tips well? Gold.

DON'T skimp on the personal hygiene. Facials and pubic waxing are, happily for you, not a requirement. But basic bodycare is not only a good idea, it's the right thing to do. Shower, trim those nails, and brush your teeth. Please.

Belle on music and books

I love music and books, always have – that was one great thing about living in London. Cruising the stacks at Foyles, followed by gigs at Barfly . . . the time when these books were written was not only a whirlwind of relationships and sex, but also of going out and loving it. Not to mention, recovering in bed with a book the next day – and all without the concern about having to get up early for work. There were some advantages, after all.

They say you are what you eat, and variety is the spice of life. I like to feed my brain big hefty chunks of French cuisine and Greek bitterness, chased with a bit of sugary pop and cheesy funk. If music be the food of love, then I love a fried, MSG-laden buffet. Okay, I think that analogy has officially swallowed its own tail now. Let me tell you about some of the songs and books that really light my metaphorical fire:

Songs

1. 'I Get Lifted' – K C and the Sunshine Band

To be honest, the original is super sexy. But this George McCrae classic 'gets lifted' by the addition of a seriously funky bass line and the long, breathy exhale in the refrain.

2. 'Ice Cream' – New Young Pony Club

Nervy, staccato, and inflected with strong New Yorkish vowels. It shouldn't be sexy, but the lyrics put this in the premier league. 'Sick like Sid and Nancy'? 'Nuff said.

3. 'Crazy on You' – Heart

Begins with a stunning acoustic solo, then rocks out. Guaranteed to raise the pulse, these hot, insistent vocals define aggressive – but still feminine – sexuality.

4. 'Walk on By' – Isaac Hayes

The superlative cover version. Hayes changes this from a lament on lost love to the sound of desire itself. Also, the album version is long. As in, 'put it on and forget about having to shuffle the playlist' long.

5. 'So Real' – Jeff Buckley

By now, 'Hallelujah' is a cliche. So eschew his covers of Leonard Cohen and go back to Buckley's own intensely passionate songwriting. This first cut off *Grace* is the perfect place to start.

6. 'My Life as a Car Crash' – Tompaulin

The first time I heard this, on John Peel's show, it stopped me dead. Like Pulp's 'Pencil Skirt', but more so. Hot tales of secret love in a small town.

7. 'All World Cowboy Romance' – Mission of Burma

Elegiac instrumental that feels like the rush of first love, available in convenient song form. A more traditional turn at composition from this recently reunited American New Wave band.

8. 'Evil' – Interpol

I defy anyone to hear this song and not want to dance. Naked. Pressed against their partner of choice. And smile.

9. 'Cursed Sleep' – Bonnie Prince Billy

Spare, country-esque ballad with longing in every note. Recorded over a long dark winter in Iceland, and the cool isolation shows.

10. 'I Wanna Be Adored' – The Stone Roses

I can't be the only person who has long associated this song, and indeed the entire album, with memories of a particularly hot – but inevitably doomed – love affair. Builds slow, just as the real thing ought.

Books

La Reine Margot, Alexándre Dumas

Less well-loved than his other masterpieces, but far more appealing to those of a romantic nature and teenage girls, that is. Margot's love of La Mole and her effect on French history has more twists and turns than a Curly Wurly. A bodice-ripper to end all bodice-rippers, and forerunner of today's historical fiction.

Of Human Bondage, W. Somerset Maugham

Extraordinary not just for invoking the authentic feel of a lonely childhood, but also the horror of obsessive love that becomes more a grudge match than a passionate affair. It ends happily after much heartbreak and shattered dreams, but that is the least memorable part of this remarkable novel.

Le Rouge et le Noir, Stendhal

What Maugham's hero would have been like with a bit more resourcefulness and swashbuckling. The silver-tongued but naïve Julien is an irresistible hero and impossible not to fall in love with. Perhaps intended as a warning against giving in to one's passions, but ironically probably the finest argument for doing so.

L'Amant, Marguerite Duras

I re-read this book almost every year, and the heartbreaking ending never fails to move me to tears. A perfectly drawn study of tragic characters and a masterclass in how the simplest writing is often the most emotionally devastating.

Lolita, Vladimir Nabokov

Whether this is an allegory or not hardly matters, as any interpretation would fail utterly if we did not believe absolutely in the love of fortyish Humbert for his prepubescent paramour. Inspiring for the quality of prose and Nabokov's ability to make the abhorrent beautiful.

Medea, Euripides

Of the set texts at school this was the one that stuck with me: the intensity of passion, the fatalities that can cause, and of course, Jason's blatant lying about Medea's future in his life. Proof that all the good plots have already been done, and done excellently.

Now I'm not anonymous . . . why?

Looking back over these diaries has been sometimes embarrassing, sometimes hilarious (often unintentionally so). After a page or two I'm right back there – living in London, keeping up a double life, with all the effort that entails . . .

Which is just too difficult to do long-term. I suppose I always thought that the part of my life I wrote about would fade away, that I could stick it in a box and move on. Totally separate it from the 'real me'.

What it took me years to realise is that while I've changed a lot since writing these diaries my life has moved on so much, in part thanks to the things that happened then – Belle will always be a part of me. She doesn't belong in a little box, but as a fully acknowledged side of a real person. The non-Belle part of my life isn't the only 'real' bit, it's *all* real.

Belle and the person who wrote her had been apart too long. I had to bring them back together.

So a perfect storm of feelings and circumstances drew me

out of hiding. And do you know what? It feels so much better on this side. Not to have to tell lies, hide things from the people I care about. To be able to defend what my experience of sex work is like to all the sceptics and doubters.

Anonymity had a purpose then – it will always have a reason to exist, for writers whose work is too damaging or too controversial to put their name on.

But for me, it became important to acknowledge that aspect of my life and my personality to the world at large.

I am a woman. I lived in London. I was a call girl.

The people, the places, the actions and feelings are as true now as they were then, and I stand behind every word with pride. Thank you for reading and following my adventures.

Love, Belle